MOUNTAIN BIKING L.A. COUNTY
(Southern   Section)

** 66 Selected Best Trips, 100 Rides **

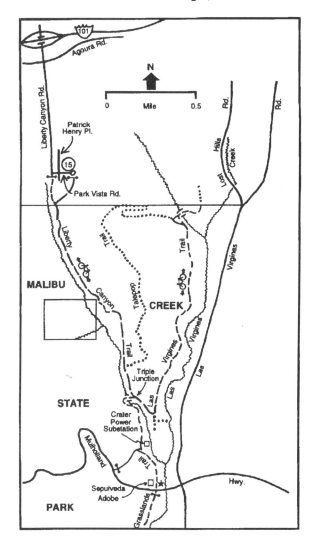

BY DON AND SHARRON BRUNDIGE

SANTA MONICA AND SANTA SUSANA MOUNTAINS   SIMI HILLS
VERDUGO MOUNTAINS/SAN RAFAEL HILLS   PUENTE HILLS
PALOS VERDES PENINSULA   SANTA CATALINA ISLAND

Other Books by Don and Sharron Brundige:
Bicycle Rides: Los Angeles and Orange Counties (Out of Print)
Bicycle Rides: San Fernando Valley and Ventura County (Out of Print)
Bicycle Rides: Orange County
Bicycle Rides: Los Angeles County
Bicycle Rides: Inland Empire
Bicycle Rides: San Diego and Imperial Counties
Bicycle Rides: Santa Barbara & Ventura Counties

Printed by Griffin Printing & Lithograph Co., Inc.
Glendale, California

Published by B-D Enterprises
122 Mirabeau Ave.
San Pedro, California 90732-3117

Photography by Don and Sharron Brundige
Maps by Sharron Brundige

We want to hear from you!
Corrections and updates will make this a better book and are gratefully appreciated. Publisher will reply to all such letters. Where information is used, submitter will be acknowledged in subsequent printing and given a free book (see above) of choice.

Front Cover: Below Sandstone Peak with Boney Mountain Backdrop
Back Cover: Zuma Canyon (Sam Nunez Photo)

TABLE OF CONTENTS

-- 100 Total Rides --

DEDICATION

To the next generation
Eric, Greta, Greg, Mark, Pete and Michelle
Who are doing it their own way
...We have faith in you!

ACKNOWLEDGMENTS

We offer our thanks to family, friends and bicycling acquaintances who gave us ideas, advice and plenty of encouragement while developing this biking book. This includes a "thank you" to the state, county and city agencies and individuals who offered their services and publications. A special thanks to Sam "The Camel" Nunez, who was a constant and valuable companion on many of these cycling tours. Additional kudos to Susan Cohen, Jill Morales, Karen Profet, Walt and Sally Bond, Rich Davis, Jim Cradduck and the folks we met on the trails, for sharing the "off-roaders." We also show particular gratitude to our venerable crew that was kind enough to review and comment on our manuscript: Susan Cohen, Jill Morales, Al Hook, Sam Nunez and Walt and Sal. Thank you Jackie Broom for helping us through so many computer crises.

We also thank Jean Bray at the Agoura Ranger Station and both Lynn Burt and Rebecca Guay of the Catalina Island Conservancy for reviewing our manuscript and offering valuable advice for improving its content. Finally, we acknowledge getting some nifty ride ideas from the following sources: *Trail Map of the Santa Monicas* by Tom Harrison, Ranger Bonnie at the Agoura Ranger Station, government agency brochures (particularly the National Park Service published guides), the Catalina Island Conservancy guides, *Mountain Biking the Coast Range*/Fine Edge Productions, *Mountain Bicycling Around Los Angeles*/Wilderness Press, *Hiking Trails of the Santa Monica Mountains*/Canyon Publishing, USGS topographic maps, Walt and Sally Bond and the many cycling comrades that we have met along the way.

BOOK TOUR

INTRODUCTION

Don   Sharron

HOW TO USE THIS BOOK

TRIP ORGANIZATION

Master Trip Matrix

Steep

Class X

TRIP DESCRIPTION/TERMINOLOGY

CHECKOFF LIST

GENERAL BIKING CONSIDERATIONS

THE BIKE TRIPS

MOUNTCLEF RIDGE/SIMI HILLS

SANTA MONICA MOUNTAINS

SANTA SUSANA MOUNTAINS

VERDUGO MTNS./SAN RAFAEL HILLS

PUENTE HILLS

POTPOURRI

INDEX

INDEX

Point of Interest   Trip #
Conejo Crest   28, 29

INTRODUCTION

As with all our books, we wanted to provide a trip guide that concentrates on trip navigation, contains a large number of well-documented trips, provides the necessary trip maps, and is reasonably priced. Hopefully, again, we have succeeded!

This guide has been developed based on biking trips taken in 1995-1996. There are over 500 <u>one-way</u> bike miles described! The document identifies 66 mountain-biking trips in the Santa Monica Mountains, Mountclef Ridge/Simi Hills, Santa Susana Mountains, Verdugo Mountains/San Rafael Hills, Whittier Hills and several other mountain biking areas scattered around the county. Each trip is written to be as complete and self-standing as possible. Many trips consist of two or more core rides which have been linked together. **100 rides are included in the book** (as noted in the "TABLE OF CONTENTS"). The authors used 18-speed bicycles (mountain bikes fitted with off-road tires) which are required for most trips.

A cross section of trips is provided. There are some short-length family trips, particularly in parks, many longer exploratory and workout trips for more experienced bikers on various quality bike routes, and a few "gut-buster" trips for the most physically fit and motivated bikers. Technical difficulty level varies from "nominal ability" to "special skills required." The trip domains include valleys, canyons, parks, rivers, lakes, hills, mountains and basins. There is a little something for everybody! **The mountain biking trips are among the best in the southern L.A. County area and most do not require exceptional technical skill or extensive physical training.** However, some are remote, physically taxing and on poor surfaces -- ride them at your own risk.

The strong emphasis in this book is "getting from here to there." This navigation is provided using detailed route descriptions in terms of landmarks, mileage, elevation contours and a quality set of trip maps. Scenery, vistas and scenic or historic landmarks are regularly noted for each trip, although detailed information about these features must be sought out in other publications. Public restrooms and sources of water are identified on those few trips where these facilities are available. Pleasant rest spots are also pointed out.

Mountain Biking -- a word to the wise. As fervent hikers, we have been agitated with mountain bikers more than once as they swooped by on narrow trails, forcing us to scatter with little warning. We have seen numerous damaged switchbacks and water bars beat to a pulp, sporting an array of bike treads. Like some hikers, there are cyclists who do not carry out their trash. We have talked to disappointed outback property owners who have graciously allowed cyclists to pass through, expecting that they will not stray off the throughway, will not disturb residents or cattle, and will not damage surrounding terrain. Cyclists sometimes enter private property despite signs warning against trespassing, to the chagrin of owners. There have been problems!

Have no doubt, there are many hikers, property owners, naturalists and other interested parties that are beginning to say "Enough!" They seek an outright ban on off-roaders in both backcountry and front-country areas or, as a minimum, want to severely limit the areas in which bikers can transit. You must understand that many of their concerns are legitimate. Learn to share the trails with your fellow outdoors men or stand the risk of losing an immeasurable freedom. A little courtesy and common sense will keep us all on the back roads and trails together!

HOW TO USE THIS BOOK

There are two ways to use this book: one way is for the person who wants to enjoy the research along with enjoying the bike ride, and another way for the biker who is just anxious to get out there "amongst em."

For the "anxious biker," follow Steps 1 through 5 below and split!

1. Check the "BEST OF THE BEST" trip summary noted on the inside cover for candidate trips or use the "Master Trip Map" in the "TRIP ORGANIZATION" section to select areas of interest for the bike ride. Note the candidate trip numbers. (Another option is to select a trip based on landmarks and sightseeing attractions referenced in the "INDEX.")

2. Go to the "Master Trip Matrices" in the "TRIP ORGANIZATION" section and narrow down the number of candidate trips by reviewing their general features.

3. Read about the individual trips and select one.

4. Read and understand the safety rules described in the "GENERAL BIKING CONSIDERATIONS" section and review the "CHECKOFF LIST" section.

5. See you later. Enjoy the ride!

For the more methodical folks, continue reading the next chapter. By the time you're through, you'll understand the trip description and maps much better than the "anxious biker."

TRIP ORGANIZATION

This bike book is organized by trip number. Trip numbers are in a general sequence governed by the mountain area (e.g., Santa Monica Mountains, Verdugo Mountains). Refer back to the "TABLE OF CONTENTS" for the entire trip list.

The "Master Trip Maps" show the general trailhead location of trips using a circled reference number (i.e., ⑦ refers to Trip #7). Alternate trailheads are described in the individual trip writeups.

The "Master Trip Matrices" provide a quick reference for selecting candidate trips and for more detailed reading evaluation. The matrices are organized by trip number. The key trip descriptors provided in those matrices are briefly explained in the footnotes at the bottom of the last matrix (page 11). A more detailed explanation of those descriptors is provided in the "TRIP DESCRIPTION/TERMINOLOGY" section which follows.

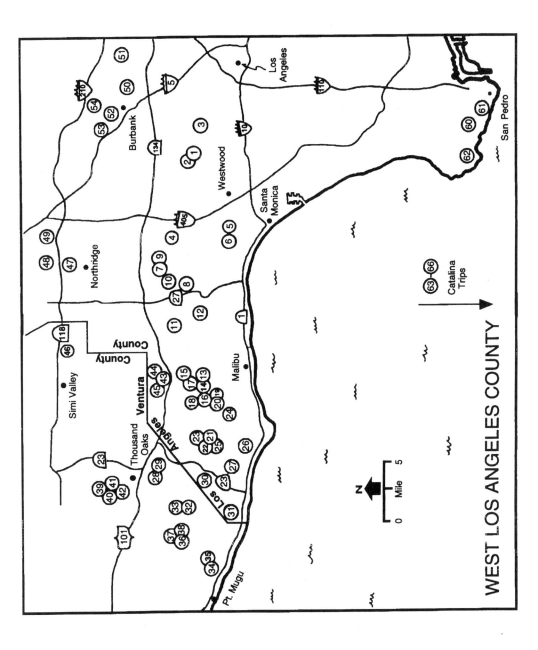

WEST LOS ANGELES COUNTY

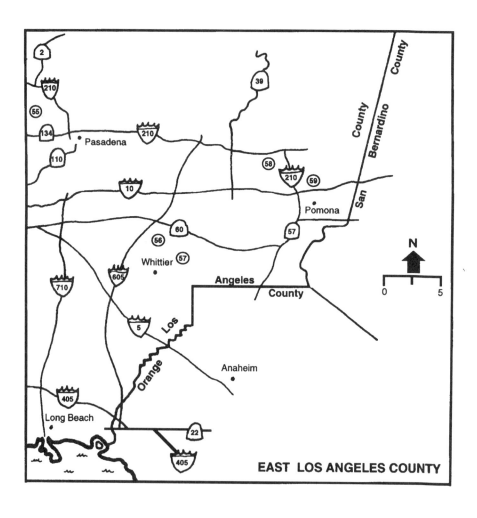

EAST LOS ANGELES COUNTY

MASTER TRIP MATRIX

TRIP NO.	GENERAL LOCATION	LEVEL OF DIFFICULTY			ROUTE QUALITY			TRIP CHARACT.[2]	COMMENTS
		L.O.D.[1]	MILES	ELEV.	BIKE TRAIL (%)	FIRE ROAD (%)	OTHER (%)		
1	Santa Monica Mtns. E. Coldwater Cyn. Dr.	M	6.6	Mod	-	90	10	S, P, L, S/A, W	Franklin Canyon (loop)
2	Santa Monica Mtns. E. Coldwater Cyn. Dr.	M	3.3	Mod	40	40	20	S, P, L, S/A, W	Wilacre Park, Iredell Canyon (loop)
3	Runyon Canyon Park	M-S	4.7	Mod-Steep	25	45	30	S, P, L, S/A	Runyon Canyon Park (loop)
4	Santa Monica Mtns. E. above Brentwood	M	9.1 (1-w)	Mod	-	100	-	S, P, L	Dirt Mulholland
5	Santa Monica Mtns. E. Mandeville Cyn.	M	9.0	Mod	-	100	-	S, P, L	Canyonback Rd., W. Mandeville Fire Road
6	Topanga State Park	M	11.2	Mod-Steep	40	60	-	S, P, L, W/C	Sullivan Fire Road, Sullivan Canyon
7	Topanga State Park	M	7.3 (1-w)	Mod	-	100	-	S, P, L	Temescal Fire Road, Trailer Canyon
8	Topanga State Park	M	5.9	Mod	-	100	-	S, P, L	Eagle Rock Loop
9	Topanga State Park	M-S	9.2	Mod	60	40	-	S, P, L, S/A, T	Will Rogers/Backbone Trail
10	Topanga State Park	M-S	9.3 (1-w)	Mod-Steep	-	100	-	S, P, L, W, T	E. Topanga Fire Road

1,2 See footnotes on page 11

5

MASTER TRIP MATRIX

TRIP NO.	GENERAL LOCATION	LEVEL OF DIFFICULTY			ROUTE QUALITY			TRIP CHARACT.[2]	COMMENTS
		L.O.D.[1]	MILES	ELEV.	BIKE TRAIL (%)	FIRE ROAD (%)	OTHER (%)		
11	Topanga State Park	S	4.5 (1-w)	Mod-Steep	-	100	-	S, P, L	Red Rock Canyon, Calabasas Peak
12	Santa Monica Mtns. Central/Calabasas	E	3.3 (1-w)	Mod	10	90	-	S, P	Summit-to-Summit Motorway
13	Malibu Creek State Park	M	7.6	Mod	-	100	-	S, P, L, S/A, W, W/C	Crags Road, Malibu Creek
14	Malibu Creek State Park	M	3.8	Mod	50	50	-	S, P, L	Grasslands Trail (up and back)
15	Malibu Creek State Park	M	6.4	Mod	40	60	-	S, L	Liberty Canyon, Las Virgenes Trail
16	Malibu Creek State Park	M	3.3	Mod-Steep	-	100	-	S, P	Lookout Loop
17	Malibu Creek State Park	VS	15.0	Steep	5	85	10	S, P, L, S/A, W, W/C	Bulldog Motorway - Castro Crest Loop
18	Paramount Park	M M-S	TBD 4.8	Mod Mod-Stp	30 30	70 70	- -	S, P, L, S/A, W, T	Flood Plains Trail, Out & Back Excursion
19	Malibu Creek State Park	M	6.8 (1-w)	Mod	-	100	-	S, P, L	Mesa Peak Motorway, Puerco Canyon
20	Santa Monica Mtns. C. Castro Crest	M-S	3.9 (1-w)	Mod-Steep	-	100	-	S, P, L	Castro Peak Motorway, West

1,2 See footnotes on page 11

6

MASTER TRIP MATRIX

TRIP NO.	GENERAL LOCATION	LEVEL OF DIFFICULTY			ROUTE QUALITY			TRIP CHARACT.[2]	COMMENTS
		L.O.D.[1]	MILES	ELEV.	BIKE TRAIL (%)	FIRE ROAD (%)	OTHER (%)		
21	Santa Monica Mtns. C. Castro Crest	S	11.8	Mod-Steep	-	100	-	S, P	Complete Castro Crest, Puerco Canyon
22	Rocky Oaks Park	M	2.1	Mod	50	50	-	S, P, L	Rocky Oaks Park (loop)
23	Santa Monica Mtns. C. Mulholland Hwy.	M-S	3.7	Mod-Steep	30	35	35	S, P	Brewster Motorway (loop)
24	Santa Monica Mtns. C. Latigo Canyon Rd.	M	5.5 (1-w)	Mod	-	100	-	S, P, L, S/A	Ramera/Murphy Mtwys.. Escondido Falls
25	Santa Monica Mtns. Central/Zuma Ridge	M-S	6.4	Mod-Steep	-	100	-	S, P	Zuma Ridge Trail
26	Santa Monica Mtns. C. Zuma Canyon	VS	14.0	Steep-Sheer	-	60	40	S, P, L, W/C	The Edison Road (loop)
27	Charmlee Park	M M-S	1.6 3.4	Mod Mod-Stp	60	40	-	S, P, L, S/A, W	Meadowlands Ride, West Ridge Road Ride
28	Conejo Crest Westlake Open Space	M-S	4.7	Mod-Steep	30	70	-	S, P, L, T	East Los Robles Trail
29	Conejo Crest Westlake Open Space	M-S	6.3	Mod-Steep	60	10	30	S, P, T	Conejo Crest, Potrero Trails (loop)
30	Santa Monica Mtns. Central/West	M	2.9	Mod-Steep	-	100	-	S, P	ETZ Moley Motorway

1,2 See footnotes on page 11

7

MASTER TRIP MATRIX

TRIP NO.	GENERAL LOCATION	LEVEL OF DIFFICULTY			ROUTE QUALITY			TRIP CHARACT.[2]	COMMENTS
		L.O.D.[1]	MILES	ELEV.	BIKE TRAIL (%)	FIRE ROAD (%)	OTHER (%)		
31	Leo Carrillo State Park	S	5.8	Steep-Sheer	-	100	-	S, P	Yellow Hill Fire Road
32	Circle X Ranch	S	7.5	Mod-Steep	-	100	-	S, P, L	Sandstone Peak, Carlisle Canyon
33	Circle X Ranch	M	3.2	Mod-Steep	-	100	-	S, P, L, S/A, W	The Grotto Fire Road
34	Point Mugu State Park	S / M	16.7 / 13.5	Steep / Mod	-	100	-	S, P, L, S/A.W. W/C	Sycamore Cyn. + Overlook Sycamore Cyn. Loop
35	Pt. Mugu State Park	S	12.7	Steep	60	40	-	S, P, L, W/C, W	Sycamore Cyn., Guadal-asco, Ovlk. Trails (loop)
36	Rancho Sierra Vista/ Satwiwa	E-M	4.9	Mod	80	20	-	S, P, L, S/A,W	Rancho Sierra Vista Trails
37	Conejo Crest Westlake Open Space	M-S	6.2	Mod-Steep	80	20	-	S, P, L, W/C	West Los Robles Trail
38	Conejo Crest Westlake Open Space	S	10.1	Mod-Steep	40	60	-	S, P, L, W/C	Los Robles Trail (West & East)
39	Wildwood Park	M-S	5.1	Mod-Steep	60	10	30	S, P, L. T	Mounclef Ridge (loop)
40	Wildwood Park	M-S	6.1	Steep-Sheer	30	70	-	S, P, L, S/A W/C, W, T	Lizard Rock Wildwood Canyon (loop)

1,2 See footnotes on page 11

8

MASTER TRIP MATRIX

TRIP NO.	GENERAL LOCATION	LEVEL OF DIFFICULTY			ROUTE QUALITY			TRIP CHARACT.[2]	COMMENTS
		L.O.D.[1]	MILES	ELEV.	BIKE TRAIL (%)	FIRE ROAD (%)	OTHER (%)		
4 1	Wildwood Park	M	2.5	Mod	30	70	-	S, P, L	Stagecoach Bluff Trail (loop)
4 2	Wildwood Park	S	6.2	Mod-Steep	90	10	-	S, P, L	Lynnmere Trail (loop)
4 3	Agoura Hills	M	9.6	Mod	35	65	-	S, P, L, W/C	Cheeseboro Canyon
4 4	Agoura Hills	S	9.2 (1-w)	Mod-Steep	10	90	-	S, P, L, W/C	Cheeseboro Canyon, Baleen Wall Trail
4 5	Agoura Hills	M-S	9.0	Steep	10	90	-	S, P, L, W/C	Palo Comado Canyon (loop)
4 6	Simi Valley	S	11.4	Steep	25	25	50	S, P, L, T	Rocky Peak, Chumash Trail (loop)
4 7	Porter Ranch	M	7.0 (r/t)	Mod	80	20	-	S, P, L, W, W/C	Limekiln Canyon
4 8	Porter Ranch	M	8.2 (r/t)	Mod	40	40	20	S, P, L, W, W/C	Limekiln, Aliso Canyons (loop)
4 9	Granada Hills	S	6.3 (1-w)	Steep-Sheer	40	40	20	S, P, L, W, W/C, T	Mission Peak, Bee Canyon (loop)
5 0	Verdugo Mountains Brand Park	S	7.0	Steep	-	100	-	S, P, L, S/A	Brand Motorway

1,2 See footnotes on page 11

9

MASTER TRIP MATRIX

TRIP NO.	GENERAL LOCATION	LEVEL OF DIFFICULTY			ROUTE QUALITY			TRIP CHARACT.[2]	COMMENTS
		L.O.D.[1]	MILES	ELEV.	BIKE TRAIL (%)	FIRE ROAD (%)	OTHER (%)		
51	Verdugo Mountains	S	6.0	Steep-Sheer	-	100	-	S, P, L	Beaudry Motorway Loop
52	Verdugo Mountains Stough/Wildwood Pks	S	11.4	Steep	-	-	-	S, P, L, S/A	Verdugo Motorway, Summit ride
53	Verdugo Mountains	M-S	4.7	Mod-Steep	-	90	10	S, N	Chandler Fire Rd. and Stough Canyon Mtwy.
54	Verdugo Mountains	M-S	7.1	Steep-Sheer	-	100	-	S, P, T	Hosteller and Whiting Woods Motorways
55	San Rafael Hills	M	5.1	Mod	-	100	-	S, P, L	San Rafael Hills Crest
56	Puente Hills	M-S	5.8	Mod-Steep	30	40	30	S, P	Skyline Trail-West
57	Puente Hills	M-S	8.0	Mod-Steep	30	50	20	S, P, L	Skyline Trail-East
58	Walnut Creek Park, San Dimas	M	3.7	Mod	100	-	-	S, P	Walnut Canyon, Walnut Creek
59	Bonelli Park, San Dimas	M-S	9.4	Mod	20	70	10	S, P, L, S/A, W	Bonelli Park
60	Palos Verdes Peninsula	M-S	5.3	Mod-Steep	20	80	-	S, P, L (T-Minor Loop)	Portuguese Bend, Major & Minor Loops

1,2 See footnotes on page 11

MASTER TRIP MATRIX

TRIP NO.	GENERAL LOCATION	LEVEL OF DIFFICULTY			ROUTE QUALITY			TRIP CHARACT.[2]	COMMENTS
		L.O.D.[1]	MILES	ELEV.	BIKE TRAIL (%)	FIRE ROAD (%)	OTHER (%)		
61	Palos Verdes Peninsula	M	4.0	Mod-Steep	80	20	-	S, P, L	Palos Verdes Bluffs (loop)
62	Palos Verdes Peninsula	M	3.3	Mod-Steep	80	20	-	S, P, L, S/A, W, T(optional)	Point Vicente Park (loop)
63	Santa Catalina, Avalon	S-VS	20.6	Steep-Sheer	-	-	100	S, P, L, S/A, W	Avalon to Airport-in-the-Sky
64	Santa Catalina, Little Harbor	S	21.1	Mod-Steep	-	100	-	S, P, L, W	Middle Canyon, Cottonwood Canyon Loop
65	Santa Catalina, Two Harbors	S	16.0	Mod-Steep	-	100	-	S, P, L, W	Two Harbors to Little Harbor
66	Santa Catalina, Two Harbors	M	13.6	Mod	-	100	-	S, P, W	West End Road

1   L.O.D. - Overall trip level of difficulty: **VS**-very strenuous; **S**-strenuous; **M**-Moderate; **E**-easy; **1-w**-one way; **r/t**-round trip

2   **TRIP CHARACTERISTICS** - General trip features and highlights: **S**-scenic; **P**-panoramas; **L**-landmarks; **S/A**-sight-seeing attractions; **W/C**-creek, river crossing; **W**-water sources available enroute; **T**-technical sections

11

TRIP DESCRIPTION/TERMINOLOGY

The trip descriptors in the "Master Trip Matrices" are described below in further detail. Several of these same descriptors are also used in the individual trip write-ups.

GENERAL LOCATION: The general location of the bike trail is provided in terms of the applicable USGS topographic (topo) map(s). The "Master Trip Map" may be useful in conjunction with this general locator.

LEVEL OF DIFFICULTY: The rides are rated on an overall basis as *very strenuous*, *strenuous*, *moderate* and *easy*, based on elevation gain, trip distance and condition of the bike route. Where technical riding expertise is required, it is noted in the write-ups.

A *very strenuous* trip can be of any length, has steep-to-sheer grades, may be very technical and is generally designed for bikers in excellent physical condition. There may be several thousand feet elevation gain. It should be noted that even on the most strenuous trip, the bike can be walked uphill or through highly technical sections for bikers in reasonably good condition. However, rather than suffer this fate, it is recommended that bikers start with the easier trips and work up. Alternately, trips are well enough described such that the biker might plan to ride the easier part of a stressing trip and link up with other easier trips. Do not attempt strenuous or very strenuous mountain-bike trips unless you are well equipped, trail wise and in good condition.

A *strenuous* trip has some lengthy steep grades and/or relatively long mileage (usually on the order of 10-15 miles total). Typically, expect 1500-2000 feet elevation gain. *Strenuous* and *very strenuous* trips are of sufficiently long duration to require trip planning and strong consideration of weather, water, food and bike spare parts. Some portions of the trip may require above-average technical biking abilities. Technical sections are noted in the trip write-up.

A *moderate* trip may have mild-to-steep grades and moderate mileage, on the order of ten miles or less. Elevation gain is typically a 1000 feet or less. The trip is typically an hour or two duration and on reasonable-condition bike route.

An *easy* trip is on the order of 5 miles or less, is relatively flat and is generally on quality fire roads or bike trails.

TRIP MILEAGE: Mileage is computed for one-way travel for shuttle trips, full-trip length for *loop* trips and trips which require an *up and back transit*. *Up and back* is specifically used for trips that share a common route in both outgoing and return directions. *Loop* means that the outgoing and return trip segments are on different routes; the degree of commonality varies with the trip. In the trip write-ups, the mileage from the starting point or "trailhead" is noted in parentheses to the nearest tenth mile, for example, (6.3).

TRIP TIME: We consider ourselves to be average mountain bikers, in good biking condition and not out to break land-speed records. Trip times assume a steady pace with time-outs for snacks and observations. A lower limit trip time of one hour is used rather than attempt to "split hairs."

TRIP ELEVATION GAIN: The overall trip elevation gain is described in a quantitative fashion in the trip write-up. In addition, a qualitative summary is provided in the Master Trip Matrix. Steepness of upgrades is loosely defined as follows: 1) *flat* indicates limited slope and little elevation gain; 2) *moderate* means more significant slope requiring use of low gears; 3) *steep* indicates workout-type grades that require low gears and high physical exertion; 4) *sheer* indicates gut-buster grades that require extreme physical exertion (and a strong will to live!).

Elevation contour plots are provided for all trips. A reference 5% (*moderate-to-steep*) grade is shown on all such maps. Cyclists in good condition can handle extended 5% grades. Lengthy 10%-and-above grades are extremely taxing, requiring extreme patience (including the possibility of walking your bike) and excellent physical condition. All elevation contours for a given mountain area are plotted on a common scale to allow trip comparison or pasting together contours from different trips to form a custom adventure.

BIKE ROUTE QUALITY: The trips are summarized with respect to route type in the "Master Trip Matrix" and a more detailed description is given in the individual trip write-ups. The following route terminology is used:

. *Trail* - single or double track (the latter includes overgrown fire roads)

. *Fire Road* - distinct dirt road (at least 4-5 feet wide, per NPS standards)

. *Other* - paved road, highway, etc.

HIGHLIGHTS: The overall highlights of the bike trip are provided in the "Master Trip Matrix" to assist in general trip selection. The trip may be scenic (*S*), with abundant tree cover, waterfalls or other interesting sights. If there are sweeping vistas and exciting overlooks, the panoramic (P) symbol is used. The trip may highlight historical or well-known landmarks (*L*) or may have one or more sightseeing attraction (*S/A*). An example of the former is Eagle Rock (Trip #8), while the latter might be the Visitor Center in Malibu Creek State Park (Trip #13). There may be creek or river crossings on the trip (W/C). Trips with reliable water sources at the trailhead or along the way (W) are also noted.

Several descriptors are unique to the individual trip write-ups. Those descriptors are defined below.

TRAILHEAD: The general location of the start of the bike path is provided for the reference trip starting point. Other trailhead options are noted where relevant. Driving directions to that trailhead and/or directions for parking are included where there is a possibility of confusion. Always check to ensure that parking is consistent with current laws. (Also, see "Parking" under "GENERAL BIKING CONSIDERATIONS.")

TRAIL DESCRIPTION: Trail or fire road connector markers and information posted on signs that are part of the described trip are noted in ***bold italics***. Those that are not (i.e. marked spur or alternate routes) are noted in *light italics*.

WATER: In the "Trailhead" description for each trip, general statements are provided about water sources if available. In the "Trip Description," available water along the route is noted, although the trip should be planned to assume that water stops may not be operational. Particular emphasis is placed on public facilities for water and use of restrooms. It is vital to take additional water for the more difficult mountain-bike trips -- you won't believe the discomfort and biking inefficiency that results from lack of water!

TRIP OPTIONS: Where trips have interesting variants or shortcuts, they are so noted. Particular emphasis is placed on spur trips which provide scenic beauty, notable landmarks or route extensions.

BIKE TRIP MAPS: Each ride in the book has an accompanying elevation contour and detailed bike map which use the symbols and features provided below.

——————	Paved Road/ Highway	— ——	Fire Road	— — — — —	Trail (Single or Double Trk.)
• • • • • •	Restricted Entry or Not Recommend.		Travel in Direction Shown		Travel is Out and Back
San Pedro	Nearby City		Lake, ocean	59	Trailhead, Trip #59
W R	Public Water Restroom		Ranger or Visitor Stat.	★	Alternate Trailhead
	Camp Site		Railroad Crossing or Overcrossing		Pass or Trip Summit
•——•	Locked Gate		Picnic Site	□ WT □ RT	Water Tower Radio Tower
	Creek or Canyon	5%	Reference 5% Grade	Mt. Orizaba (2097)	Mountain & Elev. (feet)
S.M.M.N. R.A.	Snt. Monica Mtns. Natl. Recr. Area	N.P.S.	National Park Service		Park Boundary

MAP AND ELEVATION CONTOUR SYMBOLS

GENERAL BIKING CONSIDERATIONS

The following are considerations for folks who want to make the best of traveling in the outback.

Trip Planning. We are absolute believers in advance planning. You minimize nasty surprises and have the joy of two trips for one (the anticipated trip and the physical trip itself). *Check the weather* report for anticipated temperatures, wind, and any signs of incoming inclement weather. If you have any reservations about total trip time, *start in the early morning*, which has its own advantages as far as temperature and shade. *Familiarize yourself with the trip* -- read a recent tour guide; look over the topographic maps and get a feel for the key areas of elevation change and where the key trail junctions are. Don't place total confidence in the topos with respect to trails and roads -- these maps are out of date to varying degrees as noted by the date in the lower right-hand corner. Get USFS or other area maps to complement the topos. Mark key junctions, landmarks and points of interest. Check that the trails are open and available for public travel by making advance inquiries. Bring a compass and learn how to use it in conjunction with a topo. Other smart options to minimize the chances of getting lost are to keep a sharp eye on the odometer and clock to check against known points on the map. Compare the terrain and elevation against expectations and look back frequently in the direction you came should you have to retrace your incoming route. You will do fine on most trips without all this effort; however, it's that time when you drop steeply, say 700-feet in elevation, and realize that your incorrect choice of trails means you get to retrace your steps. Or try the feeling of running out of water with night coming on and not being sure if you've got two miles of "bad road," creek crossings and more elevation gain, or a simple flat outlet (based on real-life experiences, of course!).

Safety. Always let somebody know your trip plans, your rough schedule and when and who to call should you not show up at the outlet point. *We do not recommend biking alone*, although Don will admit to doing a few solos on some of the less remote trips. Keep an eye on the weather and add or subtract layers of clothing as appropriate. If weather threatens or if you find yourself well beyond your abilities, don't be ashamed to turn back or to take a pre-planned or well-known shortcut (life is miserable in this situation when a shortcut becomes a "shortcut"). Keep your speed conservative on routes that you are unfamiliar with. Don't show off unless you really know what you are doing and you can do it safely for yourself and others -- showing off might mean making a jump, traversing difficult terrain without dismounting or biking a trail section at a faster pace than your companions.

Trail Courtesy. You will constantly be sharing trailways with other bikers, hikers and equestrians and maybe some all-terrain vehicles. *Keep your speed down* to the point that you can react quickly and safely when you encounter somebody else around that next blind turn. Always slow in the company of others. *Announce yourself* if you are coming up from behind: "Track!" says you are on the same trail and intend to pass; "on your left (or right)" says you intend to pass on the other person's left (or right) on a wide trailway. Stop and move off the trail if you encounter equestrians moving toward you. If you are coming up from behind, stop well behind and ask permission to pass. Pass slowly and steadily, holding a conversation with the rider. Why the big deal? Because horses can spook and the results can be harmful to equestrians, horses and cyclists.

Respect for the Territory. There are many ways that you can minimize your impact on the environment. *Avoid riding on wet/damp trails* -- the ruts that you

15

leave channel runout and accelerate erosion (let several warm days pass before setting out after rainy periods). *Stay on prescribed roads and trails* -- ensure trails are open and leave gates as you found them. Cross-country riding may be your "rush," but your impact on soil and vegetation may be permanent and significant. *Take care to cross water bars* (rock, log and temporary sandbags placed to divert water off of trails) by biking directly over the top or dismounting your bike and walking. Riding around the ends of water bars damages the drainage pattern and speeds erosion. *Minimize hard braking leading to skidding* -- the impact is to leave channeling which furthers erosion. Switchbacks are particularly susceptible, so slow and keep your wheels turning during negotiation. *Whether uphill or downhill, if you are consistently having trouble maintaining traction, it is time to dismount and walk your bike. Travel in a small group* -- large entourages have inherent tendencies to be less sensitive to the environment. *Pack out your trash* and take out somebody else's if you've got room.

Bugs N' Things. Learn to recognize *poison oak*, which abounds in the Southern California mountains and hills. Watch where you bike, walk and where you lay down your bike as the offending oily substance adheres to almost any surface. Wear long biking pants and long-sleeve shirts if you travel in poison-oak or tick-infested overgrown trails. Check for *ticks*, particularly around cinched areas such as cuffs, waistbands and socks. Remove ticks before they burrow into your skin. Take them off gently with tweezers -- do not pull them off or try burning them off. *Mosquitoes* can also be a problem, particularly if you bike in areas with standing water. Bring mosquito repellent if you have any doubts.

Rattlesnakes are found throughout the areas covered by this book and are most prevalent in the spring when they lie out in the sun for warmth. In summer, they tend to hide in shady places. They are usually at lower elevations and near water. Rattlers generally give ample warning if bothered and will retreat if given a chance. There are still some larger animals of prey in the Santa Monica and Santa Susanna Mountains such as *bobcats* and *coyotes* and a lesser number of *mountain lions*. Posted signs will let you know if there have been any problems with these species, ever-more threatened and sometimes reacting to man's encroachment.

Logistics. Many of the trips included are one-way trips requiring a car shuttle or that require significant on-road bike segments to complete the loop. Although we are avid on-road bikers, something is generally lost when, after completing a "killer" mountain bike trip, you must then get on the highway and deal with automobile traffic. So here are a few suggestions applicable to car shuttle trips in general and loop trips in some cases. Visit the outlet point so that both you and your shuttle can clearly identify a meeting place. (This is a natural occurrence if you are leaving a car at both entry and outlet.) Agree on an outlet arrival time and a "get concerned" time, i.e., a time to notify the proper authorities that there may be a serious problem. Identify those phone numbers ahead of time. Get a telephone message recorder which allows you to play your messages from remote telephone locations or identify family or friends' phone numbers who can act as go-betweens. This is particularly useful if you return to civilization at an unplanned location (due to navigation errors or physical inability to complete the trip) -- you call and let your car shuttle know where he/she can find you. The trick is to have your shuttle start checking the message machine or go-betweens after some agreed-on time.

Parking. Park legally and pay all self-registration day-use fees, or park well off the road, ensuring not to block other motorists, residents or emergency vehicles access to equipment or roadways. We have watched illegally-parked cars towed away from trailheads. Don't make a lot of noise at the trailhead (or on the trail for that matter); do not litter and do not bug the locals for water or telephone use unless it is an emergency.

CHECKOFF LIST

Clothing. *The key considerations* are predirections, trip duration, likelihood of the extent to which you're willing to be uncomfortable if weather conditions go sour (temperature, wind, rain, etc.) or if your trip duration extends into an unplanned time of day. (This could be a life-threatening issue if an unexpected winter overnighter is required.) In general, wear layered clothing so that you can add or subtract layers as needed. The following is our minimum standard: biking pants (long pants if you need warmth, are traveling tick- or poison-oak-infested territory or want "spill" protection), lycra or wool mesh undershirt, biking jersey (long-sleeved for the same reasons as long pants), mountain biking shoes (over-the-ankle for spill protection), socks, biking gloves (full-length if needed for cold or for spill protection), helmet, windbreaker, sweatband and sunglasses.

Bike Repair Kit. *The key consideration* is how far you are willing to walk out if you lose your means of transport. Spills and biking through rocky and/or overgrown terrain can do bad things to bikes. The minimum kit (for our bikes) consists of: patch kit, tire levers, spare tube, air pump, Allen wrench set (3, 4, 5, 6mm), adjustable crescent wrench, Phillips head and flat-blade screwdrivers and tire valve cap with valve stem remover. A more complete kit might contain a chain lube, chain rivet tool, spoke wrench, channel locks, bailing wire and duct tape for temporary repairs and boot material (for exterior patching of damaged tires).

First Aid Kit. *The key considerations* are how long you are willing to suffer with untreated wounds and what chances you are willing to take of resultant medical complications. Our packaged, baggie-sealed kit has the following: sunscreen (15 SPF or greater), lip salve, aspirin, band aids, gauze (roll), ace bandage (roll) and butterfly clips, small scissors, moleskin, needle and an antiseptic such as hydrogen peroxide or iodine, and poison oak cream. Think about insect repellent if you think conditions may warrant. Take a snake bite kit if you will be a long distance from civilization.

Water. *The key considerations* are how uncomfortably thirsty you are willing to be or, in the ultimate case, whether you are willing to chance dehydration and the resultant inability to continue. A human being physically exerting himself in 90-degree temperatures needs about ten quarts of water a day! We never travel without at least a quart of water. We always err on the side of having extra water - two quarts for strenuous trips and three quarts (or more) on very hot days or very strenuous trips. Two quarts go in the bicycle cages and 1-1/2 on a water bag which straps onto your back. If there are natural water sources on the tour and you are desperate, use water purification tablets. We coughed up the money for a compact, light-weight mini-water filtration system which is fine enough mesh to screen out Giardia.

Snacks. Considerably less critical than having water, nonetheless *the key consideration* is your willingness to slowly "run out of gas" on your tour. Personal favorite munchies are bananas, nuts, high-energy bars, electrolyte restorers (e.g., Gatorade -- buy the powder and mix your own), dried fruit (go easy on this one!) and trail mix (experiment and make your own special concoction).

Other. *The key consideration* of the items noted is to minimize the chance of getting lost. Put an odometer on your bike, plus bring a timepiece (or get an odometer with a timer). Take a compass and the 7.5-minute topographic maps which cover your tour. Mark the tour route on the topo and take a photographic copy of the tour writeup from this book with you (see more information in "Trip Planning" in the "GENERAL BIKING CONSIDERATIONS" section).

Mesa Peak Motorway Near Westside Entry

SANTA MONICA MOUNTAINS

GRIFFITH PARK & MOUNT LEE

Mt. Lee

At the eastern end of the Santa Monicas is one of the premier local parks, Griffith Park. It sports numerous hiking and equestrian trails, lush picnic areas, a famous zoo and observatory, golf course, Travel Town (train museum and rides), and many other offerings. Unfortunately, the entire park is strictly off-limits to mountain biking. There are officers who patrol the area and levy stiff fines for violators. Observe the rules and steer clear. **The good news is that there are numerous exciting and legal adventures westward in the Santa Monica Mountains as described beyond.**

TRIP #1 - FRANKLIN CANYON

GENERAL LOCATION: Location (Topo) - Beverly Hills, Van Nuys

LEVEL OF DIFFICULTY: Loop - Moderate
Distance - 6.6 miles; Time - 1-1/2 hours
Elevation gain - 800 feet

HIGHLIGHTS: This interesting loop trip leaves rustic Coldwater Canyon Park and dives from Coldwater Canyon Rd. to Franklin Canyon, a peaceful place buried in the Santa Monica Mountains Natural Recreation Area just minutes from the Los Angeles Civic Center. The pleasant tree- and chaparral-lined canyon is an excellent place to explore, enjoy a picnic or just pass through on a two-wheeler. The road out takes you on a moderate 500-foot winding climb through undeveloped environs and returns you to the start point.
TRAILHEAD: The best place to park is at the Tree People parking lot in Coldwater Canyon Park. The park is on the east side of the Coldwater Canyon Dr./Mulholland Dr. northernmost split (the roads fuse and also split further south). The park entrance is directly across from Franklin Canyon Dr. There are restrooms and water

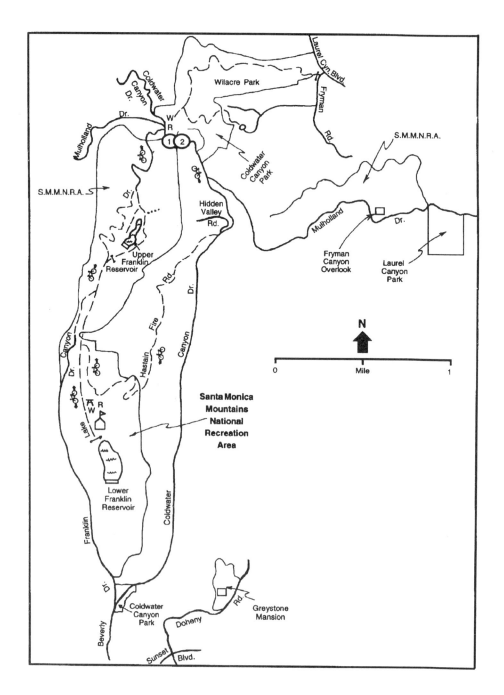

TRIP #1 - FRANKLIN CANYON

at Tree People and in Franklin Canyon. An alternative is to start from the parking area in Franklin Canyon.

The Tree People are avid conservationists, as the grounds show, and there is a Recycling Education Center, tree nursery, reference library and the famous Lectric Leopard compact car which is used to run general errands. However, the Tree People's forte is to foster the planting of trees (thousands each year around Los Angeles) to improve the environment, provide food, enhance the esthetic value of the region and to provide shade for bikers (ha!).

TRIP DESCRIPTION: **Tree People to Franklin Canyon.** Bike 0.5 mile and stay right at the southern Coldwater Canyon Dr./Mulholland Dr. split. Just below Hidden Valley Rd. (1.2) turn right at an unsigned dirt road with a large gate and follow it east through a new housing development. You work your way to a hill top and coast down a short distance on what is now the Hastain Fire Rd. Stay with the narrowing dirt road and take in the cross-canyon views. At a subsequent road divide (1.9), follow the fire road to the left which climbs a ridgeline southward above the canyon.

L.A. Civic Center from Chastain Fire Road

In 0.3 mile is the trip summit and a dynamite view of the sprawling L.A. Basin and the Civic Center! Pass up the trails which lead into the canyon and follow the clearly visible winding fire road downward, enjoying both the continued views of Los Angeles and the unblocked Franklin Canyon vistas below. Franklin Reservoir comes into view as you wind downward on dirt surface (some lightly-rutted and rocky stretches). About 0.5 mile from the summit (2.7) is a sharp switchback with an excellent vista point and a sign proclaiming *Hastain Trail: Ranger Station.* Bike past this hikers-only trail and continue the winding runout to a point where the road heads north and parallels Franklin Canyon. A short downhill places you in the canyon proper at paved Lake Dr. and a large gate (3.5). One-half mile further south is Lower Franklin Canyon Reservoir, the road terminus and the trip turnaround point. The well-groomed ranger station, picnic areas and parking are mid-way between the gate and reservoir.

Franklin Canyon is a place of peace and solitude under the spreading limbs of the sycamore trees and enveloped by chaparral-covered slopes, yet a short drive from the bustling L.A. metropolis. In times past, this was acorn-gathering and hunting territory for Indians who lived in the valleys. The Doheny family sold the land to Peter Lang and Earl Miller in 1977, two gentlemen who brought in long-horn cattle and exotic animals such as zebras, antelope, peacocks and ostriches to help them bide time while awaiting the development permits which never came. The Santa Monica Mountains Conservancy purchased the land from Lang and Miller, then sold it to the National Park Service in 1981. The canyon is now contained within the 105-acre Santa Monica Mountains National Recreation Area.

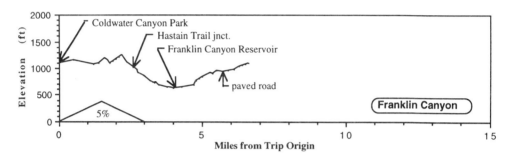

Franklin Canyon to Tree People. A steady 0.8-mile northbound upgrade takes you through the narrowing canyon to Franklin Canyon Dr. A turn right takes you to a nearby road split with the William O. Douglas Classroom and Sookie Goldwyn Nature Center to the right -- a preferred ride if the gates are open. The described route goes left (open daily from sunrise to sunset) and takes you up a sinuous deteriorating mixed asphalt, then packed dirt road through chaparral-covered hillside. While looking across the upper canyon, you see Mulholland Dr./Coldwater Canyon Dr. above and a large water tank perched high on the mountainside. You meet the road from the William O. Douglas Outdoor Classroom (5.9), return to paved surface, pass through a road gate into residential environs and pedal the final uphill to the end of Franklin Canyon Dr. Directly across the highway is the entry to the Tree People parking lot (6.6).

TRIP #2 - WILACRE PARK/IREDELL CANYON

GENERAL LOCATION: Location (Topo) - Beverly Hills, Van Nuys

LEVEL OF DIFFICULTY: Loop - Moderate
                         Distance - 3.3 miles; Time - 1 hour
                         Elevation gain - 450 feet

HIGHLIGHTS: This modest ridge and canyon tour provides gorgeous San Fernando Valley overlooks and a transit of both tree-covered Wilacre Park and partially-shaded Iredell Canyon. The common 0.3-mile inlet and outlet Coldwater Canyon Park segment is a serene stretch which may slow your progress in either direction as you check out the varied and abundant foliage.

TRAILHEAD: The best place to park is at the Tree People parking lot in Coldwater Canyon Park. The park is on the east side of the Coldwater Canyon Dr./Mulholland Dr. northernmost split (the roads fuse and also split further south). The park entrance is directly across from Franklin Canyon Dr. There are restrooms and water at Tree People and in Franklin Canyon. An option is to park on Fryman Rd. just south of Laurel Canyon Blvd. near the Maxwell Fire Rd. trailhead.

TRIP DESCRIPTION: **Tree People to Fryman Road.** From the northwest end of Coldwater Canyon Park (alongside the highway), maneuver your bike along the steps which drop down to the fire road. Turn right (the road left dies out in a few hundred feet) and follow the pleasant dirt path 0.3 mile beneath a mantle of varied tree cover. The road directs you to a wide-open plateau with an unobstructed view of Iredell Canyon and the Santa Monica Mountains. A turn left places you on Maxwell Fire Rd. with a short, gutsy climb ahead. From the level trip high point (0.5) is one of many grand looks into Coldwater Canyon and the sprawling San Fernando Valley.

Beyond is a one-mile winding downhill on a good dirt surface which gives way to a weathered asphalt path. On the way, the narrow fire road swings north and then east along a declining ridgeline, passing a mix of treed sections and more open areas with more great San Fernando Valley scenery. The lower road section leads you south, then east again through a lush mini-forest. The fire road reaches an abrupt end at a paved Fryman Rd. at a metal gate just south of Laurel Canyon Rd. (1.65).

Maxwell Fire Road

Iredell Canyon Return. Turn right and cycle a leisurely 0.2-mile asphalt uphill to Iredell St. where an earnest 0.6-mile upgrade greets you. (The road is lightly used and you can zig-zag your way across both lanes if the going gets tough.) On the way, up you pass a well-groomed hiker's trail before reaching the end of Iredell Ln. at a cul-de-sac. Pass through the gate onto ***Barker Fire Rd.*** and crank steeply uphill on a sturdy dirt surface with some rutting on the road's inside track. The tree-lined section gives way to chaparral-covered hillsides and the grade moderates as you wind your way back under tree cover. In 1/2-mile from the start of

Iredell Ln. you see the Maxwell Fire Rd. just above and to the right and realize that you have conquered most of the return uphill. The grade further flattens as you return to the overlook point junction (3.0). All that remains is the easy and shaded return to the start point in 0.3 mile.

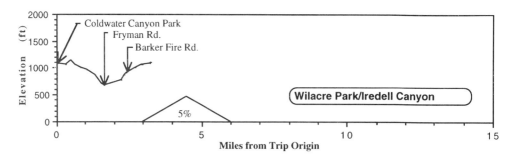

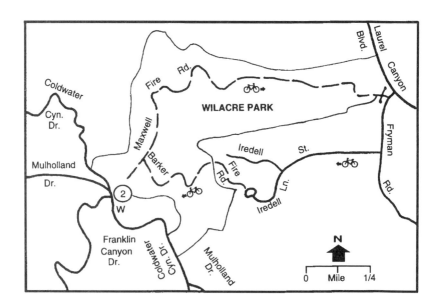

TRIP #2 - WILACRE PARK/IREDELL CANYON

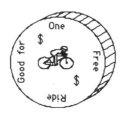

TRIP #3 - RUNYON CANYON PARK

<u>GENERAL LOCATION</u>:   Location (Topo) - Hollywood

<u>LEVEL OF DIFFICULTY</u>: Loop - moderate
Distance - 4.65 miles; time - 1-1/2 hours
Elevation gain - 1050 feet

<u>HIGHLIGHTS</u>: The moderate rating for this trip belies that fact that there is a tough initial assent and a smattering of technical riding -- however, the mileage is low. A taxing climb up scenic Runyon Canyon Rd. takes you to Mulholland Dr. From here you venture into lesser-used back trails, then visit two spectacular city overlooks before coasting back down to the trailhead.

Heading for the High Overlook

<u>TRAILHEAD</u>: From the Hollywood Fwy. (State Hwy. 2), exit west at Hollywood Blvd. and drive 1/2 mile past La Brea Ave. to Vista St. Turn right (north) and motor to street's end. From the Santa Monica Fwy. (Interstate Hwy. 10), turn north at La Brea Ave., drive to Hollywood Blvd. and continue as described above.

<u>TRIP DESCRIPTION</u>: **Runyon Canyon Road to Mulholland Drive.** Pass around the gated entrance and follow the narrow paved road to the left (right is a dirt path to the canyon bottom). Make an air-sucking climb past numerous canyon overlooks on an exposed road which follows the westside canyon contour. You cross above the top of the canyon, then swing around a ridge and continue climbing to the dirt junction to the right (south) which takes you to a superb Los Angeles Basin "lower" lookout (0.8). Save the overlook visit for later and continue climbing, when you can look down into an adjoining, highly-developed canyon. In a short distance, you pass a trail junction to the left (a future return route), a locked gate with a walker/biker

25

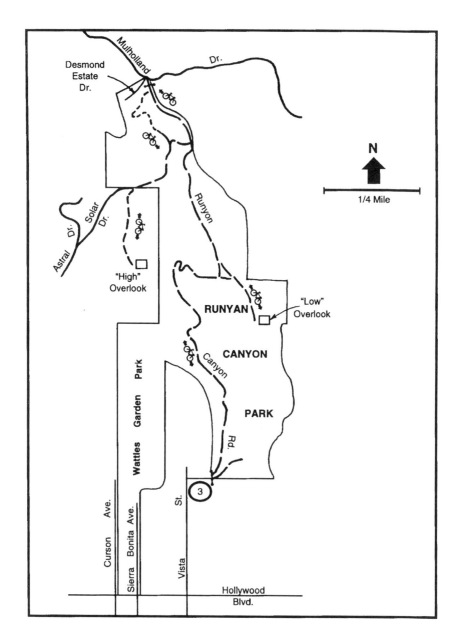

TRIP #3 - RUNYON CANYON PARK

passage, and enjoy a moderating climb. The winding road meets an attractive open wrought iron gate near Mulholland Dr. with a *Runyon Canyon Rd.* sign for southbound bikers (1.5).

The Wandering Return to Runyon Canyon Road. Follow the steep, rocky trail to the left (west) of the gate and pump up to the ridgeline. At the first trail junction, stay left and follow a very steep and sometimes badly-carved out path (biking for experienced, technical riders only -- otherwise walk your bike). At the left of the trail is a large power line structure and dirt Solar Dr. where you turn right. A little further downhill is a dirt road junction to the left (south) which you will visit later (1.8).

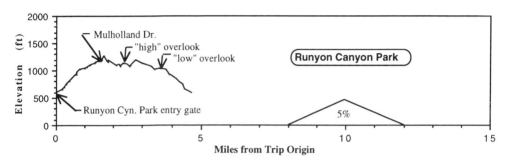

Follow Solar Dr. under the power lines about 0.3 mile and turn left onto a dirt road which takes you out to the trip's "high" overlook point at a massive rock structure. From here you get an impressive look at the "low" overlook below and across Runyon Canyon, as well as the incoming route from the trailhead (2.35). Return 0.55 mile to the junction mentioned above and turn right, dropping back to paved Runyon Canyon Rd. in 0.1 mile. Return to the "lower" overlook junction and veer left onto the dirt trail to that popular view point. To the east is a great view of the Hollywood sign on Mt. Lee and the Griffith Park Observatory beyond. Retrace your path to Runyon Canyon Rd. and enjoy a well-deserved coast back to the trailhead (4.65).

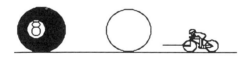

TRIP #4 - DIRT MULHOLLAND

GENERAL LOCATION: Location (Topo) - Van Nuys, Canoga Park

LEVEL OF DIFFICULTY: One-way - moderate
Distance - 9.1 miles; Time - 1-1/2 hours
Elevation gain - 750 feet

HIGHLIGHTS: We suggest that you explore the dirt eastern spine of the Santa Monica Mountains before taking on the nifty trails that spin off from it. Consider this as familiarization with the territory, as well as a nine-mile stint with the entire San Fernando Valley continuously laid out north and below you. Entirely on fire road (mixed-quality surface), the route immediately climbs to San Vicente Mountain,

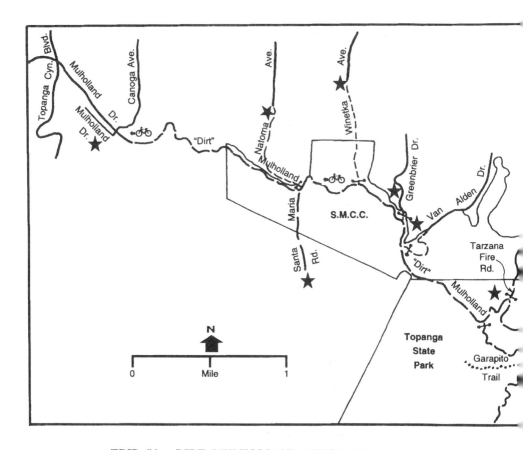

TRIP #4 - DIRT MULHOLLAND (WEST SIDE)

passing below a retired Nike missile site. It then follows a high-line traverse to the trip's high point just east of San Vicente Mountain Park and winds its way east seven more miles to an outlet at Topanga Canyon Blvd. There is one testy upgrade on the westside trip segment just east of the Temescal Canyon Fire Rd. junction.

TRAILHEAD: From the San Diego Fwy., exit at Mulholland Dr., turn west and continue 2.1 miles to a "Y" junction at Encino Hills Dr. Turn left and uphill, finding parking alongside the dirt/broken asphalt road. There is no dependable source of water on this tour until you reach Topanga Canyon Blvd. at trip's end.

TRIP DESCRIPTION: **Eastside: Trailhead to Temescal Canyon Fire Road.** An immediate uphill takes you past the gated (and typically unsigned) *Canyonback Rd.*

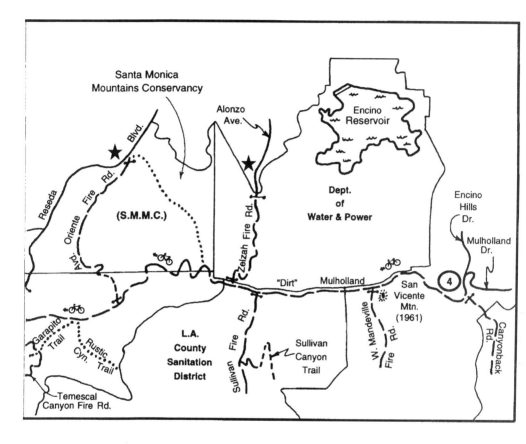

TRIP #4 - DIRT MULHOLLAND (EAST SIDE)

entry (0.1), a large concrete blockhouse and a winding climb to a summit near the *W. Mandeville Fire Rd.* entry (1.0). There is a Nike site just south, which is open to the public and has a restroom. You share the road with numerous bikers and some motorized traffic (legal along the full length of Dirt Mulholland) in this area. The relatively-exposed ridge ride, with a steady diet of canyon and San Fernando Valley vistas, is characteristic of the entire ride. You climb again to unimproved San Vicente Mountain Park where there is a very steep uphill off-shoot trail which leads south to a great Sullivan Canyon overlook. Near the trip crest is the *Sullivan Fire Rd./Farmer's Fire Rd.* (Sullivan Canyon trail gate) (1.9). On the ensuing 1.9-mile downhill, you pass entries to *Zelzah Fire Rd.* (2.1), *Farmer Ridge Fire Rd.* (2.2) (no outlet), *Avd. Oriente Fire Rd.* (Caballero Canyon) (3.6), and *Garapito Trail* (no bikes)/*Rustic Canyon Trail* (not maintained) (3.8). A 0.7-mile, 250-ft, climb winding from this low point on a saddle leads past the *Tarzana Fire Rd.* junction (4.4) to the *Temescal Canyon Fire Rd.* entry (4.7).

Near San Vicente Mountain Park

Westside: Temescal Canyon Fire Road to Topanga Canyon Blvd. The remaining 4.4-mile segment drops steadily 700 ft. along the ridgeline, dumping into Calabasas at Topanga Canyon Blvd. alongside a treed open area that makes for a pleasant tour-ending stop. Along this more exposed segment, you pass a massive water tank with Owen Brooks Rd. (dead end) just to its west (5.4), a graded parking area with the *Van Alden Rd.* extension just north (5.7) and a fork at paved *Greenbrier Dr.* (5.8) (stay left on the dirt road). The route pulls back away from the edge of civilization, passes the *Winnetka Ave.* dirt extension (6.2), *Santa Maria Ave* (marked with a hand-painted sign when we passed through) and *Natoma Ave.* (6.8), and enters the south edge of residential Calabassas at Trinidad Rd. (7.7). Stay left at the fork with Alhama Dr., return to pavement and cruise downhill to Topanga Canyon Blvd.

Trip Option: Dirt Mulholland "Play Area." For experienced technical riders in excellent shape, there is a network of trails just east of the Natoma Ave./Santa Maria Rd. entries. The sometimes-overgrown single tracks criss-cross the area on the ridges at the head of Santa Maria Canyon, accessible just off of Dirt Mulholland. No route is defined here -- pick your direction as you go. Beware, there are numerous steep drops on rocky and sporadically-rutted trailway.

Access to Dirt Mulholland:

Access from West Los Angeles. The access routes from the south are described as an integral part of the *Santa Monica Mountains-East* tours.

Access from San Fernando Valley. From east to west, the access routes to Dirt Mulholland are as follows -- distances measured from Ventura Fwy. (U.S. 101):

Zelzah Fire Rd. Exit south at White Oak Ave. and drive one mile to Valley Vista Blvd. Turn west (right), drive 0.1 mile to Alonzo Ave. and turn left. Follow Alonzo

Ave. south to a fire gate at road's end. Pass through the neatly rolled-back section of the chain-link fence to enter DWP property. From the gate, bike a sandy-surfaced road to a steep set of switchbacks 0.8 mile and 400 feet to Dirt Mulholland.

Avd. Oriente Fire Rd./Tarzana Fire Rd. Go southbound on Reseda Blvd. Just south of Golf Course Rd. (alongside Braemar Country Club), park off the road near the **Caballero Canyon Trail** sign. Follow the trail below Reseda Blvd. South and track Caballero Canyon 1.5 miles (the last 0.8 mile is very steep) for the Avd. Oriente Fire Rd. access (550 feet elevation gain). An easy alternate is to continue driving south 1.2 miles on Reseda Blvd. to a dead end and bike 0.1 steep mile on Tarzana Fire Rd. to the crest. There is a porta-pottie at the latter trailhead.

Van Alden Rd. Exit south on Tampa Ave. and turn left (east) at Wells Dr. in 1/4 mile. Head south on Van Alden Ave. to a dead end in 2-1/2 miles. Follow the trail at the south end of the cul-de-sac 0.3 mile and 150 feet to Dirt Mulholland.

Greenbrier Dr. Follow Van Alden Ave. above, turning right (west) in 1-1/2 miles from Wells Dr. on Gleneagles Dr., then left on Greenbrier Dr. to a fire gate at the end of the cul-de-sac (one mile total from Van Alden Ave.). A 0.1 mile, 50 foot, climb on a dirt road leads to Dirt Mulholland.

Winnetka Ave. Entry/Exit

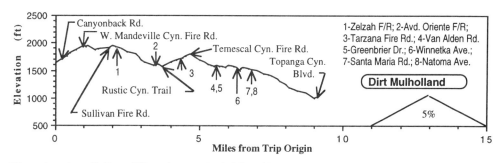

Winnetka Ave. Follow Winnetka south 1-3/4 miles to road's end at a large blocking guard rail. Pass around the guard rail and follow a very steep short drop to a saddle. Both trails at the nearby trail fork climb sharply to the ridge which intersects with Dirt Mulholland. This entry is 0.7 mile and has 300 feet elevation gain.

31

Natoma Ave. Take Serrania Ave. (De Soto Ave. north of the Ventura Fwy.) southbound as it transitions into Wells Dr. In 1-1/2 miles is Natoma Ave., where you turn right (south) and go 3/4 mile to its paved terminus. Bike a steep 0.4 mile where the single track levels somewhat. In 0.8 total mile and 350 feet elevation gain is the Dirt Mulholland entry.

Access from Topanga Canyon Boulevard. *Santa Maria Rd.* The signed entry is 3/4 mile north of Cheney Dr. and 3/4 mile south of Entrado Dr. Park off the road and keep well clear of all driveways. The mixed paved/dirt road climbs 400 feet in 2-1/4 miles to Dirt Mulholland.

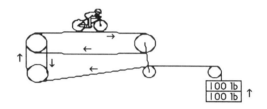

TRIP #5 - ABOVE MANDEVILLE CANYON

GENERAL LOCATION: Topos - Beverly Hills, Van Nuys, Canoga Park, Topanga

LEVEL OF DIFFICULTY: One way - Moderate
Distance - 9.0 miles; Time - 2 hours
Elevation gain - 1100 ft.

HIGHLIGHTS: This ridge-runner special follows good-quality fire roads above Mandeville Canyon on its east and west sides with a short visit to Dirt Mulholland. The east side tour on Canyonback Rd. passes through the upscale Mountaingate development, then crosses an extended saddle before climbing to a peak above Dirt Mulholland. A brief downhill and an ensuing climb along Dirt Mulholland takes you to a retired Nike missile site along W. Mandeville Canyon Fire Rd. A couple of short climbs along this view-laden road are followed by a long downhill runout back to the upper reaches of Brentwood. An option to visit Mandeville Canyon is also provided.

TRAILHEAD: From Sunset Blvd., turn north on N. Kenter Ave. Continue 2.2 miles up that steep road to a locked fire gate and park on the street.

If a true loop is exercised, cyclists must return via surface streets -- Westridge Rd. to Mandeville Canyon Rd. to Sunset Blvd., then repeat what is a tiring 2.2-mile, 750-ft, climb on N. Kenter Ave. to the Canyonback Rd. trailhead. (This becomes the toughest segment of the tour!) The full loop is 15.6 miles. The easier option is to leave a vehicle at the fire gate on Westridge Rd., 2.3 miles north and up from Sunset Blvd.

TRIP DESCRIPTION: **North Kenter Road Trailhead to Mountaingate.** An immediate short, steep upgrade on the wide fire road gives way to a brief downhill, then a steady 1.8-mile workout uphill which crests at a water tank above the posh community of Mountaingate. On the way, you pass through an open gate on a saddle (1.2) and an open chain link fence. The exposed ridge ride provides an array of views into Mandeville Canyon to the west (with the W. Mandeville Canyon Fire Rd. return route clearly evident on the paralleling ridge) and Kenter Canyon eastward. There are numerous spurs off to the nearby electrical transmission towers, however

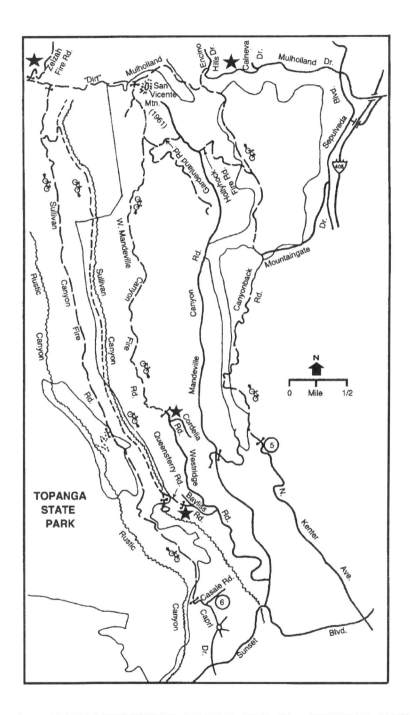

TRIP #5 - ABOVE MANDEVILLE CANYON; TRIP #6 - SULLIVAN CANYON

Canyonback Rd. is wide and easy to follow. The graded dirt road turns to pavement just above the water tank and buzzes downhill to a locked gate (2.1).

Mountaingate to Dirt Mulholland. Turn left (north), pedal 0.5 mile to the end of paved Canyonback Rd. and pass through another locked gate on the northside of the tennis court. A steep climb takes you to a flat overlook of the Mountaingate Country Club and golf course below, where there also is a full, unobstructed sweeping view from the San Fernando Valley to the eastern Santa Monica Mountains to West Los Angeles (2.8). Pass through an open gate and follow a moderating grade on the ridge. Near a large rock pile below a small rise to the east is the *Hollyhock Fire Rd.* junction (3.1), which wanders off to the left (west) into Mandeville Canyon. Continue straight ahead to a ridgeline summit in about 0.2 mile and observe the old Nike missile site on the ridge across the canyon head -- this is at the destination summit. Cross a saddle at the upper eastern edge of Mandeville Canyon (3.8), take in the great San Fernando Valley panorama from a flat turnout 0.1 mile on the ensuing upgrade, and follow the semicircular traverse up the side of the mountain to a view-laden summit in 0.2 mile. A short downhill follows which leads you to *Dirt Mulholland* (4.2).

Canyonback Road below Mulholland Crest

Dirt Mulholland and the W. Mandeville Canyon Fire Rd. Return. A winding 0.6-mile, 320-ft. upgrade takes you to the locked fire gate at the head of the return ridge route (see "Dirt Mulholland" for detail of that segment). Pass through the gate and cycle alongside the decommissioned Nike air defense missile site, a symbol of the "hottest" part of the Cold War in the '50's and '60's. A hasty broken-paved section gives way to a turn SSW onto a graded dirt fire road and the first glimpses of the upcoming ridgeline traverse. Pass a locked gate to the right (5.3) which drops to the power transmission towers below and dead ends. A clear view of the developed upper section of Mandeville Canyon pops into view to the left (east), then you bike directly below the power lines and pass the fenced *Gardenland Rd.* junction to the left (5.7).

A 0.4-mile, 180-ft. uphill is followed by a drop along the west side of the ridge and a clear view of Sullivan Fire Rd. across Sullivan Canyon -- you will roughly parallel this high road for the trip's remainder. Just past a saddle with a clear Mountaingate

34

vista, you make a short climb, then coast another two miles on the west side below the spine of the ridge. This brings you to the last of many overlooks of West Los Angeles before you return to civilization and the Westridge Rd. fire gate (9.0).

Retired Nike Missile Site

Hollyhock Fire Rd. and Gardenland Rd. A moderate route variation is to take the *Hollyhock Fire Rd.* junction (3.1) and drop 430 ft. into Mandeville Canyon, then bike up Gardenland Rd. to *W. Mandeville Canyon Fire Rd.* (440 ft. ascent). Hollyhock Fire Rd. winds downward 0.8 mile before passing through a pleasant tree grove to a fire gate near a private residence (street sign *3700 N. Hollyhock Pl.*). To reach Gardenland Rd., turn right (north) on Mandeville Canyon Rd. and go 0.3 mile. Follow the fire road at the left side of the cul-de-sac and stay right at the road junction at 0.5 mile (the other is a power tower junction leading steeply downhill with no outlet). Climb past another power line access road (staying right) before reaching W. Mandeville Canyon Fire Rd. 0.9 mile from the Mandeville Canyon Rd. entry.

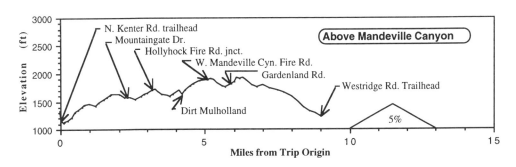

35

TRIP #6 - SULLIVAN CANYON

GENERAL LOCATION: Location (Topo) - Topanga, Canoga Park

LEVEL OF DIFFICULTY: One way - moderate; Time - 2-1/2 hours
Distance - 11.2 miles
Elevation gain - 1300 ft.

HIGHLIGHTS: A combination ridge route (Sullivan Fire Rd.) and canyon traverse (Sullivan Canyon Trail), this dandy route is named after one of the most scenic canyons in the Santa Monica Mountains -- Sullivan Canyon. The ridge ride is a good workout and chock-full of unobstructed mountain and canyon views. The canyon trail is steep and lightly technical on the upper reaches, but settles into a marvelous, good-quality, single-track as it plies the rustic tree-canopied canyon.

TRAILHEAD: From Sunset Blvd., turn north at Monaco Dr./San Remo Dr. (next intersection west of Allenford Ave.), branch left immediately on Monaco Dr. and continue to a small traffic circle. Follow Capri Dr. to Casale Rd. and park along that street, being mindful of the numerous tow-away signs. The trailhead is at the west end of Casale Rd. at a locked fire gate, where signs note the entry to Topanga State Park and warn travelers of mountain lions in the area. The trailhead is 3/4 mile and 230 ft. above Sunset Blvd. Bring water as there are no reliable sources on the tour. Do not save this ride for a rainy day!!

If you want to bike the full loop, including the paved route between inlet and outlet trailheads, return up Queensferry Rd. to Bayliss Rd. and coast down Westridge Rd. to Mandeville Canyon Rd. A right turn (west) on Sunset Blvd. and retracing your way up Monaco Dr./San Remo Dr. makes this a total 14.6-mile loop with about 300 ft. added elevation gain. Otherwise, park your shuttle vehicle near the fire gate/road gate along Queensferry Rd. at the outlet point.

Lower Sullivan Fire Road

TRIP DESCRIPTION: **Sullivan Fire Road.** Beyond the gate, you follow a graded-dirt fire road 0.9 mile to a crest with views left (west) into Rustic Canyon. A 1/2-mile downhill greets you before you begin the long steady pull to Dirt Mulholland. While traveling below the west side of the ridge, you pass one of several single tracks heading to Rustic Canyon (1.6), then take in the view across Sullivan Canyon to the W. Mandeville Fire Rd. trailhead area -- this road will parallel your route for most of the uphill.

You pass the Camp Josepho (Boy Scouts) portal /roadway at 2.4 miles, then begin a butt-kicking, two-mile upgrade with a scattered set of short flats along the way. A 0.4-mile pedal along an exposed saddle is followed by a continued steep traverse on the west side of the ridge spine. A look up Rustic Canyon frames the first San Fernando Valley vistas (4.6) as the trail moderates, then levels -- Dirt Mulholland looms in the distance. A long and level saddle takes you past the *Sullivan Canyon Trail* junction (5.5), followed by a mild uphill to the locked fire gate at *Dirt Mulholland* (6.0).

Sullivan Canyon

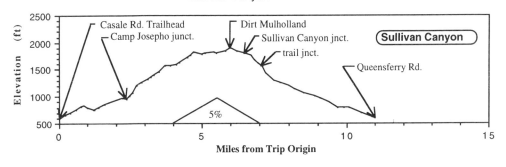

Sullivan Canyon Return. Retrace the route and turn east at the paved *Sullivan Canyon Trail* entry. The single track plummets downhill on a more technical, rocky surface (a rugged uphill, should you decide to reverse the route), switchbacking to a sharp turn south on a terse concrete section (7.1). The trail north (left) at this point has no outlet, so you continue downhill alongside a creek bed and enter the ever-more-lush canyon bottom. The trail drops through an unforgettable mix of overhanging oaks, smaller tree cover and vegetation as you hop in and out of the creek bed. The canyon walls reach down closer to the trail as you bike directly into the creek bed (there was an inch or two of flowing water when we passed

37

through a week after the last prior winter rain). The canyon widens as you cycle on a light shale surface before reaching a wide trail split (11.0). On the right is the Sullivan Canyon Dam and a blocking chain link fence. Your route goes left on a steep paved uphill which is Queensferry Rd. A 0.2-mile crank deposits you at the fire gate/road gate entry where you return to residential Brentwood. (Note the posted signs on the road gate which announce, *Private Road* and *No Trespassing*. These apply to motor vehicle entry only.)

Helmet   No Helmet

TRIP #7 - TEMESCAL RIDGE AND TRAILER CANYON

GENERAL LOCATION: Location (Topo) - Canoga Park, Topanga

LEVEL OF DIFFICULTY: One way - moderate
                                Distance - 7.3 miles; Time - 1-1/2 hours
                                Elevation gain - 500 feet

HIGHLIGHTS: Starting from Dirt Mulholland, this tour follows good-quality Temescal Fire Rd. on a winding ridgeline tour up to the "Hub," the focal point junction for local tours. Beyond is a continued mild uphill which takes you by Cathedral Rock, a superb perch and Temescal Peak, the highest point in Topanga State Park. More scenic ridge running leads you to the Trailer Canyon Fire Rd. junction where you enjoy a steep winding runout on fire road of variable quality and width. The descent provides interesting views into Quarry Canyon and the developed environs of Santa Ynez Canyon, the trip outlet.

TRAILHEAD: From the San Fernando Valley, enter Dirt Mulholland via the 0.1-mile steep and rutted Tarzana Fire Rd. entry (see the "Dirt Mulholland" tour). Turn right (west) and climb 0.3 mile to the fire-gated entry to Temescal Fire Rd. at the local summit. The sign at the gate reads *Topanga State Park*. There is also a warning sign about mountain lions. (The trip mileage noted below in the "Trip Description" starts from the parking area at the end of Reseda Blvd.)

From the Malibu/Pacific Palisades area, turn off Pacific Coast Hwy. (PCH) onto W. Sunset Blvd. and continue 0.6 mile to Palisades Dr. Turn left (north) and follow the road 2.5 miles, then go left on Vereda de la Montura and right almost immediately at Michael Ln. The *Trailer Canyon* sign is about 0.5 mile further just to the east of a small reservoir. The trip is strenuous in this direction. (A hearty addition is to take the 3.1-mile, 700-ft. paved climb from W. Sunset Blvd. to the trailhead).

TRIP DESCRIPTION: **Dirt Mulholland to the "Hub."** The good-condition fire road takes you 0.4 mile downhill to a scenic saddle where the *Garapito Trail* (hiking only) crosses, then back uphill to a second saddle below a steep incline (2.1). A 0.3-mile testy climb below a ridge to the west guides you up to *Hub Junction* or the "Hub," a flat on the ridge top with porta-pottie and posting board describing the local environs. To the hard right is a marker stating *Eagle Rock Loop/North Loop Trail* (uphill), the next right has a marker noting *To Backbone Trail/Eagle Springs* (downhill) (see the "Eagle Rock Loop" ride for the full loop description). Continuing roughly straight ahead (south) is a third posting proclaiming *T e m e s c a l Ridge/Backbone Trail,* which is the destination route (2.45).

Hub Junction

The Hub to the Trailer Canyon Junction. A few hundred yards beyond is Cathedral Rock; a classic diversion is to pass the monolith, take a short and steep path back toward the summit through a gap in the rocks and enjoy the Rustic Canyon Vista from its broad shelf top.

You continue on a nearly flat ridgeline traverse taking in continued canyon vistas, pass the *Will Rogers Trail* entry (newly opened to bikers) on a saddle (2.9) and reach a hiking path on the left which leads to the Temescal Peak summit, the highest point in Topanga State Park. More ridgeline biking takes you under roughly-paralleling power lines and past several smaller trails which access those poles. In 2.1 miles from Hub Junction is an open metal gate and then a short off-shoot trail to the right leading to a superb vista point. In 0.2 mile is a view south of an antenna-spiked facility on a mountain top (known as "Radio Peak") and an unsigned road split (4.75).

Trailer Canyon. Temescal Fire Rd. continues along a series of ridges and turns to a hikers-only trail in 1-1/2 miles. That trail outlet is at Temescal Gateway Park. Our route turns right onto the *Trailer Canyon Fire Rd.* and begins an immediate descent toward the bowels of Trailer Canyon. The next 1.6 miles of downhill take you on good quality fire road to a closed gate. There is a mountain lion warning sign here. Along the way are numerous looks down the sheer drops into Quarry Canyon and across into developed Santa Ynez Canyon and a sharp switchback at 0.9 mile from the trail entry. Far across the canyon is the "Wirebreak," a cleared swath near the power lines which hikers dread -- 800-ft. elevation change in less than a half mile. The next 0.8 downhill mile is on a varying width road with a couple of short

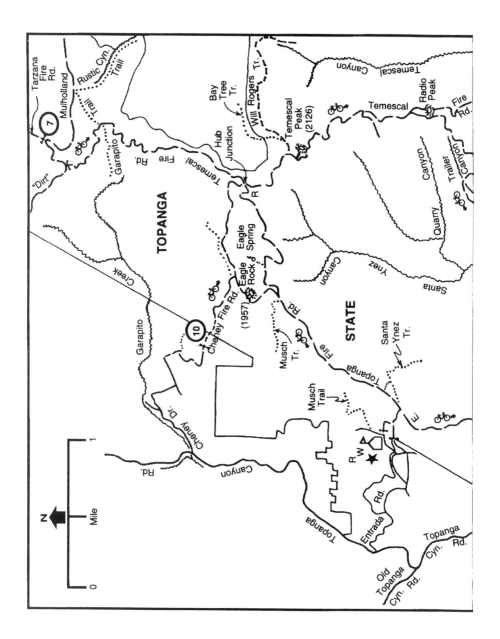

TRIP #7 - TEMESCAL RIDGE AND TRAILER CANYON &

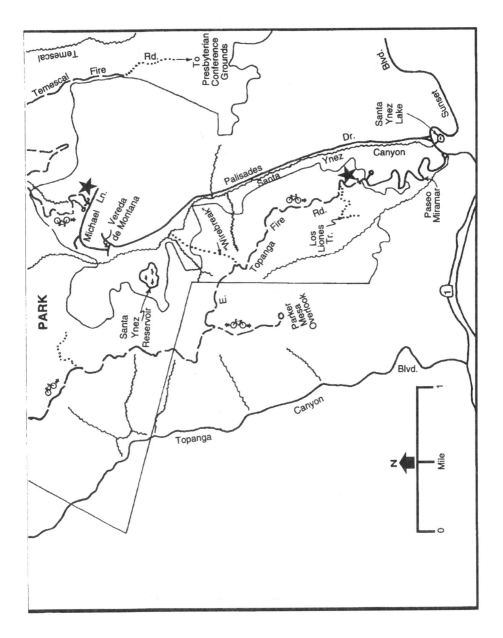

TRIP #10 - CHENEY FIRE ROAD/EAST TOPANGA FIRE ROAD

rocky segments and along the canyon creek. The locked outlet gate is at paved Michael Ln. where the dirt tour ends (7.1).

Trailer Canyon

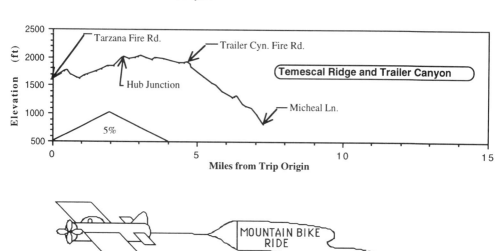

TRIP #8 - TRIPPET RANCH/EAGLE ROCK LOOP

<u>GENERAL LOCATION</u>:   Location (Topo) - Topanga

<u>LEVEL OF DIFFICULTY</u>: Loop - moderate
Distance - 5.9 miles; Time - 1-1/2 hours
Elevation gain - 950 ft.

<u>HIGHLIGHTS</u>: The highlight of this modestly-challenging tour is the close-up visit to Eagle Rock. To get there, you enjoy an easy rolling-ridge run, a visit to Eagle Springs, a testy climb to the "Hub," and a scenic ride around the "rock" itself. A scenic downhill returns you to E. Topanga Fire Rd. and the trip origin at Trippet Ranch.

<u>TRAILHEAD</u>: The loop can be accessed from Trailer Canyon Fire Rd. ("Temescal Ridge/Trailer Canyon" trip), Cheney Fire Rd. ("Cheney Fire Road/E. Topanga Fire Road" tour) or Trippet Ranch as is described here. From Topanga Canyon Blvd. turn right (east) at Entrada Rd. (just north of Greenleaf Canyon Rd. and 0.3 mile north of the Old Topanga Rd. junction). Wind uphill to the park boundary and pass two lower parking lots. At the next junction, bear left on Entrada Rd., then left again into the pay parking lot. The fire road entry is at the southeast end of the lot.

Eagle Rock Loop

<u>TRIP DESCRIPTION</u>: **Trippet Ranch to Eagle Springs Junction.** Bike to the junction with E. Topanga Fire Rd. at the plentifully-treed "Latitude." The sign here notes: *2 miles to Eagle Rock, 2.2 to miles to Waterfall Santa Ynez Trail* (no bikes), *4.8 to Mulholland, 8 miles to Temescal Conference Grounds* (no bikes); *8.7 miles to Will*

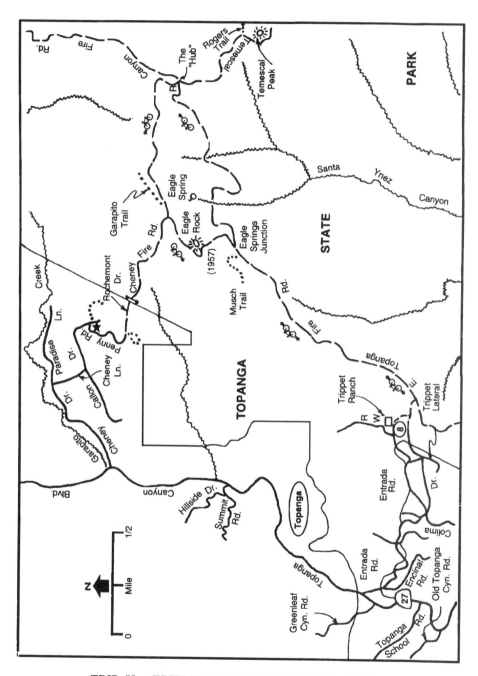

TRIP #8 - TRIPPET RANCH/EAGLE ROCK LOOP

Rogers (no bikes), *3 miles to Parker Mesa Overlook, 4.8 miles to Pacific Palisades* (Paseo Miramar). Turn left (north), pass the marked *Santa Ynez Trail* junction (0.5), bike above the Trippet Ranch area and follow a modest up and down leading to the *Eagle Springs Junction* (1.6). At the junction is a sign which reads: *Backbone Trail to Eagle Springs - 1/2 mi.* The trailway off to the left just before reaching the road split is the Musch Trail (hiking only).

Eagle Rock Loop and Back. Turn right and follow a curving route downhill with nice views into the very upper reaches of Santa Ynez Canyon. There are interesting views of Eagle Rock. The mildly-rutted road makes a sharp turn and drops to a low point where Eagle Springs intersects our route near a deteriorating water tank. When we visited in Feb. 1995, the springs drainage had carved out a 1-2 foot wide, several-feet deep trough across the road, forcing us to divert above the normal route. A hiking couple had also spotted a large rattlesnake on the road just before we arrived.

A one-mile, 470-foot winding and exposed climb from Eagle Springs takes you to *Hub Junction* or the "Hub" (2.9). On this flat you'll find a porta-pottie, probably several other riders and/or hikers, and a bevy of trail signs. The trail just north of our outlet from Eagle Springs is marked *Eagle Rock Loop - North Loop Trail - 1.1 Km.* Follow that route up and onto a scenic ridge and continue to a flat with a grand view of Eagle Rock and the canyons to the south. A steep and sometimes rough and rocky downhill takes you further west where you pass the *Garapito Hiking Trail* and *Cheney Fire Rd.* (3.9) junctions.

You have "front-row seats" to view Eagle Rock as you pedal uphill and around to the marked backside hiking entry to this monolith. Consider a walking diversion and join the hikers at the top of the "rock." Continue on and follow the fire road on a steep scenic downgrade which soon places you back at the *Eagle Springs Junction* (4.3). All that remains is to retrace your incoming route on E. Topanga Fire Rd.

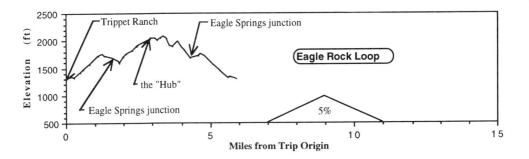

45

TRIP #9 - WILL ROGERS/BACKBONE TRAIL

GENERAL LOCATION: Location (Topo) - Canoga Park, Topanga

LEVEL OF DIFFICULTY: One way - moderate-strenuous [patchy technical sections]
Distance - 9.2 miles; time - 2 hours
Elevation gain - 900 feet

HIGHLIGHTS: From the San Fernando Valley, a short climb to Dirt Mulholland and diversion to the Temescal Ridge Fire Rd. leads you to Hub Junction, the entry point to the Topanga State Park universe. A half-mile traverse leads you to the Will Rogers Backbone Trail junction where you start 5.3 miles of "single track heaven." A series of climbs and drops provide gorgeous canyon vistas as you swing east and then south. A fantastic overlook that is the congregation point for both hikers and bikers is followed by a short bridge crossing and a nose-dive down to the end of the Backbone Trail at the Inspiration Point Loop Trail. A 0.9 mile runout on this downhill dirt road leads to the trip terminus at Will Rogers State Park. Pat yourself on the back, stroll the grounds and enjoy a well-deserved picnic!

Upper Will Rogers Trail

TRAILHEAD: From the San Fernando Valley, enter Dirt Mulholland via the 0.1-mile steep and rutted Tarzana Fire Rd. entry (see the "Dirt Mulholland" tour). Turn right (west) and climb 0.3 mile to the fire-gated entry to Temescal Fire Rd. at the local summit. The sign at the gate reads *Topanga State Park*. There is also a warning sign about mountain lions. (The trip mileage noted below in the "Trip Description" starts from the parking area at the end of Reseda Blvd.)

From the Malibu/Pacific Palisades area, turn off Pacific Coast Hwy. (PCH) onto W. Sunset Blvd. and continue 4.6 miles to Will Rogers State Park Rd. Turn left and continue to the pay parking area. The most convenient trail entry is near the east side of the main parking lot. Follow the asphalt road north along the white fence to the first intersection in 0.2 mile. Turn left or a hard right and uphill -- either direction on this Inspiration Loop Trail takes you to the Will Rogers/Backbone Trail. When biked in this direction, the ride is rated as strenuous.

Will Rogers moved to the Sunset Blvd. area in 1928 and expanded the family's small weekend cottage into the current 31-room estate. The grounds and ranch buildings are maintained as they were when the family lived there, including Will's

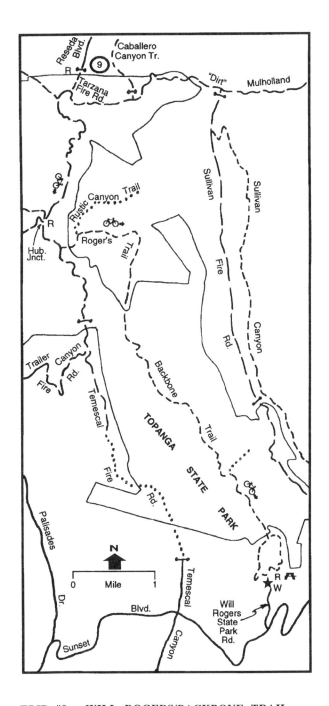

TRIP #9 - WILL ROGERS/BACKBONE TRAIL

local polo grounds. The actor-philosopher-good-will spokesman died in a plane crash in 1935. The ranch became Will Rogers State Historic Park in 1944 after his widow died. The park sports ranch tours, nature trails, a nature center, horse stables and plush lawns under scattered tree cover. Picnic tables are available for post-ride wind down. Water and restrooms can be found near the Visitor Center.

TRIP DESCRIPTION: Dirt Mulholland to the "**Hub.**" The good-condition fire road takes you 0.4 mile downhill to a scenic saddle where the *Garapito Trail* (hiking only) crosses, then back uphill to a second saddle below a steep incline (2.1). A 0.3-mile testy climb below a ridge to the west guides you up to **Hub Junction** or the "Hub," a flat on the ridge top with porta-pottie and posting board describing the local environs.

Signed Overlook

Hard right is a marker stating *Eagle Rock Loop/North Loop Trail* (uphill), the next right has a marker noting *To Backbone Trail/Eagle Springs* (downhill) (see the "Eagle Rock Loop" ride for the full loop description). Continuing roughly straight ahead (south) is a third posting proclaiming *Temescal Ridge/Backbone Trail*, which is the destination route (2.45).

The Hub to the Will Rogers/Backbone Trail. A few hundred yards beyond is Cathedral Rock; a classic diversion to is pass the monolith, take a short and steep path back toward the summit through a gap in the rocks and enjoy the Rustic Canyon Vista from its broad top shelf. You continue on a nearly flat ridgeline traverse taking in continued canyon vistas, then reach the *Will Rogers/Backbone Trail* entry on a saddle (2.9).

Will Rogers/Backbone Trail to the Inspiration Point Loop Trail. The sign on the trail continuation south says *Temescal Ridge Trail/Conference Grounds -*

48

7 Km; back the way you came, a posting notes *Backbone Trail/Eagle Junction - 2.9 Km*. Left (east) is your route and a sign noting **Backbone Trail to Will Rogers - 9.6 Km**. This trail, recently-opened to bikers, is a hiker's favorite. It is also narrow and deserves your undivided attention and courtesy to other users in order to keep it open!

A short steep drop and follow-up climb on a single track leads you eastward with grand views north to the feeder canyons of Rustic Canyon. There are also over-the-shoulder views of Cathedral Rock and the Hub. The narrow trail flattens and continues east, providing striking Rustic Canyon views, then bends south and crosses above the head of Temescal Canyon below and to the right (3.9). Across and above the canyon is the imposing Temescal Ridge. (See "Temescal Ridge and Trailer Canyon" tour.) You traverse below a ridge to the east on a generally-steep downhill for 1.5 miles, pulling away from Temescal Canyon. This segment is on good single-track surface with scattered sections of rutting and a little slate.

A short, steep climb atop an east-west ridge (5.5) is followed by a small saddle crossing and a traverse through a lush area where the trees and brush have been cut away from the narrow trail. Rustic Canyon appears to the left (east) and Sullivan Ridge (see the "Sullivan Canyon" ride) beyond. At (6.8), pass above a small canyon, head to the right and traverse for 0.4 mile, following the contour of the mountain on your left. You climb to a cutaway mountain section and pass above a rock pile on a very short, testy section of trail. Consider walking your bike here as a spill might give you a first-hand look at the geology 20-30 feet further downhill!

The first peek at the Santa Monica area opens up and you climb to a majestic flat with a signed overlook (7.6). This is a favorite hiker and biker collection point. You are required to walk your bike down the steep switchback beyond, crossing the first of many scattered railroad-tie water bars to come, and cross a wooden walking bridge. About 10 yards beyond is a trail split; take the left fork and switchback southeast and downhill, crossing more scattered water bars on a ridgeline. Leaving the ridge, you take a very steep downhill (keep a lookout for hikers) and drop down to a large dirt road. This is the effective terminus of the Backbone Trail (8.2).

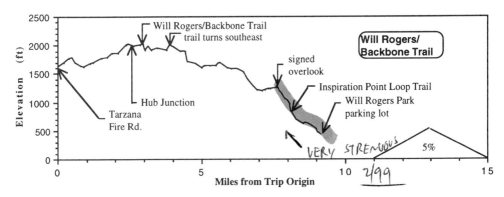

Inspiration Loop Trail to Will Rogers State Park. Looking back the way you came is a sign noting *Entering Topanga State Park* and a mountain lion warning. Across the road is a marker with ***Inspiration Point Loop Trail*** pointing either left or right (they meet further downhill) and Inspiration Point (Betty Rogers Trail) pointing due south (hikers only). If you turn left, there is a *Bone Canyon Spur* marker in a short distance pointing right (hiking) with ***Inspiration Loop Trail/Nature Center - 0.7 mi.*** leading you straight ahead and east. Follow the main dirt road as it winds downhill (the major road split beyond

49

leads to a common junction). Enjoy the eucalyptus-lined "freeway" as it dumps out at an asphalt, three-way junction (9.0). Left leads to the Inspiration Point Loop entry, while you turn hard left and follow alongside the white fence on tree-shaded asphalt road to the parking area. (9.2).

TRIP #10 - CHENEY FIRE RD./E. TOPANGA FIRE RD.

GENERAL LOCATION: Location (Topo) - Topanga

LEVEL OF DIFFICULTY: One-way - moderate to strenuous [technical section]
Distance - 9.3 miles; Time - 2-1/2 hours
Elevation gain - 1600 ft.

HIGHLIGHTS: One of our favorite rides in Topanga State Park, this one-way tour works its way up testy Cheney Fire Rd. to the Eagle Rock Loop, passes around and above that stark monolith, then coasts down to the Eagle Springs junction. Here we pick up the E. Topanga Fire Rd. and follow that roller-coaster route over to the "Latitude," across the Topanga Fault and down a super-scenic runout into Pacific Palisades. The trip includes a "can't miss" diversion to Parker Mesa Overlook where you are treated to one of the really outstanding South Bay coastal overlooks.

TRAILHEAD: From Topanga Canyon Blvd., turn east on Cheney Dr. (3/4 mile south of Santa Maria Rd. and 3/4 mile north of Hillside Dr.) and follow several linked roads: 0.7 mile to Callon Dr., turn left; 0.2 mile to Penny Rd., turn right (the road is not signed but there are residence address signs); 0.3 mile to Rochemont Dr. Continue 0.4 mile to near road's end and park well enough off the road to allow fire truck passage. We started from below Penny Rd. because of lack of adequate parking space. (From Topanga Canyon Rd., the Cheney Fire Rd. entry is 1.6 miles and a 750-foot climb for those looking for added challenge.)

From the Malibu/Pacific Palisades area, turn inland on W. Sunset Blvd. and proceed 0.6 mile to Paseo Miramar and turn left. Follow the road signs (carefully, or you'll miss) uphill 1.3 miles and 500 ft. to a fire gate at road's end. The cross street there is Vista Pacifica. The tour from this direction is strenuous due to the unforgiving 1.3-mile, 800 ft. climb from the trailhead.

TRIP DESCRIPTION: Cheney Fire Road. Immediately climb a steep mixed paved/dirt Penny Rd. and follow that winding uphill on what becomes (unmarked) Rochemont Dr. In 0.4 mile is road's end and a locked gate to the right below the largest water tank. A sign post beyond the gate notes that this is a multi-use (hikers, equestrians, bikers) road. You begin a climb on a rocky, badly chopped-up narrow road and continue for 0.3 mile on this almost unbikeable surface (technical experts, maybe) where the road stays narrow but improved. The grade lessens, the road surface improves further, then you cross a small saddle and traverse a "full-fledged" fire road on the north side of, and below, a ridge. (From this point to trip's end is reasonably high-quality fire road.) You climb to a "T" junction at a wide fire road (*Eagle Rock Loop - North Loop Trail*) and immediately face imposing Eagle

Rock to the right (southwest) (1.1).

Topanga Fire Road/On the Ridge

To the Eagle Springs Junction. Turn right and climb to the backside and above Eagle Rock where there is a signed hiking trail junction. A downhill coast takes you past numerous viewpoints down to the Eagle Springs area and the South Loop Trail. There is a particularly majestic overlook point in 0.3 mile. The 180-degree plus view includes a look at the winding E. Topanga Fire Rd. to the southwest, our destination route. Another 0.3 mile of let-it-out downhill brings you to a junction with the *South Loop Trail* to Eagle Springs.

To the "Latitude"/Trippet Ranch Junction. Turn right, immediately pass the Musch Trail entry to the right (hiking only) and follow a short climb below ridge 1531. A wandering downhill ridge run leads you above the developed Trippet Ranch area past the marked *Santa Ynez Trail* junction (Santa Ynez Canyon Trail - hikers only) (2.8).

You pass a cozy flat within a grove of Coast Live Oak (a nice rest stop) and several small hiking trails to the right before reaching the "Latitude" (3.1), a junction leading west to the Trippet Ranch trailhead with a sign stating: (pointing north, our incoming direction) -- *Eagle Rock-1.8 miles; Waterfall Santa Ynez-2 miles; Mulholland Dr.-4.6 miles; Temescal Conference Grounds-7.8 miles; Will Rogers State Park-8.5 miles;* (pointing south) -- *Parker Mesa Overlook-2.8 miles; Pacific Palisades-4.6 miles.*

To Parker Mesa Overlook. The 2.9-mile trek to the overlook follows a sinuous ridgeline route on a mixed series of ups and downs. Initially, a short passage on an oak-shaded segment takes you uphill and onto a ridge with Topanga Canyon to the

Off-shoot Trail to Parker Mesa Overlook

west and Santa Ynez Canyon to the east. The geology changes from the sandstone formations of the earlier route to primarily basalt (fine-grained rock) as you cross the east-west tending Topanga Fault. There are interesting rock formations and patterns in the cuts into the mountainsides along the roadway in this segment. At the 5.2-mile point is a portal which gives you a dandy view directly down into the Santa Ynez Reservoir and one of the many overlooks into the densely developed Santa Ynez Canyon. After attaining a crest below peak 1614, you coast down to the signed *Parker Mesa Overlook* junction and turn right. A 1/2-mile roller-coaster ride takes you out to one of the premier overlooks of the South Bay coastline out to the Palos Verdes Peninsula.

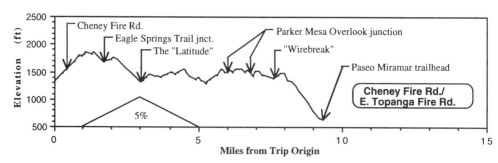

The Finale. After returning to the E. Topanga Fire Rd., turn right and coast downhill along a ridge with an east-facing exposure, then pump the final upgrade, passing the "Wire Break" just before the crest (7.8). The "Wirebreak" is a 1/2-mile murderous 800-ft. drop clear cut trail below the power lines. It plummets into Santa Ynez Canyon and is better left for the very few hikers who use it! What follows is an exhilarating, snaking ridge-running blowout with continuous views of the coastline, Westwood and Pacific Palisades directly below. The finale is punctuated by the Los Liones Trail (hiking only) junction and comes to a sharp halt at the gated road entry at the head of Paseo Miramar (9.3). At the gate is a sign stating that this is a bonified biking trail, as well as a mountain lion warning posting.

52

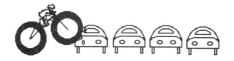

TRIP #11 - RED ROCK CANYON/CALABASAS PEAK MTWY.

GENERAL LOCATION: Location (Topo) - Malibu Beach

LEVEL OF DIFFICULTY: One-way - moderate to strenuous
Distance - 4.5 miles; Time - 1-1/2 hours
Elevation gain - 1200 feet

HIGHLIGHTS: This scenic adventure takes you through Red Rock Canyon with its unforgettable multi-colored and -shaped, sandstone rock formations. After a workout uphill out of the canyon, you follow the Calabasas Peak Motorway on a very steep 1.1-mile climb to just below the Calabasas Peak summit. The scenic vistas on the summit approach continue beyond the trip's high point as you enjoy a 1.2-mile downhill runout to the trip's end at Old Topanga Canyon Rd.

Rider North of Calabasas Peak

TRAILHEAD: From Mulholland Hwy., turn south onto Old Topanga Canyon Rd. and continue four miles, passing on a bridge over Red Rock Canyon Creek and turn right (west) on Red Rock Rd. Continue 0.7 mile on a narrow dirt road to the Santa Monica Mountains Conservancy (SMMC) sign near the Old Boy Scout Camp (Camp Slauson). For access from the south, the Red Rock Rd. turnoff is two miles northwest of the Old Topanga Canyon Rd./Topanga Canyon Rd. junction.

For access from the opposite end of this trip, see the trailhead directions in the "Summit-to-Summit Motorway" tour. The road entry is on the west side of Old Topanga Rd. at the fire gate. (Do not take the private road entry just south which is marked with a sign stating *Deep Creek Ranch, 2695 Old Topanga Canyon Rd.*)

TRIP DESCRIPTION: **Red Rock Canyon.** Consider the option of biking an extra 200 feet and 0.7 mile from Old Topanga Canyon Rd. to the trailhead at the SMMC sign.

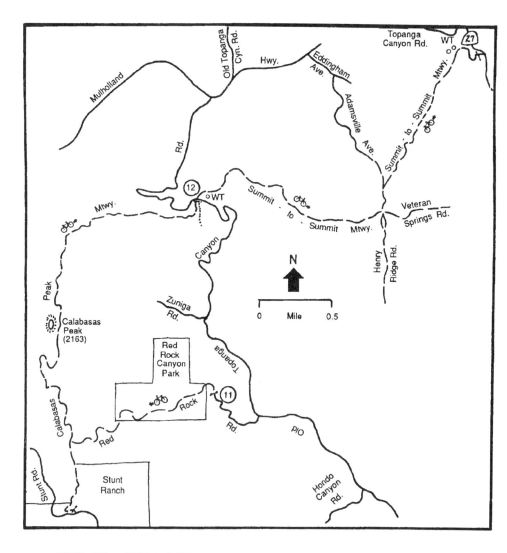

TRIP #11 - RED ROCK CANYON/CALABASAS PEAK MOTORWAY
TRIP #12 - SUMMIT-TO-SUMMIT MOTORWAY

You climb under a luscious tree canopy alongside Red Rock Canyon Creek through a sparse area of rural residences (keep clear of the marked private road entries). Near the SMMC sign (0.0) is a posting noting, among other things, a 10 mph speed limit. As you continue along and above the creek, you almost immediately bike under a large sandstone ledge, pass a new wood structure (which was surrounded by sandbags when we biked through after the January 1995 rains), and pass into an opening canyon. Here you see the first of many huge slabs of sandstone which have been tilted on edge and have been weathered into a variety of spectacular shapes. These formations are highly evident all the way up to Calabasas Peak. The slightly-rutted road follows the creek course, swings away and begins a steep winding and exposed traverse in a southwesterly direction, rising above the canyon. Enjoy over-the-shoulder canyon views as you work your way up and below power lines to the *Calabasas Peak Motorway* "T"-junction (1.35). There is an unobstructed view of dominant, tower-bedecked Saddle Peak to the south, the developed valley floor to the west and the destination "Fossil Ridge" to the north (right). This name originates from the large number of older bikers, like us, who ply this ridge (just kidding).

Fossil Ridge from the Southward Switchback

Calabasas Peak Motorway. The route to the left drops down to Stunt Rd. in 0.6 mile to the parking pullout near the Stunt Nature Trail (hiking only) trailhead. So you make the fateful decision to turn right and begin the 1.1-mile very steep climb to Calabasas Peak. The challenge begins immediately as you sweat your way up the west side of a ridge on a fire road of continuously varying surface. Navigating uphill between ruts on sections of gravel top is particularly challenging. A single, short flat section crosses a badly-eroded draw which had swallowed up a pickup truck when we passed through in February 1995.

Take a break and enjoy the numerous overlooks as you swing east, then follow a steep switchback southward to the ridgeline. The view back down to the sandstone formations and the Red Rock Canyon junction is awesome! A final push along the ridge brings you below a peak just south of Calabasas Peak and onto a welcome flat saddle. The distant San Gabriel Mountains, the San Fernando Valley and surrounding canyons are visible.

You transit below and east of Calabasas Peak (2.5), pass the signed (hikers only) *Calabasas-Cold Creek Trail* junction in 0.6 mile, then continue on a scenic ridgeline with a few ups and downs. In another 0.2 mile, you start a steady, serious downhill and get the first glimpses of Old Topanga Canyon Rd. amongst the scenic canyons.

The water tank you see near the road is across from the fire road outlet at a closed metal gate, which you reach at 4.5 miles from the trip start.

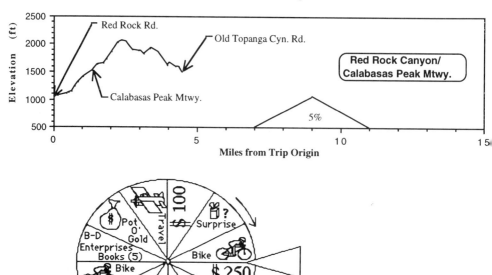

TRIP #12 - SUMMIT-TO-SUMMIT MOTORWAY

GENERAL LOCATION: Topos - Malibu Beach, Calabasas, Canoga Park, Topanga

LEVEL OF DIFFICULTY: One-way - easy
Distance - 3.3 miles; Time - 1 hour
Elevation gain - 300 feet

HIGHLIGHTS: This short ride takes you from the high point of Old Topanga Rd. across Henry Ridge and deposits you at onto Topanga Canyon Blvd. The road is sprinkled with scenic vista points. The motorway provides modest segments on fire road, double track and single track which may appeal to less experienced bikers who want to hone their technical skills.

TRAILHEAD: From the north, follow Old Topanga Rd. 1-1/2 miles south of Mulholland Hwy. to the road's summit. Turn left (east) onto the Summit-to-Summit Mtwy. and drive a short distance to a makeshift parking turnout. The fire road entry is just to the north of and below a water tower. From the south, the trip origin is 4-1/2 mile northwest of the Topanga Canyon Rd. junction (also 1-1/2 miles north of Zuniga Rd.). This is the western access.

The eastern access is just north of Navajo, off of Topanga Canyon Blvd., 1-3/4 miles south of Mulholland Dr./Mulholland Hwy. and one mile north of Entrado Dr. Look for a locked metal gate which provides paved-road access to the water towers above. Park in the scenic overlook pullout on the east side of Topanga Canyon Blvd.

TRIP DESCRIPTION: You begin an upgrade on quality fire road that is open to motorized traffic. The dirt bikers that you see use the road for access to the many spur trails scattered along the road. In one mile on the mildly-winding motorway, you stay left at a major fork -- the road right drops to a nearby canyon. Just beyond is a crest where you can view the plush homes on Henry Ridge. After a short coast, you work your way up to a four-way junction at Henry Ridge Rd. (1.5). A right turn leads up private Henry Ridge Rd.; straight ahead is Veteran Springs Rd. (dirt) which takes you 1/2 mile and steeply downhill to paved Alta Dr. within a housing development. That route outlets on Entrado Dr. in 0.8 mile to Topanga Canyon Blvd.

Above Old Topanga Road Entry

Our route goes left (north) and uphill to a scenic summit, then follows an easy-to-miss trail about 100 yards further on the ensuing downhill (a dirt berm hid the entry when we biked through). In 0.2 mile, you get a clear view of two water tanks on a small knoll to the northeast which is just above the trail outlet to Topanga Canyon Blvd. That highway is clearly viewed in the canyon below. The road deteriorates to a rougher double track, then passes through a metal gate (2.4) above a housing development, and follows a slightly choppy single track to a large log which blocks the trail. Turn left (north), make a short climb and turn right at a "T" junction in about 50 yards. Next you pass a spur trail to a nearby outlook on the right, bike below the set of water towers, and bomb downhill 0.2 mile on a paved segment which outlets at a locked metal gate at Topanga Canyon Blvd. (3.3).

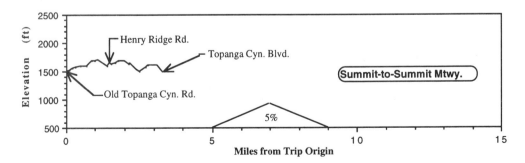

57

TRIP #13 - CRAGS ROAD/MALIBU CREEK

GENERAL LOCATION: Location (Topo) - Malibu Beach, Point Dume

LEVEL OF DIFFICULTY: Up and back - moderate
Distance - 7.6 miles; Time - 1-1/2 hours
Elevation gain - 300 feet

HIGHLIGHTS: A can't-miss tour for bikers at all skill levels, this passage along the only creek which fully transits the Santa Monica Mountains is a scenic treat! Once onto Crags Rd., you follow the general contour of lush Malibu Creek, pass mystical Century Lake with its overpowering backdrop, and navigate a rock-strewn treed segment which gives way to the old M*A*S*H TV series site. Having passed between the striking volcanic Goat Buttes, you swing north along the creek and reach trail's end at the Malibu Lake spillway. About face and return to the start point and enjoy a well-deserved picnic.

M*A*S*H TV Series Site

58

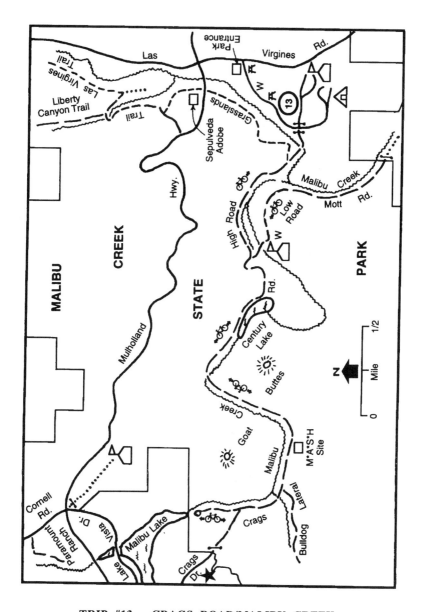

TRIP #13 - CRAGS ROAD/MALIBU CREEK

TRAILHEAD: From Pacific Coast Hwy., turn inland on Malibu Canyon Rd. and proceed 6-1/2 miles to the Malibu Creek State Park entry, about 1/4 mile south of Mulholland Hwy. From the San Fernando Valley on U.S. Hwy. 101, exit south at Las Virgenes Rd. and continue four miles to the park's entrance 1/4 mile beyond Mulholland Hwy. There is a day-use fee for entry. Drive to the second parking area along the paved entry road. The trailhead is accessed from the northwest corner of the parking lot. Water is available at the visitor center/ranger station.

59

Near Century Lake

There are other free parking accesses. The westside entry is achieved by turning south from Mulholland Hwy. at the western terminus of Lake Vista Dr., south again (right) onto Crags Rd. and continuing to a parking area in 0.8 mile at the park boundary. Also, there are entries from Mulholland Dr. and Liberty Canyon. (See "Grasslands Trail" and "Liberty Canyon/Las Virgenes" trips, respectively.)

Malibu Creek originates in the Simi Hills to the north of this 10,000-acre park and has the largest watershed in the Santa Monica Mountains. The area was inhabited by the Chumash Indians for several thousand years, then Spanish explorers and their attendant missionaries arrived. The local population dwindled in the Mission era, as the Native Americans contracted European diseases or migrated to the missions. A limited number of Chumash returned to the area after the breakup of the missions. Ranchers populated the area in the late 1800's, then part of the park was acquired by a group of businessmen, who built the Crags Country Club in the 1920's. The land was bought by 20th Century Fox in 1941 and many films were shot in the area. The State of California purchased the studio's land in 1974, together with the Hope Ranch, Reagan Ranch and other holdings. With these acquisitions, Malibu Creek State Park was formed, which was opened to the public in 1976.

TRIP DESCRIPTION: **To Century Lake.** Cross the entry road and locate the nearby locked gate, where there is a sign with a hiker's caricature. Cross Las Virgenes Creek on a small concrete apron and parallel the creek. Just beyond is a sign noting: *Crags Road: Visitor Center-0.7 mi.; Century Lake-1.33 mi.; M*A*S*H Site-2.3 mi.; Reagan Ranch-2.6 mi.* Pass a sign which points right (east) and notes *Grasslands Trail*. In 0.2 mile, you reach a broad fork and go left for the Low Road, right for the High Road. These roads are at roughly the same elevation and fuse later. The High Road has a *Backbone Trail* marker on a small vertical post. The described route goes left and crosses Malibu Creek on a broad concrete apron (which

60

is submerged after rains, although generally shallow). Follow under a line of oaks to marked Mott Rd. to the left, with a sign that says *Park Boundary-0.7 mi.* -- this is a diversion route to the Mott Adobe Ruins, once a posh vacation home for L.A. lawyer Johnny Mott (0.75).

First Malibu Creek Crossing

You continue past the off-shoot road to the Visitor Center and recross Malibu Creek. Among the many marked hiking trails along the way is the *Rock Pool Trail*, which comes up shortly and to the left. This is a 0.2-mile easy scramble to a pool at the mouth of a gorge, an idyllic spot where segments of the "Tarzan" series and "Swiss Family Robinson" were filmed. Next the High Road comes in from the right just before you begin an earnest 1/2-mile, 200-foot climb above Century Lake, where you are treated to picture-postcard views of the lake and an impressive mountain backdrop. The distinctive Goat Buttes on the lake's west end were produced under the sea by volcanic action, then upthrust when the Santa Monica Mountains were formed. A short downhill segment takes you to the western tip of the lake (2.1).

To Malibu Lake. The fire road crosses Malibu Creek and traverses a 0.7-mile rock- and boulder-strewn flat section that was created by the January 1995 rains (thus the "moderate" trip rating). However, the abundant tree cover does shelter the "road," compensating for the slow and bumpy ride. You continue between the Goat Buttes and return to quality fire road just before reaching the *Lost Cabin Trail* and the burned out military vehicles (victims of the 1982 brush fire) below the helicopter pad used in the M*A*S*H series opening scene. You are treated to a couple of fun crossings at Mendenhall and Fern Creeks with the westbound *Bulldog Lateral Junction* just short of the latter crossing. At that fire road junction, the sign states *Park Boundary*-4.3 mi.; *Castro Peak Motorway-3.4 mi.* The road swings north into a wider canyon and follows Malibu Creek to a road junction. To the left is a 0.3-mile trek that takes you to the park's western edge at paved Crags Dr., while the reference tour follows Malibu Creek 0.3 mile to the fenced-off spillway and a small turnabout near a picnic table (3.8). Return the way you came, then branch left at the High Road junction, following an oak-lined passage on the north side of Malibu Creek. Once you have fused with the Low Road, retrace your tire tracks back to the start point (7.6).

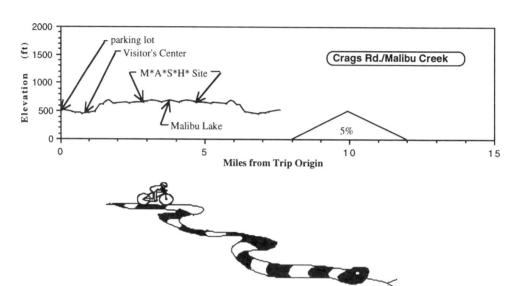

TRIP #14 - GRASSLANDS TRAIL

GENERAL LOCATION: Location (Topo) - Malibu Beach

LEVEL OF DIFFICULTY: Up and back - moderate
Distance - 3.8 miles; Time - 1 hour
Elevation gain - 450 feet

HIGHLIGHTS: The Grasslands Trail takes you from the Malibu Creek State Park entry area up through the rolling grasslands to Mulholland Hwy. The trail continuation to the north of the highway takes you past the Sepulveda Adobe, through a scenic meadow and deposits you at the Grasslands/Liberty Canyon/Las Virgenes Trail junction ("Triple Junction"). An easier return drops you back to the park's picnic area.

TRAILHEAD: From Pacific Coast Hwy., turn inland on Malibu Canyon Rd. and proceed 6-1/2 miles to the Malibu Creek State Park entry, about 1/4 mile south of Mulholland Hwy. From the San Fernando Valley on U.S. Hwy. 101, exit south at Las Virgenes Rd. and continue four miles to the park's entrance 1/4 mile beyond Mulholland Hwy. There is a day-use fee for entry. Drive to the second parking area along the paved entry road. The trailhead is accessed from the northwest corner of the parking lot. Water is available at the visitor center/ranger station.

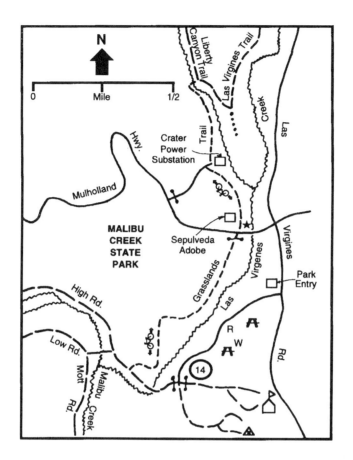

TRIP #14 - GRASSLANDS TRAIL

TRIP DESCRIPTION: **To Mulholland Highway.** Cross the entry road and locate the nearby locked gate, where there is a sign with a hiker's caricature. Cross Las Virgenes Creek on a small concrete apron and parallel the creek. Just beyond is a sign noting: *Crags Road: Visitor Center-0.7 mi.*; *Century Lake-1.33 mi.; M*A*S*H Site-2.3 mi.; Reagan Ranch-2.6 mi.* In a short distance, you spot a marker which points right (east) and notes *Grasslands Trail.* Bike a 0.3-mile steep upgrade (the toughest climb of the trip). From this initial crest, enjoy the views into the Malibu Creek drainage, spotting the assemblage of hikers and bikers on Crags Rd. below. Pass an unmarked trail junction which beelines down to Crags Rd. and enjoy a short downhill through the grasslands. Another climb takes you past a *"Crags Rd. - 0.7 mi."* sign (visible to bikers heading in the opposite direction) to Mulholland Hwy. (1.15).

Mulholland Highway to the Liberty Canyon/Las Virgenes Trail Junction. Turn right (east) and cycle a short distance on the highway to a trail continuation marked by a *Grasslands Trail* sign on the north side of the road. This single track through high grass (tick country) takes you past the fenced-in Sepulveda Adobe, a small structure with a wood exterior over the partially-exposed adobe bricks. Originally, this was the home of Pedro Alcantara Sepulveda, a local charcoal maker and merchant.

A 0.35-mile sinuous route takes you to an asphalt road, turn right and bike towards the Crater Power Substation. You swing left just before reaching a large metal substation entrance gate and track a fire road northbound. Another 0.35-mile of cruising takes you through a serene meadow with scattered valley oaks. The route follows a hairpin west-to-east turn, drops down through a lush woodland to a small bridge across a Las Virgenes Creek feeder stream and then climbs to Triple Junction (1.9).

Creek Crossover Near Triple Junction

The Return. Retrace your incoming route and enjoy a bash in the Malibu Creek State Park picnic area.

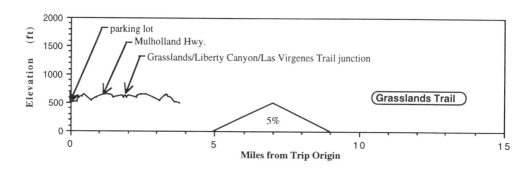

TRIP #15 - LIBERTY CANYON/LAS VIRGENES TRAIL

GENERAL LOCATION: Location (Topo) - Calabasas, Malibu Beach

LEVEL OF DIFFICULTY: Up and back - moderate
Distance - 6.4 ; Time - 1-1/2 hours
Elevation gain - 450 feet

HIGHLIGHTS: This up-and-back ride takes you south through broad, oak-studded Liberty Canyon and back north on grassy trail above and along Las Virgenes Creek. There are 3.2 miles of mild rolling terrain on fire road, single and double track along Las Virgenes Trail. Taken in the spring, this is a flower lover's delight.

TRAILHEAD: From U.S. Hwy. 101 in the San Fernando Valley, turn south onto Liberty Canyon Rd. and proceed one mile to a deadend at Park Vista Rd. Here there is a wrought iron fence with a walker/biker/rider entry. This is the trailhead for the trip described below.

From Las Virgenes Rd. and Mulholland Hwy., drive west on the latter road and park along the north side of the highway about 1/4 mile beyond the intersection. The Grasslands/Liberty Canyon/Las Virgenes Trail junction (we refer to it as "Triple Junction") is 0.75 mile north of the marked *Grasslands Trail* trailhead on Mulholland Hwy. as described in the "Grasslands Trail" trip.

TRIP DESCRIPTION: **Park Vista to Triple Junction.** Pass through the entry gate and cycle alongside a horse stable on an asphalt path 0.1 mile to its terminus. Follow the single track on the left for a short distance to a dirt road and turn right (south). You follow a wide canyon on generally good quality surface passing scattered impressive valley oaks which will greet you throughout the tour. In 0.7 mile, at a private property fence line, follow the single track left on a short and steep incline to a scenic crest below a particularly striking oak. You follow a series of small ups and downs with a Las Virgenes Creek feeder stream coming near and parallel to the fire road. Pass the marked *Talepop Trail* junction (hikers only) (1.3), which is to the left, and reach Triple Junction in 0.2 mile.

Las Virgenes Trail. Continue straight ahead (the marked *Grasslands Trail* is a hard right) and follow the Las Virgenes Trail on quality fire road. What follows is a 2.1-mile series of ups and downs on a fire road which narrows to a single track. Taken in the spring, you will ride on a narrow swath through high grass and flowering plants. Be prepared for ticks! At 0.15 mile from Triple Junction is a junction with a sign that points back to the way you came and announces *Liberty Canyon*. Another marker points left (north) and states *Talepop Trail* (the Talepop

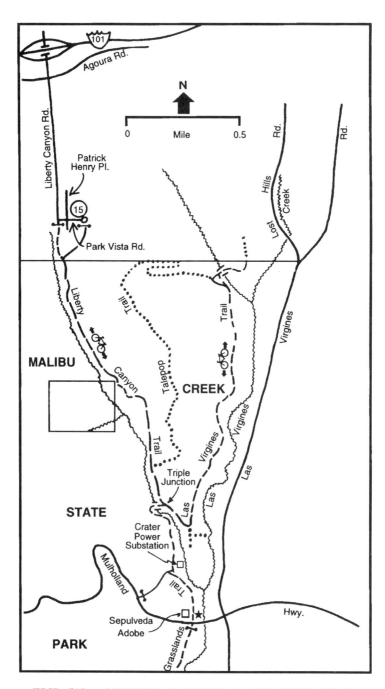

TRIP #15 - LIBERTY CANYON/LAS VIRGENES TRAIL

Trail junction is 1.2 miles further north), while a turn right leads you towards the private White Oak Farm.

Near the End of Las Virgenes Trail

Turn left and follow a light roller-coaster route which keeps you in view of Las Virgenes Creek at the canyon's bottom and Las Virgenes Rd., both to the right. You pass an out-of-place yellow fire main (2.5), then bike another 0.4 mile to a "Y" junction where a marker about 50 feet up to the left states *Talepop Trail* (no bikes); *Liberty Canyon-0.5 mi.* and *White Oak Farm-1.3 mi.* You take the right fork, cross a wooden bridge over a Las Virgenes Creek feeder, and follow a meandering path around a knoll to the park boundary (3.2). Beyond, a criss-crossing group of fire roads lead you to private property in the form of new developments -- stay out! Turn your two-wheeler around and retrace your incoming path (6.8).

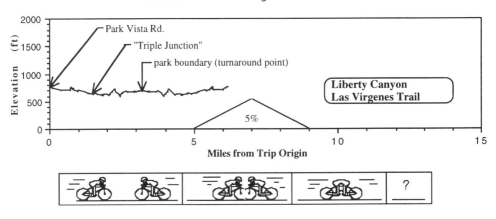

67

TRIP #16 - LOOKOUT LOOP

GENERAL LOCATION: Location (Topo) - Malibu Beach, Point Dume

LEVEL OF DIFFICULTY: Loop - moderate
Distance - 3.3 miles; Time - 1-1/2 hours
Elevation gain - 600 feet

HIGHLIGHTS: This low-mileage route provides short uphill challenges at both the beginning and end segments. There are numerous scenic vistas on both the Bulldog Lateral and Bulldog Mtwys. in the middle section, plus a short ride on Crags Rd. along serene Malibu Creek.

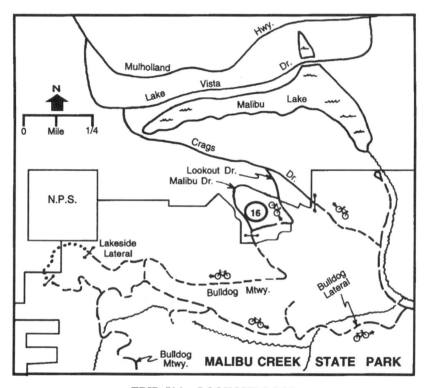

TRIP #16 - LOOKOUT LOOP

TRAILHEAD: From the San Fernando Valley, exit on Kanan Dume Rd. in Agoura Hills and continue 1/2 mile south to Cornell Rd. where you turn left. Continue on Cornell Rd., cross Mulholland Hwy. and follow what is now Lake Vista Dr. one mile to Crags Dr. Turn left and continue about 1/2 mile to Lookout Dr. Follow Lookout Dr. 1/4 mile to Maquoketh Trail and find parking. The trailhead is to the left on that road at an open gate which is marked with a sign stating *State Park Boundary*.

From Pacific Coast Hwy., take Kanan Dume Rd. north to Mulholland Hwy. and turn right (east). Drive 1-1/4 mile to Lake Vista Dr., turn right and proceed 1/2 mile to Crags Dr. Turn right again onto Lookout Dr. and continue as noted above.

TRIP DESCRIPTION: **Bulldog Motorway to Bulldog Lateral Junction.** From the trailhead, you start steeply uphill on a poorly-surfaced fire road. There are interesting canyon and valley vistas along this entire segment. You face rocks and ruts for 0.5 mile until the road swings west just beyond a graded turnout to an overlook. In 0.15 mile, the grade moderates and you follow a ridgeline on little ups and downs above the Bulldog Lateral.

Bulldog Motorway near Lakeside Lateral

At 0.9 mile is the junction with the *Lakeside Lateral*, where a sign announces *Motorway ends 1/8 mile.* This diversion to the right used to take you on a scenic one-mile loop. Now the loop is blocked off by two gates which close off about 1/4 mile of the road where there is a private residence. You turn left and buzz 0.1 mile downhill to a junction with the *Bulldog Lateral* (0.95).

Bulldog Lateral to Crags Road. In the next 1.3 miles, you dive downhill on good quality fire road (with a few wide ruts to slow your progress) passing road junctions at 1.2 and 1.4 miles, both offshoots are power pole access roads. At 1.85 is a Fern Creek crossing in a lush wooded area, followed by a winding, more-exposed runout which brings you to *Crags Rd.* (2.25). You will see a sign which points back in the direction you came proclaiming *Park Boundary-4.3 mi.* and *Castro Peak Motorway-3.4 mi.*

Crags Road to the Trailhead. Turn left and cycle along Malibu Creek, looking east to the flat and marshy waterway and the Goat Buttes above. Don soloed this trip and listened to something large crackle through the brush to the west, paralleling his path and heading in the same direction. (He set a land-speed record on this segment!) Turn left at the next (unsigned) junction (2.55) and pump uphill to a blocking gate where you encounter paved Crags Dr. In 0.15 mile is Lookout Dr.

69

where you turn left and challenge a 200-ft. paved upgrade to return to the original trailhead (3.25).

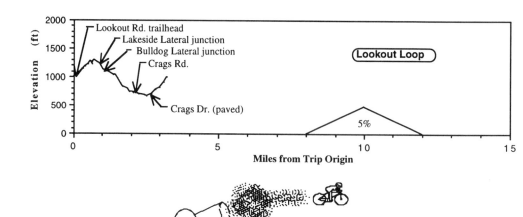

TRIP #17 - BULLDOG LOOP

GENERAL LOCATION: Location (Topo) - Malibu Beach, Point Dume

LEVEL OF DIFFICULTY: Loop - very strenuous
Distance - 15.0 miles; time - 4 hours
Elevation gain - 2450 feet

HIGHLIGHTS: There are few better rides than this grand loop. You follow Crags Rd. through the marvelously-scenic park along Malibu Creek. Next is a heart-pounding, panorama-filled 3.4-mile climb up Bulldog Lateral and Bulldog Mtwy. to the Castro Crest. Almost four miles on ups and downs along Castro Peak and Mesa Peak Mtwys. are filled with additional distant scenic views, as well as intriguing rock formations. The payoff is a steep downhill on Tapia Mtwy. with a few technical segments thrown in for variety. A short segment on Malibu Canyon Rd. returns you to the start point at Malibu Creek State Park.

There are options to start this trip from the top of Corral Canyon Rd. or from Tapia Canyon Park. In the latter case, should you start by biking up Tapia Mtwy. (not a preferred option unless you enjoy steep uphills on poor surfaces), the trailhead is a couple hundred yards south of the Tapia Canyon Park's parking area. The shaded parking turnout is on the west side of the road.

TRAILHEAD: The Malibu Creek State Park trailhead described for the "Crags Rd./Malibu Creek" trip is used here. There is water at the visitor center/ranger station and at Tapia Canyon Park. There are several creek crossings on the way up Bulldog Lateral and Bulldog Mtwy.; however, these are not reliable year-round water sources. (The water should be treated, if used.) Best bet is to bring an excess water supply along with you.

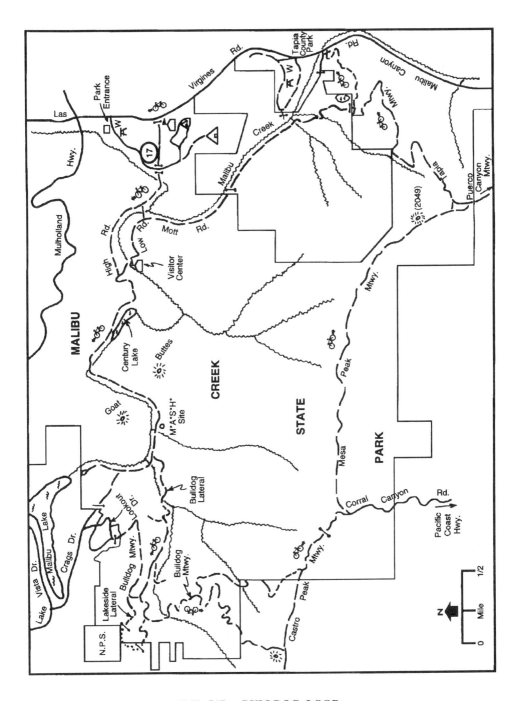

TRIP #17 - BULLDOG LOOP

TRIP DESCRIPTION: **Trailhead to Bulldog Motorway**. The first 3.2 miles of the tour are on Crags Rd. as described in the "Crags Road/Malibu Creek" tour.

Bulldog Motorway to Castro Crest. At the signed Bulldog Lateral junction, turn left (southwest) and cycle above Fern Creek on a generally steep upgrade. The road wiggles westward, makes two crossings of the creek (3.55) within a shaded glen, then passes a little-used off-shoot road on the right (most off-shoots lead to the evident power poles). Continue on a more exposed road with some light rutting on an unrelenting upgrade with a canyon to the left. Ignore a small fire road which splits off to the left near the top of the canyon and continue another 0.15 mile to a "T" junction (4.3).

On the Climb to Castro Crest

To the right is *Bulldog Mtwy.* (north segment)/*Lookout Rd.*, however you turn left onto *Bulldog Mtwy.* (south segment), noting the signpost which states that you are heading for the **Backbone Trail**. You cross above the incoming canyon and are treated to the first of many scenic vistas that you will enjoy both on Bulldog Mtwy. and Castro Crest. In 0.25 mile from the Lookout Rd. junction, the signed *Lakeside Lateral* comes in from the right. Shortly, you reach a false summit and coast downhill to cross a small feeder to Fern Creek. From here is a rugged 1.9-mile, 1140-ft. (11.5% average grade) switchbacking climb to the Castro Crest. On the way up in this panorama-filled segment, you pass a spur road to the left (5.2) and a sign announcing **Bulldog Motorway** with an arrow pointing directly ahead. You pass under some power lines at the end of an east-facing ridge and reach a super overlook in 0.25 mile. Malibu Lake can be seen to the north and distant Saddle Peak to the east. Tower-bedecked Castro Peak comes into view to the west, then becomes blocked as you transit an east-facing ridge above a steep canyon. The grade moderates as you make a final push to a "T" junction at Castro Peak Mtwy. near the crest (6.6). Bikers coming from the east on the crest see a sign which says: *Backbone Trail* and *Latigo Canyon Road* (arrow points west), and *Bulldog Motorway* (arrow points north).

Tapia Motorway Obstacle Course

Castro Crest to Mesa Peak Motorway. Turn left (east) at the junction. A 0.85-mile downhill on a mildly rocky and rutted surface takes you under some power poles and drops you at a gate on the west edge of the parking lot at the northern terminus of Corral Canyon Rd. A sign notes *Castro Peak Mtwy.* and points west. You follow a 0.3-mile stretch west on paved Corral Canyon Rd. looking for a point where a power line breaks across the road. Cross the road (east) to a wooden structure below the power lines with a sign noting *Backbone Trail to Puma Trailhead.* This is the entry to the *Mesa Peak Mtwy.* (7.6).

Mesa Peak Motorway to Tapia Motorway. This pleasant ridge run provides 2.9 miles of moderate ups and downs with the final upgrade taking you just below Peak 2049 and 0.25 mile further to the Tapia Mtwy. junction. On the way, you transit near an interesting sandstone monolith whose face has been weathered into a series of caves and pinnacles, cross a lovely meadow, and pass the marked state park boundary (9.1). Soon after, a steep, curving downgrade with some rocky and washboard surfaces drops you below a sharp unnamed peak -- keep your speed in check. There are periodic looks down into Tapia Canyon Park, part of your destination route, starting about 1.8 miles from the Mesa Peak Mtwy. entry. The signed Tapia Mtwy. junction announces: *Tapia Canyon Park-2 mi.* (left); *Pacific Coast Hwy.-3.5 mi.* (via Puerco Canyon) (right). (Note that Mesa Peak is reached via Puerco Canyon Mtwy. and not Mesa Peak Mtwy. as you might expect.) You go left.

Tapia Motorway to Malibu Canyon Road. In about 0.1 mile, Puerco Canyon Mtwy. comes up from the right at another signed junction. As seen by a cyclist

73

coming up Tapia Mtwy. from Malibu Canyon Rd., it reads: *Corral Canyon Trail-2.6 mi.* and *Castro Peak-4.0 mi.* (arrow points right, i.e., in the direction you came from); *Pacific Coast Highway-3.5 mi.* (arrow points left). Stay on Tapia Mtwy. by keeping to the left (north), then follow a mild downhill which gives way to a steep switchbacking run on slightly rocky surface. You enter a wooded area (the first real shade for miles) and parallel above a creek for a short distance. Next you plummet downhill through scattered steep rock-strewn, rutted zones where you must slow considerably or walk you bike.

In this area, we were forced to portage our bikes across a large dirt/boulder/tree slide when we cycled through in March '95 (11.7). The motorway crosses a steep ridgeline where there are views down the sheer canyon to Malibu Canyon Rd. You pass a chain-link fence to the left on a steep, hairpin switchback and reach a signed junction just beyond. Staying on the fire road takes you to a dead end at a fence around a reservoir. Instead, you follow the arrow on the sign which says *Tractors Only*, turning right and following the trail uphill. (We're still trying to figure out this sign.) The brief but rutted uphill leads you above the reservoir through mild rolling terrain under scattered tree cover. In the last 0.3 steep mile, the surface deteriorates and you must navigate various size ruts, gravel and exposed rocks before reaching Malibu Canyon Rd. (13.1).

Malibu Canyon Road to Malibu Creek State Park. The remaining 1.9-mile ride north on paved road is anticlimactic. Both the excellent traction and passing motor traffic take some getting used to. Climb a couple hundred feet in about a mile, then coast past Virgenes Canyon Rd. to the Malibu Creek State Park entrance and pedal back to your car (15.0). Both congratulations and a post-ride picnic are called for!

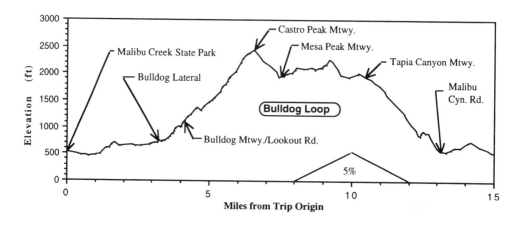

TRIP #18 - PARAMOUNT RANCH

<u>GENERAL LOCATION</u>:   Location (Topo) - Point Dume, Thousand Oaks

<u>LEVEL OF DIFFICULTY</u>: **Flood Plains Trail** - moderate
Distance - 3.1 miles; Time - 1 hour
Elevation - 400 feet
Out and Back Excursion - moderate to strenuous
[technical section]
Distance - 4.8 miles; Time - 1-1/2 hours
Elevation gain - 620 feet

<u>HIGHLIGHTS</u>: Paramount Ranch has a little something for everybody. There are short and easy rides on the east side of Medea Creek starting from the parking area. More challenging rides through the hills are found in the criss-crossed roadways and trails out beyond the "backside" of Western Town, west of the creek. Most demanding is the "Out-and-Back Excursion" over a scenic crest to Kanan-Dume Rd. and back. Pick the right (or wrong, depending on your tastes) day and you may be treated to a television shoot or an open-invitation fiddle contest in Western Town.

<u>TRAILHEAD</u>: From U.S. Hwy. 101 in the San Fernando Valley, exit south at Kanan Rd., veer left at the Cornell Rd. junction in 1/2 mile and continue 2-1/2 miles south to the park's entrance. If you reach Mulholland Hwy., you've gone 1/2 mile too far. Turn right (west), then follow the road left to the dirt parking area. From Pacific Coast Hwy., proceed up Malibu Canyon Rd. seven miles to Mulholland Hwy., turn left (west) and proceed 2-1/2 miles to the Cornell Rd./Lake Vista intersection. Turn right (north) on Cornell Rd. and drive 1/2 mile to the park's entrance.

Western Town

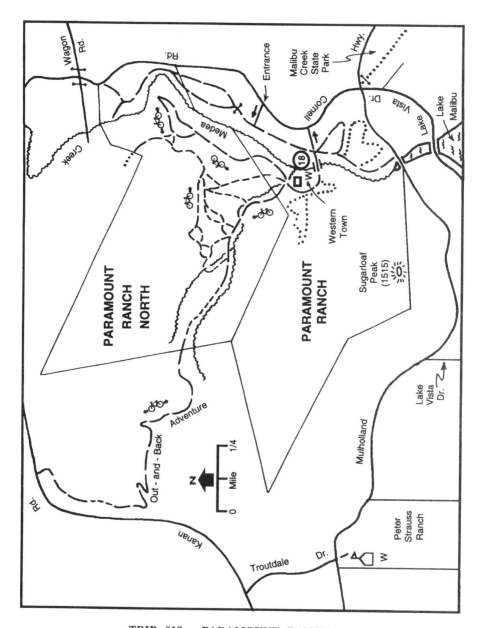

TRIP #18 - PARAMOUNT RANCH

The 436-acre Paramount Ranch is part of the Santa Monica Mountains Recreation Area and sports many multi-use trails, the Western Town movie set, picnic areas, restrooms and a ranger station. You must honor signs and the Paramount brochure noting which trails are open to bikers -- the area is patrolled.

In 1927 Paramount Pictures purchased 2700 acres of the old Rancho Las Virgenes, moved in several sets and shot films here for 20 years. With the advent of television and because of other business setbacks, the ranch was sold to Elser Wickholm. Sets were torn down and crops planted before William Hertz bought the southeast portion of the ranch in 1952. His family built their own western town and it came to be used for many 50's and 60's T.V. series. The ranch was sold to the Paramount Sportsman's Club a few years later, and then acquired by the National Park Service in 1980, all the while supporting television shoots. The Western Town, in its current form, was revitalized in 1984 and is still used by independent production companies.

TRIP DESCRIPTION: Trails interweave the entire ranch. There are short rides in the area east of Medea Creek; however, the major trail network is accessed by crossing the creek at the Western Town entry and proceeding to the town's western edge. Follow the routes described below or free-wheel around the network -- it is difficult to get lost due to the large number of distinct landmarks.

Flood Plain Trails: Zero your odometer at the Medea Creek crossing and follow the dirt road through Western Town, turning right and staying on the east side of the railroad tracks, and proceed past the "Colorado Springs Railroad Station."

Flood Plain Trail/Paramount Ranch North

Just beyond the station, turn left and travel along the wide road past the *Coyote Trail* marker (no bikes) on the left (0.3). Cross an intermittent stream, follow the road sharply left, and pass a large sign inscribed **_Paramount Ranch/Phase II_**. Next is a "Y" junction with a stately oak occupying the center (0.45). Bear left and follow the deteriorating road WSW across another intermittent creek and reach a dirt road junction on the right (0.7) -- continuing ahead takes you on a quickly narrowing and steep trail (the "Out and Back Excursion" described below). Turn right and cycle the narrowing trail as it becomes a single track and passes below a couple of broad oaks. Stay to the left on the serpentine trail which leads below the hillside to the left (north). A series of modest ups and downs takes you into the hills and down into the small separating draws and normally-dry creek beds. From here you get a grand sweep of the oak and brush meadow lands and Medea Creek to the east.

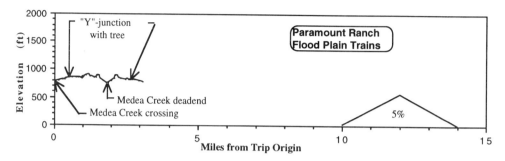

You pass small trails which drop off to the right of the flood plains below, including one at (1.55) that is a decision point. Turn right for an easy 2.5-mile loop or continue left for an interesting up-and-back segment. Turning right leads you on a continued traverse, passing a "No Trespassing" sign which keeps you from turning left to a horse corral. Veer right and bike down to Medea Creek, passing a junction to the left that climbs a small knoll and leads to residences. Enjoy the creek-side flora, then return to the "decision point" junction. You veer left and drop to the flood plain, heading west below the incoming hillside traverse route. The trail swings southwest and crosses a couple of interesting dirt paths. You continue on the route that takes you toward the "Y" junction with the stately oak that you passed at (0.45). (If you miss the described route, any of several paths will lead you back. The wide-open view makes it impossible to get lost.) Once back at the "Y" junction (2.65), you swing left and reverse the incoming route, returning to the parking area (3.1).

Out and Back Excursion: An option at the 0.7 mile junction described above is to follow the deteriorating, narrowing trail left. You bike on a rutted surface with sections of loose gravel and some exposed rock, surrounded by high abundant growth; however, the route is light on tree shade. The butt-kicking climb covers about 3/4 mile and takes you up 350 feet where the grade lessens and you have a 1/4-mile flat before reaching a saddle (1.6). To the north are distant mountain ranges with spectacular "Ladyface" in the foreground. South is the Castro Crest and the Mulholland Hwy./Kanan-Dume Rd. intersection.

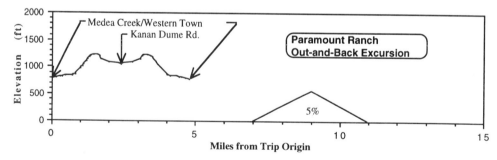

Continue on a flat, round the ridgeline and follow a switchback which reverses your direction to the south. The outlet at Kanan-Dume Rd. comes into view as you coast steeply downhill and sharply change direction westward on the last 0.7 mile, coasting traverse (2.4). You can ride the asphalt roads, mostly downhill, back to the Paramount Ranch parking lot (south and west on Kanan-Dume Rd., south on Troutdale Dr., east on Mulholland Hwy. and north on Cornell Rd. -- there is one steep climb on this return) or reverse your incoming route. We like the latter option because, other than for one very steep, chopped-up trail section near the crest (experienced technical riders only), there is a mildly challenging downhill to hone your riding skills (4.8).

Out and Back Excursion on the Climb

Trip Option: 5K Run Trail. The run trail is generally used by runners and hikers, but also open to bikers. Sections of the trail are described below. The northeast park section is easy and wide, while the southeast trail is a moderate single track. (We have included the latter. However, there are so many biking trails in the park, you might consider leaving this to the folks on foot. Avoid any spur with a "no bikes" symbol.)

Northeast Trail Section. From the north end of the parking area, head north to a fenced entry and a trail to its left marked *Run Trail*. Passing through the fenced entry takes you onto a flat, wide trail which heads northeast through an oak restoration area and parallels Cornell Rd. You stay right at a wide junction (0.3), leaving the Run Trail and continue north 0.3 mile along Medea Creek until you reach the trail terminus at the creek itself. Turn around and return to the wide junction, turning right to complete the small loop and exit at the *Run Trail* sign (2.0).

Southeast Trail Section. From the bridge across Medea Creek which leads to Western Town, bike south on the east side of the creek and turn onto a side dirt trail in about 100 yards. In 0.1 mile is an unmarked fork. Right goes below the Mulholland Hwy. bridge and leads to Malibu Lake. You go left on a single track and climb to a ridge which parallels the highway. Stay on the widest trail until you come to a marker (0.4). Right goes toward Cornell Rd., but you turn left, following the *Medea Creek Western Town* direction. This splits again (both marked *Medea Creek Trail*) and you go right and downhill through heavy foliage and tree cover, returning to a wide dirt road and a *Medea Creek Trail* sign pointing back the way you came. A short downhill returns you to the first junction of this segment and a 100-yard pedal returns you to the bridge.

TRIP #19 - MESA PEAK/PUERCO CANYON

GENERAL LOCATION: Location (Topo) - Point Dume, Malibu

LEVEL OF DIFFICULTY: One way - moderate; up and back - strenuous
Distance - 6.8 miles (one-way); time - 1-1/2 hour
Elevation gain - 450 feet (one way)

HIGHLIGHTS: From the paved Corral Canyon Rd. terminus, this moderate ride along the scenic Castro Crest and Puerco Canyon Mtwy. is a "cheater's special." For about 500 ft. elevation gain, you experience one of the finest downhill rides in the Santa Monica Mountains. Exotic sandstone formations, lovely canyon vistas and a nearly 2000-ft. drop along the mountain ridgelines are your rewards. Done in the opposite direction, this is a scenic and challenging workout.

Sandstone Formations/Mesa Peak Motorway

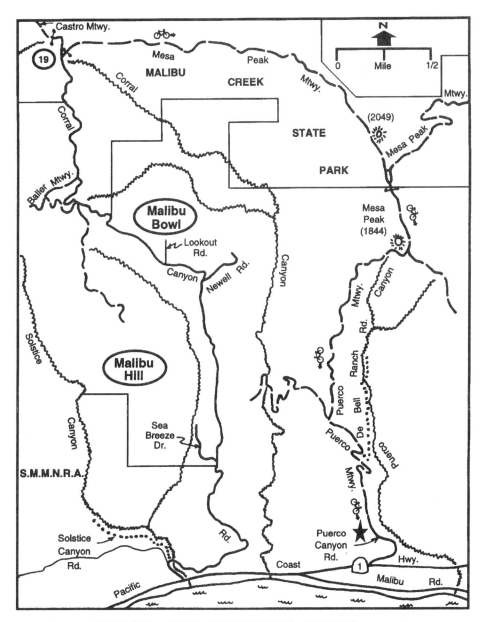

TRIP #19 - MESA PEAK/PUERCO CANYON

TRAILHEAD: From Pacific Coast Hwy. (PCH), turn north onto Corral Canyon Rd. (between Latigo Canyon Rd. to the west and Malibu Canyon Rd. to the east) and drive 4.9 miles and 2050 ft. to road's end at the parking area. From the San Fernando Valley, follow Las Virgines Rd./Malibu Canyon Rd. to PCH. Turn right (west), motor 2-1/2 miles to Corral Canyon Rd., then continue as described above.

To start from the described outlet, turn north on Puerco Canyon Rd. (about halfway between Malibu Canyon Rd. and Corral Canyon Rd.) and drive 1/3 mile to the end of the paved road, where there is ample parking. From the Puerco Canyon Rd. trailhead to the Mesa Peak Mtwy. junction is 3.7 miles at an average 8.4% grade on fair-to-good surface fire road. The uphill ride from Puerco Canyon is rated as strenuous.

Near Peak 2049

TRIP DESCRIPTION: To Puerco Canyon Motorway. Backtrack down Corral Canyon Rd. 0.3 mile to a point where the telephone lines cross the road. Pass through the wooden gate onto Mesa Park Mtwy. The 2.7-mile ride along the crest is peppered with several challenging but short climbs followed by downhills. At 0.3 mile, the Backbone Trail comes up from the left and below and, in another 0.1 mile, are some intriguing caves and pinnacles worn into a large sandstone monolith. Beyond, you are treated to views down into Malibu Canyon, followed by an array of vistas southward of the Pacific Ocean and the local coastline. Beyond the 2.5-mile point, you pass a water tank on your left which signals the Puerco Canyon Mtwy. junction just beyond (3.1). At the junction is a sign which states: *Pacific Coast Hwy.-3.5 miles (arrow to right); Tapia Canyon Park-2.5 miles (left).*

To the Puerco Canyon Trailhead. You go right and pass a second junction in 0.1 mile. As seen by a biker coming up from PCH, the sign reads: *Mesa Peak-1.6 mi., Corral Canyon Trailhead-2.6 mi.* (sign points left); *Malibu Canyon Rd.* (Tapia Canyon Park)-*2.5 mi.* (right). (The Mesa Peak reference must be to some official start point of the motorway since Mesa Peak is about 0.4 mi. south in the direction you are heading!) You are treated to a view of the steep canyon which drops east (left) into Malibu Canyon and a less dramatic view into Corral Canyon (right) on a small saddle. Just beyond is an open metal gate (3.4) and a mildly-rutted, sometimes rock-exposed surface, which will force you to keep your speed down -- this is typical of the entire route. Across Corral Canyon is Corral Canyon Rd., which you will track for most of the downhill until you divert from the ridge to Puerco Canyon.

You get a nice look down to Malibu Canyon Rd. and north-east to Saddle Peak in the distance, pass below Mesa Peak and then meet a road junction (3.7). The road left

Puerco Canyon Motorway Looking across Corral Canyon

(east) climbs a ridge and dies in 3/4 mi. Stay right and look ahead to your destination route on the ridgeline well below. Continue downhill along the chaparral-covered slopes, turning west above the head of Puerco Canyon, then follow a serpentine fire road on the western slope of a ridge above Corral Canyon. On the downhill, take the time to gaze back up at the crest that you rode early in the trip.

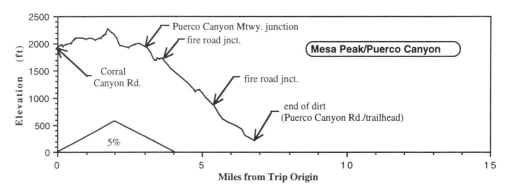

You top the ridge a couple of times getting views into both canyons. The increasing sea breezes tell you that the coast is near. Pass a junction (5.35) where a turn right drops you down into Corral Canyon to a dead end in about a mile. Stay left and look ahead and down to a series of switchbacks which take you to the outlet trailhead. Pass a couple of burned-out stretches and reach a "T" intersection (5.7) where the gated road to the left is private property. The described route goes right and switchbacks about 400 ft. down to paved Puerco Canyon Rd. (6.8), generally following the power lines past a couple of off-shoot tracks.

83

TRIP #20 - CASTRO PEAK MOTORWAY (WEST)

GENERAL LOCATION: Location (Topo) - Point Dume

LEVEL OF DIFFICULTY: One way - moderate to strenuous
                            Distance - 3.9 miles; Time - 1-1/2 hours
                            Elevation gain - 800 feet

HIGHLIGHTS: The Castro Crest is a scenic gem. This route plies the western portion of the crest starting from the Corral Canyon Rd. trailhead. A heart-pounding 1.8 mile, 725-foot climb (average 8% grade) to Castro Peak takes you through a continuos vista-laden stretch past intriguing rock formations. The route crest places you below the antennae-bedecked Castro Peak. Castro Peak Mtwy. then heads downhill with some short climbs, passing through scattered residential pockets in a serene valley before reaching Latigo Canyon Rd.

West of Bulldog Motorway Junction

TRAILHEAD: Drive up Corral Canyon Rd. to the road's end to bike Castro Crest Mtwy. westward. Follow the "Mesa Peak/Puerco Canyon" trip trailhead description to the parking lot. To start from the west end and bike east, drive to the Kanan-Dume Rd./Latigo Canyon Rd. intersection (0.6 mile south of Mulholland Hwy. on Kanan-Dume Rd.). Turn east onto Latigo Canyon Rd. and continue 1-3/4 miles to a dirt road entrance on the left, dead-center within a wide, sweeping 180-degree road turn. The

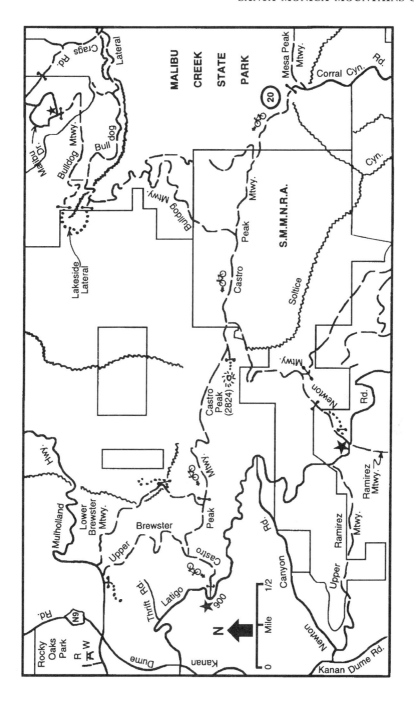

TRIP #20 - CASTRO PEAK MOTORWAY (WEST)

85

address of the nearest home is 900 Latigo Canyon Rd. Park across the street (west side) in the wide dirt turnout.

Castro Peak

TRIP DESCRIPTION: To Castro Peak. Leave the parking lot through the open metal gate at the north end and begin an immediate steep climb on the reasonable quality dirt fire road, pass a stanchion marked *Castro Peak Mtwy.* The rock formations on the hills are typical of the many that you will see on this segment. You pass a junction with a fire road that veers off to the left (south) and dumps into the valley floor below. At 0.3 mile, as you pass around a ridge outcropping, is the first of many long-distant vistas to the north. Later, you see Bulldog Mtwy. coming up across the canyon, reaching that road junction at 0.9 mile. The signpost says *Backbone Trail/Latigo Canyon*, pointing straight ahead, and *Bulldog Mtwy.*, pointing right (north).

Continuing straight ahead, the grade lessens as you pass above some interesting rock formations, then start another steep climb with the towers on Castro Peak looming ahead. Next is a ridgeline traverse between a cluster of weathered rock monoliths.

Beyond, a marked junction appears with *Castro Peak Mtwy.* inscribed on a stanchion to the right, marking the *Newton Mtwy.* turnoff (left or south). (This route option is described below.) Coming up shortly on Castro Peak Mtwy. is the junction with the blocked road to Castro Peak (1.8) to the left. The road leads to the massive antenna farm on the peak itself.

Castro Peak to Latigo Canyon Road. A rewarding downhill on a sometimes-rocky surface provides unblocked views northward. A short climb and more downhill brings you to an open gate with a marker noting *Castro Peak* on its opposite (downhill) side. In less than 0.1 mile is a five-way intersection. Four roads lead up to visible residences. The last (unmarked) turnoff to the right is *Lower Brewster Mtwy.* You continue on the wide **Castro Peak Mtwy.** 0.25 mile and pass another fire road which cuts back sharply to the right -- this is *Upper Brewster Mtwy.*, as noted on a yellow stanchion at the northeast corner (2.9).

Bike past numerous marked private driveways to scattered trailers and homes on rolling hills. Pass another gate with a marker pointing back the way you came, noting *Castro Peak M/W* Stay on the main fire road, passing through higher density residential areas and reach Latigo Canyon in another 0.85 mile (3.9).

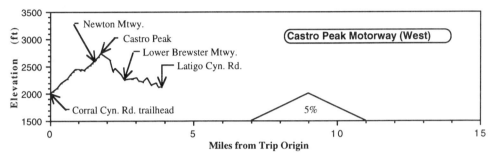

Newton Motorway Option. At the marked *Newton Mtwy.* junction (1.6), turn left (south) and bike over the small Castro Peak lower ridge and follow a sweeping turn west. You traverse the Castro Peak massif 0.25 mile and reach a switchback which turns you back east -- the unblocked views south on this segment are spectacular! A short pedal takes you to a very steep and exposed southward downhill which races down to a small saddle where the unmarked *Backbone Trail* crosses. A quick workout uphill takes you through the remnants of a gate and past a dirt road junction that dumps downhill and to the left (this road joins with a range of other dirt routes that continue all the way to upper Solstice Canyon). You opt for the right fork. Another short upgrade gives way to a 0.4-mile downgrade which takes you out of the prior barren trip segment and sends you through a lightly-treed zone to a locked gate (1.55). In 0.2 mile of pleasant coasting, you reach Latigo Canyon Rd. at the site of two large, abandoned yellow and red trucks. (The trail exit point is described in the "Ramera/Murphy Motorways" trip.)

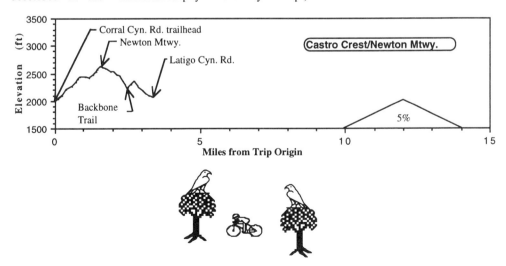

87

TRIP #21 - CASTROMAX

GENERAL LOCATION: Location (Topo) - Point Dume, Malibu Beach

LEVEL OF DIFFICULTY: One-way - strenuous
Distance - 11.8 miles ; Time - 3 hours
Elevation gain - 1900 feet

HIGHLIGHTS: This has got to be one of the finest trips in the Santa Monica Mountains! By linking the Upper Brewster Motorway ("Brewster Motorway Loop"), the "Castro Peak Motorway (West)", and the "Mesa Peak/Puerco Canyon" rides, this dandy adventure transits the entire Castro Crest, then drops down 1800 feet through Puerco Canyon to the coast. Another option is to exit via Tapia Motorway into Tapia Canyon Park (see the "Bulldog Loop"). Taken in reverse, this tour is rated very strenuous.

TRAILHEAD: Start from the "Brewster Motorway Loop" trailhead. To do the reverse, very strenuous route, start from the exit point of the "Mesa Peak/Puerco Canyon" trip.

TRIP DESCRIPTION: **To Corral Canyon Road.** From Rocky Oaks Park, follow the "Brewster Motorway Loop" 1.95 miles to the five-way residential intersection. Continue on the main road, reversing the route described in "Castro Peak Motorway (West)" east of the same five-way intersection. This route takes you to Castro Peak, then downhill past the Bulldog and Newton Mtwys. junction to the trailhead/parking area at the head of Corral Canyon Rd.

   The Finish. The remainder of the trip is identical to that described in the "Mesa Peak/Puerco Canyon" tour.

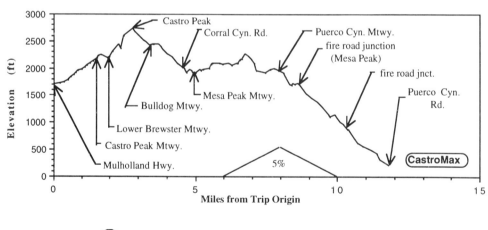

TRIP #22 - ROCKY OAKS PARK

GENERAL LOCATION: Location (Topo) - Point Dume

LEVEL OF DIFFICULTY: Loop - moderate
Distance - 2.1 miles; Time - 1 hour
Elevation gain - 250 feet

HIGHLIGHTS: This is a great area for beginners and more experienced bikers looking for highly scenic trailways. The pond and sculpted rock formations, found throughout the park, are delightful sights along the way. There are restful shady tree groves, lovely meadows and delightful vista points. The loop described is only one of several ways to see the park and is the most challenging. Wander around the park as your heart sees fit -- there are far too many easy-to-recognize landmarks in this compact area to get lost.

TRAILHEAD: From U.S. Hwy. 101 in the San Fernando Valley, turn south at Kanan Rd. and continue six miles to Mulholland Hwy. Turn right (west) and then right again into the park in a few hundred yards. Park in the lot or along Mulholland Hwy. well off the paved road From Pacific Coast Hwy. turn north on Kanan-Dume Rd. and proceed six miles to Mulholland Hwy. and turn left and enter the park. There is a compost toilet in the parking area, as well as picnic tables and a water fountain just beyond the trailhead.

Near the Park Entry

The area was settled by the Thompson family near the turn of the century. The family had extensive ranch holdings, unfortunately, the remaining structures and

89

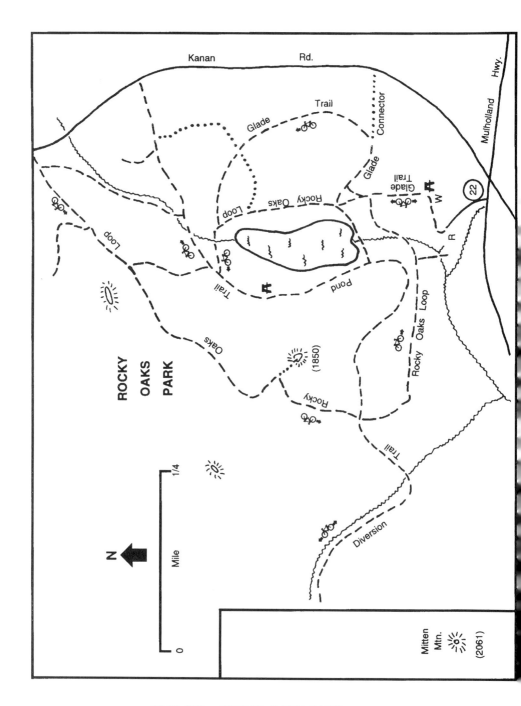

TRIP #22 - ROCKY OAKS PARK

90

farm machinery were destroyed by the 1978 Agoura fire. The park got its name from Vernon and Heriott Brown who lived on their ranch and farm holdings for 30 years before selling the property to the National Park Service in 1980. The Browns planted an orchard and built the pond as a watering source for cattle. The extensive land use is thought to have wiped out any trace of the Chumash Indians who are speculated to have harvested the abundant acorns in the oak grove and to have hunted animals who visited the spring just west of the site. The caves among the rocks in this western zone may have offered temporary or possibly permanent shelter to the Chumash.

TRIP DESCRIPTION: **Wanderings.** Bike north (away from the park entry point) under the verdant tree grove on a sandy trail, staying on the right as you cross many small paths. You pass an amphitheater and water fountain. A sign points in your direction of travel, showing *"Glade Trail."* After passing some picnic tables, cross over to a paralleling trail which leaves the grove (0.2) and heads out into an open meadow, then returns under the shade of a line of trees. At a pronounced fork, bear right and aim towards the wide-open meadow and Kanan Dume Rd. beyond. The Glade Trail bends and returns west.

Pond Overlook

Rocky Oaks Loop Trail. At a "T" intersection is a sign proclaiming *Rocky Oaks Loop Trail* (either direction) (0.35). Turn right and follow a little downhill to an intersection with *Pond Trail*, pointing left -- this leads to a little loop alongside the pond itself, which is now visible. You go right, heading uphill toward Kanan-Dume Rd. on a mildly rocky and rutted surface, then switch direction and head west. After passing a junction with a trail that heads back for Kanan-Dume Rd. (a dead end in a short distance), you begin some serious uphill on a mixed quality narrowing trail that traverses below one of the many rock-formation-studded hills in the park.

The half-mile uphill lets up, the trail widens and you continue through the chaparral enjoying views of the pond below (0.95). A short downhill takes you past a marked *Overlook Trail* (hikers only) junction and presents clear views of the multi-faceted rock formations in the area. The trail drops toward the pond's southern end, then meets an unsigned junction in 0.1 mile.

Loop Diversion. A turn right takes you off the loop, down into an idyllic meadow and back uphill through the dense tree cover to the marked park boundary. This is a slightly technical section where you must dodge road ruts and climb some sections with loose gravel. It is also one of the prettiest sections of the park. This up-and-back diversion adds about 1/2 mile to the basic loop.

Loop Continuation. Back at the junction you turn right and follow the *Rocky Oaks Loop* markers, passing alongside the parking lot which is separated from the trail by lush, dense vegetation. At 0.3 mile from the "diversion junction" is a junction with a *Pond Trail* marker just ahead and to the left. You make a hard right here and return to the parking area (2.1)

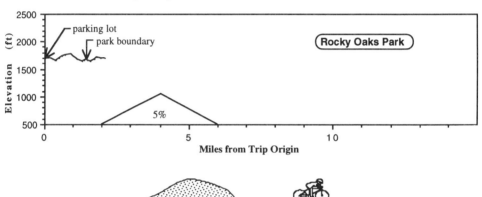

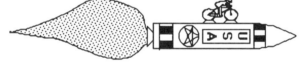

TRIP #23 - BREWSTER MOTORWAY LOOP

GENERAL LOCATION: Location (Topo) - Point Dume

LEVEL OF DIFFICULTY: Loop - moderate to strenuous
Distance - 3.7 miles; Time - 1-1/2 hours
Elevation gain - 550 feet

HIGHLIGHTS: Though short on distance, the described loop trip is long on variety. A one-mile ridge climb on Upper Brewster Mtwy. takes you through an exposed mountain stretch with distant scenic views which improve with altitude. A short up-down segment on Castro Peak Mtwy. drops you to the Lower Brewster Mtwy. entry. From here you are treated to a refreshing runout through overhanging tree cover, followed by a short, challenging climb back to Mulholland Hwy. within a few hundred feet of the loop entry point.

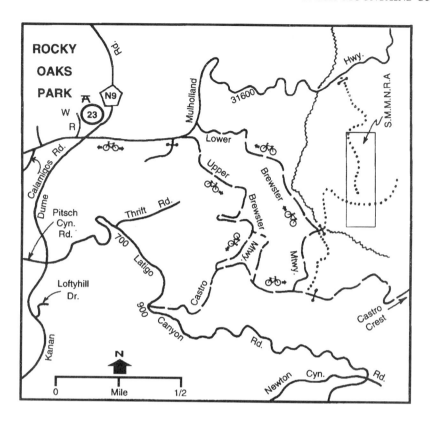

TRAILHEAD: See the Rocky Oaks Park trip and start at that point. There is a porta-pottie near the parking lot and a water fountain beyond the parking area within the park proper.

TRIP DESCRIPTION: Upper Brewster Motorway. At the park, set your odometer to 0.0 and bike across Kanan-Dume Rd. on paved Mulholland Hwy. Continue 0.5 mile to a yellow metal gate with *Brewster M/W* imprinted on the stanchion on the gate's right side. You start steeply on a good quality fire road and power uphill. In 0.2 mile, you get a clear view of the destination ridgetop to the south with a lower ridgeline, which trails off to the northeast. You climb steadily on a sparsely-shaded winding road with mixed sections of packed dirt, gravel, sand and "all of the above," gaining steadily improving views to the north. A wide curve takes you above and to the left of an undeveloped flat site and past an overgrown road to the left (1.2). Beyond is a steady traverse to a short, deeply-tilled road section (no traction) that deposits you at the intersection with packed, graded *Castro Peak Mtwy.* The stanchion on your left points back the way you came and states *Brewster M/W* (1.55). Turn left (east), climb to the trip's crest and coast down to a five-way residential intersection, 0.4 mile from the Upper Brewster Mtwy. junction.

Lower Brewster Motorway. Take the first unmarked road to the left (all others lead to clearly visible residences) and begin a downhill passage past the first of many scattered home sites, marked private junctions off the main road and thickening tree cover. The steepening downgrade takes you over a creek which drops down and stays alongside the road below and to the left (2.25). In 0.35 mile is a

93

small creek ford, a short upgrade through continued tree cover and a quick drop to the loop's low point. A healthy 0.4-mile climb returns you to Mulholland Dr. where you swing left, pass the Upper Brewster Mtwy. entry junction and return to Rocky Oaks Park (3.7).

Castro Peak from the Top of Upper Brewster Motorway

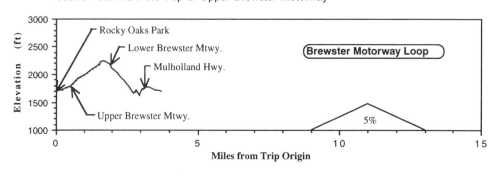

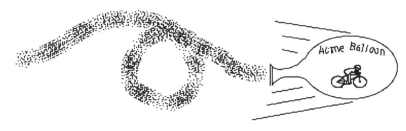

TRIP #24 - RAMERA/MURPHY MOTORWAYS

GENERAL LOCATION: Location (Topo) - Point Dume

LEVEL OF DIFFICULTY: One way - moderate
Distance - 5.5 miles; Time - 1-1/2 hours
Elevation gain - 250 feet

HIGHLIGHTS: This little-known ridge run provides a scenic-laden downhill in the mountains between and above Kanan-Dume and Latigo Canyon Rds. The route starts at the upper reaches on Latigo Canyon Rd. on a quality double track, transits almost 1-1/2 miles on asphalt road on a spate of small crests and continues to plummet downhill. A winding passage into a small canyon and a short climb give way to a let-it-out ride into the upper reaches of Malibu. This is a strenuous trip when done in the opposite direction.

Ramera Motorway Near the Entry

TRAILHEAD: From Pacific Coast Hwy. drive north 6-3/4 miles on Latigo Canyon Rd. to the first major plateau. On your right is a dirt road (Newton Mtwy.) with two large abandoned yellow and orange trucks parked to the side Directly across the road is the entry to Ramera Mtwy. From U.S. Hwy. 101 (Ventura Fwy.) in the San Fernando Valley, turn south on Kanan Rd. and drive six miles to Mulholland Hwy. In another 0.6 mile on the left is Latigo Canyon Rd. where you drive 2-3/4 miles to the trailhead. Park off the Newton Mtwy.

TRIP DESCRIPTION: **Ramera Motorway.** Just beyond the trailhead, follow the wide dirt double track on the left (right is private - 1875 Latigo Canyon Rd.). In 0.15 mile is a stanchion on the left marked **Ramera Mtwy.** You follow the good-quality, packed-dirt route downhill with a view to the left of Latigo Canyon and its namesake road above. In 0.4 mile from the trailhead, in a locale filled with chaparral and

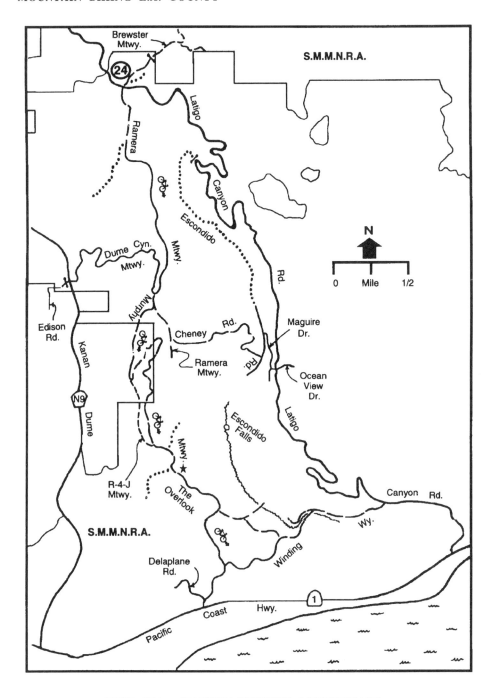

TRIP #24 - RAMERA/MURPHY MOTORWAYS

scattered low tree cover (typical of this exposed route), you reach an asphalt road.

Murphy Motorway

Just past a "Road Narrows" sign is a faint trail off the right which heads south and west for 1/2 mile and dies. Pass that by and follow a view-laden ridgeline on a mini-roller-coaster ride, cruising for 1.4 miles on asphalt. At this juncture is the Dume Canyon Mtwy. which dives right (west) and snakes its way down to Kanan-Dume Rd. Proceed left and pass two stanchions, one noting you are leaving Ramera Mtwy. and the other being faintly marked saying that you are now on **Murphy Mtwy**. Immediately beyond is a road split, the left junction (1.9) wandering off east to Escondido Canyon and our route proceeding uphill and right past a short power pole access road to the right.

More ridge-running on small ups and downs and continued good road surface takes you east around a bend. There is a hard-to-see uphill trail (R-4-J Mtwy.) to the right which you pass up. You follow a sharp turn north which leads to a series of quick turns that dump you down into a canyon bottom (3.0) We passed under a large beehive which Don, in the lead didn't notice, but which partner Sam observed as an active hive stirred up by Don's motion. The analogy is the old "hiking in the desert creek bed" maxim which says, "The first hiker through steps on the buried snake and the second hiker gets the aroused snake's greeting!"

You traverse the barren canyon's east side and climb along the west side 0.2 mile to a scenic level area where you get a clear view of the developed Malibu/Point Dume area. After passing a private road entry to the left, you see an unreadable trail marker on a metal stanchion to the left and continue 0.2 mile to a major road split (3.85). Right and uphill leads to a private residence and a power line road which dumps down to gated Ramirez Canyon (do not take!). Veer left, starting on the main road, and begin a no-worries 0.55-mile downhill on paved road on The Overview, with interesting canyon views to the left. At the road's easternmost point (4.6) is a small trail to the left which drops down to a dirt road that takes equestrians and hikers over to the Escondido Falls area. You continue on pavement and outlet at a "T" intersection with the road right heading into restricted-entry Ramirez Canyon and your route left dropping 0.1 mile to Pacific Coast Hwy. on W. Winding Wy. (5.5).

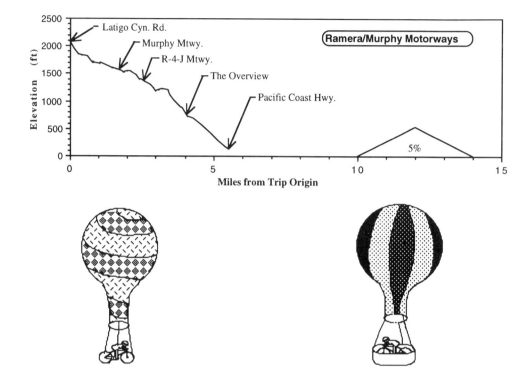

TRIP #25 - ZUMA RIDGE TRAIL

GENERAL LOCATION: Location (Topo) - Point Dume

LEVEL OF DIFFICULTY: Loop - moderate to strenuous
Distance - 6.4 miles ; Time - 2 hours
Elevation gain - 850 feet

HIGHLIGHTS: A ridge runner's delight, Zuma Ridge Trail starts from Encinal Cyn. Rd. and climbs 1.8 scenic workout miles with great views of Zuma Canyon, Castro Peak, Saddle Rock, Malibu Country Club, Sandstone Peak and Trancas Canyon. At the summit is the private entry to Buzzard's Roost Ranch but, more important, there is shade and a couple of rocks to perch on. Beyond is a 3.6-mile, 2000-foot elevation runout which puts you onto both east and west sides of Zuma Ridge, takes you by the Edison Rd. East and West entries and provides you with charming vistas that change with every major turn. Near trail's end is a switchbacking downgrade that lets you out within the "walls" of the Point Dume area civilization. An option to divert to a strenuous route on Edison Rd. W. is also provided in the trip description.

TRAILHEAD: From the San Fernando Valley, follow Kanan-Dume Rd. south to Mulholland Hwy. and turn right (west) continuing one mile and veering left at Encinal Canyon Rd. Proceed 0.7 miles to the Zuma Ridge Mtwy. entrance near a *Buzzards Roost Ranch* sign. There is parking for 2-3 cars just east of the entrance. From PCH drive six miles north on Kanan-Dume Rd. to Mulholland Hwy., turn west and continue as described above.

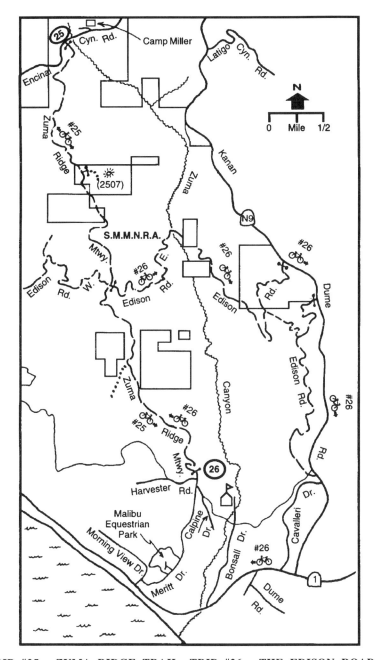

TRIP #25 - ZUMA RIDGE TRAIL; TRIP #26 - THE EDISON ROAD

To start from the south end, turn north from PCH onto Busch Dr. which is one mile west of Kanan-Dume Rd. Proceed 0.8 mile, jog right to stay on that street and

99

find parking above Cuthbert Dr. near where the road turns to dirt. The ride, when taken in this direction, is strenuous.

TRIP DESCRIPTION: **Climb to Buzzard's Roost Ranch.** Begin an immediate climb and pass a gate and *Zuma Ridge Trail, Busch Dr.-5.7 miles* sign at the top of the first rise. The destination ridgeline summit is visible to the south and 700 feet above in the form of a road cut into the mountain. The grade lessens, you enjoy a short downhill, then begin a steady 1.5-mile workout climb to the trip's crest. On the winding packed-dirt road you pass mostly barren slopes, gaining views eastward to Castro Peak and down into Zuma Canyon, northeast to Saddle Rock and northwest to the Malibu Country Club. Sandstone Peak, the highest peak in the Santa Monica Mountains, stands out in the distance to the west. At (1.4) you cross a small saddle with a single tree to remind you that there is such a thing as shade! The road flattens in another 0.3 mile and you propel another 0.1 mile to a crest at a saddle. The Buzzard's Roost Ranch wooden arch and entry road are to the left (private) and a road to the right climbs to a nearby flat. Before taking the middle road with the stanchion marked *Zuma* which points the way, stop and enjoy the shade of the grand oaks and the first Pacific coastline glimpse (1.8).

Initial Climb with Saddle Rock Backdrop

On to Edison Road. The road degrades in quality somewhat with some exposed rock and gravel from here to E. Edison Rd. You drop rapidly, working down the mountain's west face, viewing low scrub on the surrounding hills and Trancas Canyon below and to the right. The ocean views open significantly. You can look back and up to a magnificent residence perched high on the peak just south of Peak 2507 and Sandstone Peak still looms in the distant west. You pass a small National Park Service (NPS) marker (2.55) and take in the first Point Dume views.

Descend from the ridge, pass through patchy areas of red clay soil, then wind down the ridge's west side where you look across a wide canyon to Edison Rd. W. At (3.1), you get your first clear look at the switchbacking Edison Rd. E. that plummets into Zuma Canyon and a 12% grade, "slash" traverse that is the "escape route" out -- this is The Edison Rd! At a saddle and the trip's crest beyond is a metal gate and roads to the left with a sign noting *Zuma/Edison Rd. - Kanan Rd. 5 mi.* (3.5). Off to the right is a short spur trail to the power poles. A look back north reveals the now-more-distant house near Peak 2507 and ever-present Sandstone Peak to the northwest.

South of The Edison Road Junction

On to the Outlet. The improved quality main (middle) road continues ahead and switches from the east to west side of the scrub-laden ridge. In 0.1 mile is a small sign to the right which is readable to uphill bikers and notes *Trancas/Edison Rd. 1.5 miles to end.* This is the northern entry to Edison Rd. W. In another 0.2 mile of downhill is a flat former building site with the southern Edison Rd. N. entry "hiding" below. You continue coasting with improving views of Pt. Dume and Trancas Canyon, gain the ridgetops again, then reach a marked road junction (4.5). The fainter road to the left follows a short ridge and dies while the stanchion before the junction notes *Zuma Mtwy.* and points to the right which is your route.

More downhill keeps you within view of Trancas Canyon as you pass a small hiking trail on the right which outlets at Morning View Dr. at its western end and is marked *trail not maintained.* In 0.5 mile of downhill on a good road surface is another road split, with the fainter right fork heading directly up to an evident overlook point (5.3). Civilization is creeping closer as you see more and more structures and roof tops. Recross Zuma Ridge to the east and bike above a small, steep feeder canyon that meets Zuma Canyon further downstream and later pass through an open metal gate with an unreadable marker (6.0). You come up behind some homes, switchback downhill past a large water tank and continue to the trail's exit (6.4). On the other side of the gate is a sign pointing back uphill which notes *Zuma Ridge Trail.* The trail off the left is marked *Zuma Canyon* and leads directly to that destination (no bikes). Ahead is an information board with paved Cuthbert Dr. beyond and to the south.

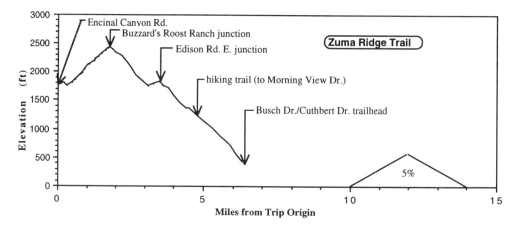

Trip Option: Edison Road West. A few very adventurous folks have explored the western road segment which can be entered at (3.6) in the described trip. You drop about 1100 feet in 1.5 miles (14%+ grade!) and reach a point not too far from the Trancas Canyon floor. Since private property blocks further travel, options are to gut it out back the way you came or follow a "no-nonsense" connector near the terminus which takes you on a more southerly route almost directly up the ridgeline. Do not attempt this very strenuous option unless you are in excellent condition and capable of route finding over the sometimes-overgrown southerly return route.

TRIP #26 - THE EDISON ROAD

GENERAL LOCATION: Location (Topo) - Point Dume

LEVEL OF DIFFICULTY: Loop - very strenuous
Distance - 14.0 miles; Time - 4 hours
Elevation gain - 3000 feet

HIGHLIGHTS: You won't find many better, or more difficult, rides in the Santa Monica Mountains. A stiff climb up Zuma Mtwy. on 2.8 miles of mildly-sinuous, good quality fire road affords a variety of scenic views. Across Zuma Canyon you see "The Climb," your gut-busting outlet on this tour. A steep, tight-winding 2.1-mile downgrade drops you to the lush and scenic canyon depths at Zuma Creek. The 1.9-mile climb out of the canyon along the eastern wall is moderate at first, then turns downright gut-wrenching until you reach the low southern end of the ridge. A graceful "U"-bend leads to the top of the ridge and then you get a well-deserved coast down to Kanan-Dume Rd. Closing the loop involves 5.9 miles of pedaling on paved road with the last mile giving you a chance to test for your tired legs.

TRAILHEAD: From the San Fernando Valley, take Kanan Rd. south (it becomes Kanan Dume Rd.) to Pacific Coast Hwy. Turn north from PCH onto Busch Dr. which is one mile west of Kanan Dume Rd. Proceed 0.8 mile, jog right to stay on that street, and find parking near Cuthbert Dr. just before the road turns to dirt.

Another option is to start the trip from Encinal Canyon Rd. as described in the "Zuma Ridge Trail" ride. You significantly reduce the elevation gain required to reach the Edison Rd. E. trailhead. A car shuttle is required for this option.

Just Before the Dive into Zuma Canyon

TRIP DESCRIPTION: **Trailhead to the Edison Road Turnoff.** Pass around the blocking gate with the sign noting *Zuma Ridge Trail*. Start an immediate steep climb past a large water tower and begin the first of several sweeping turns on good fire road. In 0.5 mile pass through an open metal gate and later cross over to the western side of Zuma Ridge. Pass a metal stanchion marked *Zuma M/W* near a concrete-surrounded fire hydrant and a "trail not maintained" sign on the left just beyond (1.6). (This no-bikes trail outlets at Morning View Dr.) Pass two unmarked road spurs in another 0.2 mile and another *Zuma M/W* stanchion. The steep eastern wall outlet from Zuma Canyon comes into distant view in this area giving you advanced notice of your impending heart-pounding climb. In succession, pass another road spur and a *Zuma M/W* sign on an outcropping on the left and a trail and marker noting *Trancas Edison Rd.-1.5 miles to end*, (2.7). Another 0.1 mile leads to a chain link fence on the right (east) with two markers, one noting that there is water for horses in 0.5 mile and another stating *Kanan Rd.-5.0 mi. into Zuma Canyon*. This is the Edison Rd. turnoff. If you are tired at this point, turn around!

Into Zuma Canyon. A wide fire road takes you steeply downhill on a tight-winding fire road with scree patches, some small rocks and sections of loose dirt. This road down the mountain face fronts you with views northwest to Castro Peak, north to the residence perched on the mountain cliffs in the Buzzard's Roost and east across Zuma Canyon. There are numerous chances to "study" the ominous road on the canyon's eastern wall, which is your exit route. Also in view across the canyon are the gnarly bulges of the rocky face of Peak 1918. As advertised you pass a white water tank marked "not for human consumption" in 0.5 mile of hell-bent downhill, then are greeted by a surprise short, steep upgrade after crossing a small ravine (3.4). This crossing puts you on a ridge coming down from Peak 1791.

Zuma Creek With Peak 1918 Backdrop

You pass under the power transmission lines in another 0.4 mile. In 1.3 miles from the gate, point north and recross the ravine that was further up the mountain. More steep winding downhill, a modest climb and a last gasp downhill drops you into the lush sycamore-studded bowels of the canyon and Zuma Creek (4.9). As witnessed by the trip photo and the photo on the back cover, it doesn't get any better than this!

"The Climb." After enjoying the spectacular neck-craning views, cross the creek and get lulled by a short flat and modest climb, following the contour of the canyon wall on quality fire road. You pass an off-shoot road to the left, then bike under the power lines (5.8). The road veers east, then starts a heart-pounding one-mile, super-steep traverse with scattered sections of shale. There are sharp canyon drops to your right (west).

We took several "vista breaks" in this area which included eyeballing the down-canyon views to the Pt. Dume area. You reach the southernmost point of The Edison Road at the end of a ridge, then follow a slow-winding "U" turn to the top of the ridge in another 0.1 mile (6.9).

The Outlet to Kanan-Dume Road. Pat yourself on the back, take in the sweeping view and follow the ridge to a second and higher crest. Beyond is a newly-opened single track off to the right marked *Zuma Canyon Connector Trail.* (The trail drops down to the easternmost segment of Edison Rd., which parallels Kanan-Dume Rd. -- see the "Trip Option" below.) Another short climb to a ridgetop gives way to the start of a 0.9-mile steep, winding downhill on fire road which lets out at a mesh metal gate at Kanan-Dume Rd. (8.1). On the downgrade are views of the local scrub-filled mountains and ravines, pass again under the power lines coming over from

Zuma Canyon and exit through a densely-wooded area just above the highway.

   The Paved-Road Return. A hang-it-out 3.3-mile downhill on Kanan-Dume Rd. drops you to Pacific Coast Hwy. A right turn here and easy climb to Heatherview Rd. are followed by a downhill to Busch Rd. (12.6). Turn right and follow your incoming automobile route 380 feet and 1.4 miles uphill to the trailhead (14.0).

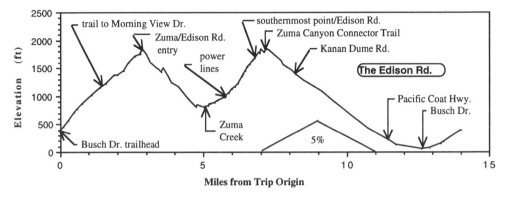

   Trip Option. Edison Road Extension. At the return to Kanan-Dume Rd. (8.1), bike south on that road as before. However, in about 1/2 mile (before reaching paved Dume Canyon Mtwy. on the left), leave Kanan-Dume Rd. at a fire road on the right with a chain across its entry. (Mileage below is measured from the chained entry.) In 0.2 mile is a mini canyon crossing, followed by a short winding climb which takes you above and parallel to Kanan-Dume Rd. in 0.5 mile. At 0.9 mile the *Zuma Canyon Connector Trail* comes down from the right and soon the road begins a southward descent. Roughly tracking Kanan-Dume Rd. below, cross another canyon (2.4) and pass equestrian trails which drop into Zuma Canyon on your right (west). Below Peak 705 is the Ocean View Trail which was being considered for access to cyclists in the summer of 1996 -- stay off these trails unless specifically marked for bike use. The road drops sharply to paved Cavalleri Dr. (3.1) then continues to descend to Pacific Coast Hwy. Turn right (west) and cycle back to the trailhead as described above.

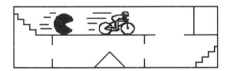

TRIP #27 - CHARMLEE COUNTY PARK

GENERAL LOCATION: Location (Topo) - Trifuno Pass

LEVEL OF DIFFICULTY: Meadowlands Loop - moderate
[West Ridge Rd. - moderate to strenuous]
Distance - 1.6 [3.4] miles ; Time - 1 hour [1-1/2 hours]
Elevation gain - 250 feet [800 feet]

HIGHLIGHTS: Charmlee County Park is touted as a natural preserve and was named for private owners Charmaine and Leonard Swartz. The park has a history of

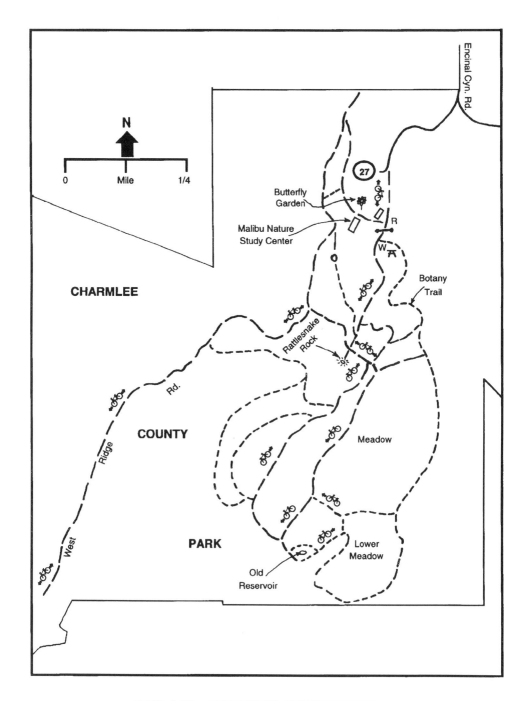

TRIP # 27 - CHARMLEE COUNTY PARK

ranching use as evidenced by the many criss-crossing trails and paths and the old cattle reservoir near the southern edge of the predominant meadow. The land was purchased by the county and opened to the public in 1981.

This compact 460-acre park sports ten miles of hike-and-bike trails and is an area locally revered by both plant and animal naturalists. The springtime blooms in the upper meadow are spectacular. Cyclists can ply the meadows and hills on packed open trailway, challenge both open- and four-foot high brush-enclosed single tracks. Though a sample tour is provided, we recommend that you select the combination of trails that suit or challenge your skills -- it is nearly impossible to get lost in this landmark-strewn area. There is a physically challenging up-and-back ride on West Ridge Rd. which lets you coast south 0.8 miles to the lower park boundary, then will challenge your stamina on the return 500-foot uphill return.

TRAILHEAD: From Pacific Coast Hwy., turn north on Encinal Canyon Rd. and drive 4.5 miles to the park entrance on the left (west). Follow the signs to the parking area on the right. There are water spigots at the picnic sites and a restroom. Encinal Canyon Rd. is 4-1/4 miles west of Kanan-Dume Rd. and 1/2-mile east of Decker Rd. (State Hwy. 23).

From the San Fernando Valley on U.S. Hwy. 101, turn south on Westlake Blvd. (State Hwy. 23) and continue seven miles to a fusion with Mulholland Hwy. In 1-3/4 miles at Decker Rd., bear left, staying on Hwy. 23, and continue 1-1/4 miles to Lechusa Rd. Turn left and pass the eastbound segment of Encinal Canyon Rd. (on the left). Continue on the southbound segment of Encinal Canyon Rd. 1-1/4 miles to the park entrance.

Overlook Near the Old Reservoir

107

TRAILHEAD: **Meadowlands.** From the parking area, bike back to the entry road and turn right (south) to a blocking gate. Set your odometer to 0.0 at the gated entry to the southbound dirt road (there are shaded picnic sites immediately to the left). A right turn on paved road takes you up to the Malibu Nature Study Center. However, you continue through the gate. A 0.2-mile shaded climb and a short flat takes you to a four-way junction with West Ridge Fire Rd. to the right (more later) and Rattlesnake Rock (scenic vista and an immediate chance to scope out the southern meadows) a short distance directly ahead. Our route goes left and drops to another (five-way) junction, with the road hard left going back to the picnic area, left to the park's eastern edge. The single track coming up on the right is your return path. Take the remaining option due south and dump down into the middle of a wide flower-filled meadow on the park's most evident road/path. A short climb follows taking you to a "T" intersection at a scenic overlook point (0.7).

Climb to the Five-Way Junction

Turn left and pass by an old reservoir to an area with a grand vista point and the coastline and Point Dume to the east. Just beyond is a junction to the right which takes you down a steep, well-rutted trail/single track to a lower meadow that rests above a ring of bluffs. However, continue straight on a ridge to a nearby junction with two overgrown single tracks; right takes you down onto the park's western edge and left (our choice) puts you on a "bomb-run" through high brush back to the floor of the main meadow. (Less challenged cyclists can just return west to the previously-mentioned "T" intersection.) A dinky single track on the left returns you to the main incoming trail and a return to the "T" (1.3).

A right turn here takes you west and north on a sinuous mixed-width trail below a series of low knolls and through hardpack with scattered sandy stretches. You bike past a series of single-track junctions to the left (all lead up to the knolls) and follow a nice downhill to a small creek bed. A short workout climb from here returns you to the incoming five-way intersection where you retrace your incoming route on a quick and steep upgrade that returns to the Rattlesnake Rock/West Ridge Rd. intersection (1.6). From here you can return 0.25 easy mile to the trip's origin or continue west on West Ridge Rd.

West Ridge Road. West Ridge Rd. is a very steep "down-in/up-out" ride that drops over 500 feet in 0.8 mile (roughly 12% average grade). Follow the good-condition and hard-packed curving path downhill as it bends east, flattens for a short stretch below a knoll and then continues to plummet down the ridgeline. The surrounding foliage is mainly chaparral and low bushes. On the way are spectacular Pacific Ocean views and refreshing sea breezes. The trail drops down to the park boundary at a gate near a water tank, which has a private development below it. Suck it in, put the shoe to the metal and return to the Rattlesnake Rock/West Ridge junction. From here is an easy 0.25-mile return to the trip origin (3.4).

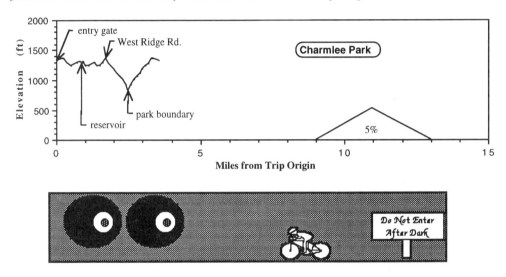

TRIP #28 - EAST LOS ROBLES TRAIL

<u>**GENERAL LOCATION**</u>:   Location (Topo) - Thousand Oaks, Newbury Park

<u>**LEVEL OF DIFFICULTY**</u>: One way - moderate to strenuous [technical section]
Distance - 4.7 miles ; Time - 1-1/2 hours
Elevation gain - 1200 feet

<u>**HIGHLIGHTS**</u>: The East Los Robles Trail can be linked with its western counterpart (see "West Los Robles Trail" and "Los Robles Trail (East and West)" trips) for a strenuous adventure or can be biked as a single segment. The eastside trail particularly reminds us of Dirt Mulholland in that it is the "main line" from which numerous accesses and trail options are available. Most of the route is on good quality fire road. The route discussed leaves the Moorpark Rd. trailhead, works back west and then splits off from the West Los Robles Trail heading south toward the Conejo Crest. A steep climb to a scenic ridge is followed by a meadow transit and crossing of several outlet junctions on the view-laden ride. A mile-long traverse below the north slopes of the crest lead to a decision junction. One route continues on the fire road exiting near the Foothill Dr./Fairview Rd. intersection. The route described here takes a very technical 0.9-mile single track which skirts the upper reaches of Trifuno Canyon, climbs an adjacent ridge and roars down to the northern edge of Trifuno Canyon Park.

109

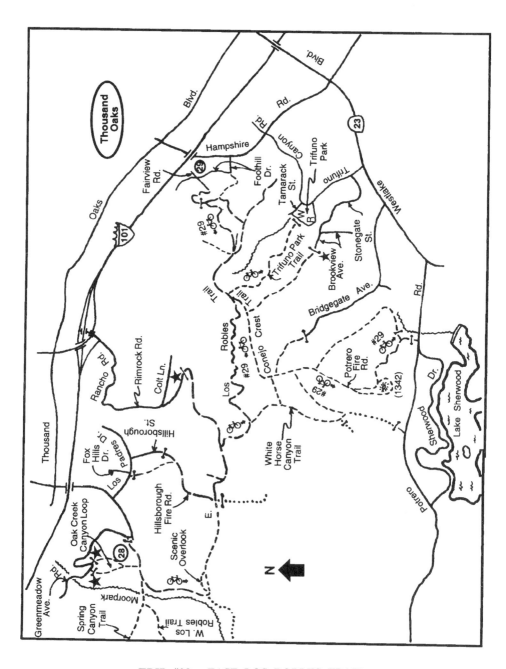

TRIP #28 - EAST LOS ROBLES TRAIL
TRIP #29 - OVER THE CONEJO CREST

TRAILHEAD: There are numerous convenient entries to the East Los Robles Trail. For the trip described, exit south at Moorpark Rd. and drive 3/4 mile to its end just beyond Greenmeadow Ave., parking in the dirt lot near the marked trailhead.

Other Entries:

Potrero Rd. - 0.6 mile west of Westlake Blvd. on Potrero Rd. just beyond Vista Oaks Way. A small road to the west of the creek leads a couple of hundred yards to a metal gate behind a fenced residence. (See "Over the Conejo Crest" outlet.)

Brookview Ave. - 0.1 mile north of Westlake Blvd. on Trifuno Canyon Rd., turn left on Stonegate St. and drive 1/2 mile to its end at Brookview Ave. Turn right and continue to road's end. This is the easiest access to the crest.

Trifuno Canyon Park - 0.4 mile north of Westlake Blvd. on Trifuno Canyon Rd., turn left on Tamarack St. and left again into the park. (See "East Los Robles Trail" outlet.)

Foothill Dr. - 0.2 mile west of Hampshire Rd. on Foothill Dr. where the Foothill Dr. turns right and uphill. Look for a hard-to-see trail on the north side of the road.

Foothill Dr./Fairview Rd. - see "Over the Conejo Crest" trail entry.

Rimrock Rd. - Exit U.S. Hwy. 101 (Ventura Fwy.) south at Ranch Rd., which becomes Rolling Hills Dr. in a short distance. The road veers left (south) and becomes Rimrock Rd. Stay right at the Colt Ln. junction and continue to road's end at an unmarked blocking gate (1-1/2 miles from the freeway).

Los Padres Dr. - 0.5 mile south of the Ventura Fwy. on Moorpark Rd., turn left on Los Padres Dr. and a few hundred feet, just short of Fox Hills Dr. The trailhead is on the right (south) side of Los Padres Dr. There is a metal gate and a marker noting "Los Padres Trail."

Hillsborough St. - As above, continue 0.2 mile past Fox Hills Dr. and turn right on Hillsborough St. continuing uphill to the cul-de-sac. On the right between residential properties is a dirt trail leading to a brown metal gate and the trail.

Greenmeadow Ave. - At Moorpark Rd.'s terminus, turn right onto Greenmeadow Ave. and continue 1/4 mile to a turnaround with a sign noting "Oak Creek Canyon Loop" on the left. A second trailhead is 1/4 mile beyond in a treed parking lot. To the left (south) is a metal gate and a sign noting "Los Robles Trail."

Captain St., Spruce Hill Ct. and Acacia Rd. - See the "West Los Robles Trail" tour.

TRIP DESCRIPTION: Trailhead to Lake Sherwood Turnoff. From the trailhead you wander west on a wide, flat expanse with scattered tree and ground cover, staring directly ahead and above to the complex of towers above the West Los Robles Trail switchbacks. In 0.3 mile is the marked *Oak Creek Canyon Loop Trail* junction to the right (to Greenmeadow Ave.). Your route is directly ahead per the sign marked *Los Robles Trail*. A short climb beyond leads to the Los Robles Trail split, where the marked *Los Robles Trail West* sign points right and your route, ***Los Robles Trail East*** aims left (south) toward some nearby hills. Follow the good-quality road uphill to a junction (0.8) where a right turn would take you across a small draw and past a shaded picnic table (the route continues south to private property in Hidden Hills).

Proceed left and uphill, then right in 15-20 feet at the ***Los Robles Trail*** marker (left is a steeper ridge climb that rejoins this marked route). Follow the steep, rutted and rocky single track up to a ridge top about 0.3 mile from the "picnic table" junction. The San Fernando Valley views northward and a long-running, east-west ridge ending at Sandstone Peak to the southwest reward you at this local crest.

East of White Horse Canyon Junction

An immediate junction left leads to the *Scenic Overlook Loop* alternate (which rejoins the Los Robles Trail at another marked junction 0.35 mile beyond). The described route continues ahead through a high meadow, passes the Scenic Overlook Loop outlet junction (1.4), then dives down to a four-way intersection. A right turn (south) leads to a gate and private property, while a left leads to Los Padres Dr. and Hillsborough St. via the Hillsborough Fire Rd. Continue directly ahead toward the hills to the east noting the large transmission lines to the east-south-east that mark your destination route. Climb the hill ahead (a rattlesnake at road's edge greeted us in this segment), pass above a water tower, and reach a crest with a paved spur road to the left (1.8). (The spur heads up the nearby ridge and dies. Proceed right, pass under the power poles and follow a flatter, packed-dirt road past another tree-shaded picnic table and a faint, wide trail which climbs the ridge to your left (north).

The reference route works basically eastward under the general line of power poles before reaching another road fork. Left leads to the top of Rimrock Rd. (2.2). The Los Robles Trail is to the right; beyond the junction is a large brown metal gate with **Lake Sherwood** and **Trifuno** marked on its face. The road continues to drop, then flattens in an area with a view down to the housing developments in the Lake Sherwood area. In 0.3 mile from the brown gate is the marked turnoff noting *Lake Sherwood-2 mi.* to the right and downhill (into White Horse Canyon) and your route directly ahead (east) marked **Trifuno Park-2 mi.; Fairview Rd.-2 mi.** (2.55).

Lake Sherwood Turnoff to Trifuno Canyon Park. Just past the junction, cross a saddle, circuit the north side of another ridgeline peak and follow the ridgeline contour. There are steady views of the San Fernando Valley below which include the Ventura Fwy. and State Hwy. 23 northbound. Directly below is a small canyon with its own network of trails. Continue the traverse eastward on a downhill, then bottom out and make a 0.6-mile workout climb to a crest, passing a northbound downhill single track (3.4) along the way. All the while you follow the power poles.

At the crest (3.7) and on the right is the unmarked access to the Conejo Crest Trail, that cuts back west and heads uphill. Pass that junction and continue 20-30 yards downhill to the *Trifuno Park* trail marker on the right. Ahead on the packed-dirt fire road takes you on a 1.4-mile route with an outlet at Fairview Rd. A challenging option, that is very technical, is to turn right. Follow the narrow, rocky single track as it crosses southeast above the head of, and then on the west side of, Trifuno Canyon. The canyon vistas and specter of Westlake far below can divert you from a difficult trail that needs your attention. In 0.3-mile climb the next ridge to the south, then follow some very steep switchbacks to the head of a small canyon. Cross over to the south side of the canyon, then coast downhill on still steep and rocky surface that outlets under scattered tree shade near a creek. A short flat leads to the northern corner of the shaded, beautifully groomed, grass-matted park (4.7).

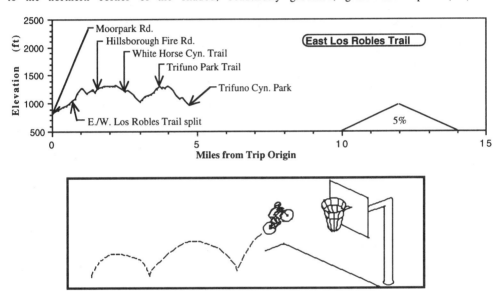

TRIP #29 - OVER THE CONEJO CREST

__GENERAL LOCATION__: Location (Topo) - Thousand Oaks

__LEVEL OF DIFFICULTY__: Loop - Moderate to strenuous [technical section]
                        Distance - 6.3 miles; Time - 2 hours
                        Elevation gain - 750 feet

HIGHLIGHTS: There are numerous trails which branch off of the East Los Robles Trail. This tour leaves the Los Robles Trail exit at Fairview Rd. and climbs several hundred feet to the Conejo Crest Trail. A rocky road on that trail follows the super-scenic ridge crest, then dives down to a lower roller-coaster ridge run which passes numerous spur trails. In 2.5 miles from the start is an option to plunge into White Horse Canyon and climb back up to the East Los Robles Trail. The reference route follows a ridge east which parallels the Conejo Crest. A series of ups and downs on the now-southbound ridge takes you to the last of several vista points. You drop down on a sinuous route above a canyon that lets out beside a creek at Potrero Rd. north of Lake Sherwood. A run on surface streets returns you to the trip origin.

TRAILHEAD: From the Ventura Fwy., exit south on Hampshire Rd. and drive 1/2 mile to Foothill Dr. Turn right (northwest) and drive 1/4 mile, parking near Fairview Rd.

TRIP DESCRIPTION: Trailhead to Conejo Crest Trail. Bike south on the packed-dirt/asphalt Fairview Rd., climbing steeply on dirt switchbacks which take you past a water tank (0.2) to a metal blocking gate in another 0.1 mile. Continue uphill past an antenna-bedecked pump house to a three-way junction (0.35); the uphill trail ahead leads steeply to a vista point, while the road left dumps out at Foothill Dr. or serves as an alternate (less desirable) route to E. Los Robles Trail. Turn right and continue to take in the San Fernando Valley views below and Simi Hills across the Ventura Fwy.

A meandering uphill takes you alongside a ridge to your south until you accede the ridge top at a five-way junction (1.2). A hard left (east) is an uphill ridge spur. Left is a fire road that works its way around the hill above to Foothill Dr. and southeast to a dead end. To the right is a single track that climbs steeply to a crest, then dives steeply (very technical) down to Rancho Rd. Modestly to the right (almost straight ahead) is a fire road which appears to disappear, then reappears in the distance across a canyon under a distant line of power poles. This is your destination route. Cycle down into the trough that is the head of Trifuno Canyon, then crank a short steep grade, passing the marked Trifuno Canyon Park Trail entry (left) just before reaching a local crest and another trail junction (1.5).

Below the Precipice/Conejo Crest Backdrop

Conejo Crest Trail. The fork right is the Los Robles Trail, the destination route for this trip is left and climbs steeply to the trip's crest. The views in the next up-and-down is a very rocky 0.7 mile and are obstructed only by scattered high brush. The Santa Monica Mountains' spine is spread along the distant south and the Simi Hills to the northeast. There are many views into the nearby canyons both north and south. Los Robles Trail follows below and to the north of the trail. Westlake Lake and Lake Sherwood are clearly evident as you reach a precipice and careen down a steep-to-shear grade heading south (experts ride, non-experts should walk/slide down this section). The White Horse Canyon Trail is evident below and to the right (west).

Pass a single track which drops west into White House Canyon (2.3), then a trail east blocked with heavy wire. In another 0.3 mile of rolling terrain is a prominent "T" intersection. One exciting option is to turn right and drop very steeply on a short, wide road into the White Horse Canyon. A junction right in the canyon bottom leads you back up to the Los Robles Trail (see "Trip Option" below).

Potrero Fire Road. However, the reference option is to turn left (east) on a dirt road and parallel the Conejo Crest on a flat. In 0.1 mile is a junction with a trail to the left (north) which works over to the Conejo Crest. At the junction is a stanchion stating *No Vehicles.* You continue ahead and follow some ups and downs along the scenic ridge to another junction -- the path left drops on an initially rocky surface to residences. Another junction follows which is marked *White Horse Canyon Loop* to the right (west) and *Equestrian Alternate* to the left, both steep single tracks. The sign pointing back in the incoming direction states *Conejo Crest Loop* (2.8). Continue ahead on the wide trail.

In 0.2 mile climb to a crest with an unblocked 360-degree view of the Conejo Crest area and "forever" views beyond. A dallying downgrade leads to a junction with a single track that climbs to the ridge of Peak 1342. Stay to the left and power downhill to a junction in 0.2 mile where the road to the right climbs back up to Peak 1342 (3.5). (The Peak 1342 climb leads to another grand vista point.) Your route left turns east on a steep traverse and on a wide, rocky trail that is severely washed out on its inside section. Below and to the left is a steep canyon drop off as the route follows the contours of the ridge to the right. The surface improves and a switchback funnels you down to an outlet above a metal gate. Beyond is private property and Heather Oaks Ln. Look for a single track which heads south (before reaching that gate) and stays above a chain-link fence. This route leads you, in a few hundred yards, to a small metal blocking gate behind a private residence which you pass through and follow a beeline alongside an outlet creek from Lake Sherwood to Potrero Rd. (4.0).

Return to Home Base. Retrace your entire route, return via White Horse Canyon (see "Trip Option" below) or take the surface streets. This route takes the latter option, with a serene 0.6-mile run east on Potrero Rd. and a 1.2-mile segment north on Westlake Blvd. (separated bike lane) to Hampshire Rd. Turn left. and bike 0.9 mile to Foothill Dr. and turn left again, returning to your car near Fairview Rd. (7.3).

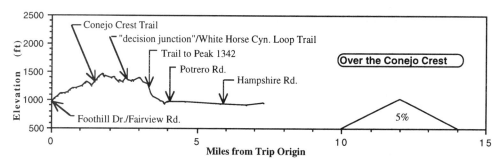

Trip Option -- White Horse Canyon Return. At 2.6 miles from the Foothill Dr/Fairview Rd. trailhead, "nurse" your bike down a steep-to-sheer grade and the canyon proper, climb to a flat and wind around a hill -- from this area the Los Robles Trail is visible above and to the northeast, and the Conejo Crest Trail sits northwest. A steep, short and rocky downhill leads past a marker noting **White Horse Loop** (3.0). Cross a normally dry creek bed in the now-evident canyon, passing through the scrub-filled domain. To your right (east) on the ridgecrest is the Conejo Crest Trail you came in on. Pass a single track that climbs to that crest, then cross the creek bed again. In the final 0.2 mile, negotiate heavily rock-exposed sections on a steep climb to the visible exit trail above. The final upward thrust is very steep and difficult, leaving you sucking air when you reach the Los Robles Trail and a sign pointing back downhill and noting *Lake Sherwood - 2 mi.* (3.6).

Los Robles Trail East Segment. Follow the Los Robles Trail east (marker notes *Trifuno Park-2 mi; Fairview Rd.-2 mi.*), cross a saddle, circuit the north side of another ridgeline peak and follow the ridgeline contour. There are steady views of the San Fernando Valley below which include the Ventura Fwy. and State Hwy. 23 northbound. Directly below is a canyon with its own network of trails. Continue the traverse eastward on a downhill, then bottom out and make a 0.6-mile workout climb to a crest, passing a faint northbound downhill single track (4.5) along the way. All the while you follow the power poles and continue another 0.3 miles to a crest. Hard right and uphill is the unmarked access to the Conejo Crest Trail. Continue straight and repeat your incoming route to the Foothill Dr./Fairview Rd. intersection (6.3).

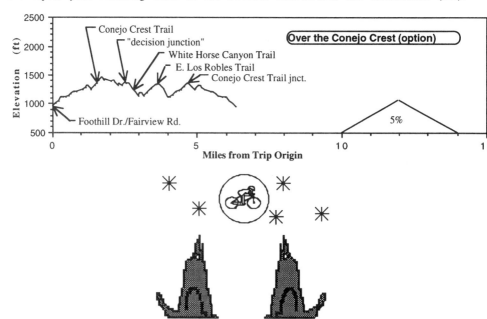

TRIP #30 - ETZ MOLEY MOTORWAY

<u>GENERAL LOCATION</u>:   Location (Topo) - Point Dume, Trifuno Pass

<u>LEVEL OF DIFFICULTY</u>: One way - moderate
                    Distance - 2.9 miles; Time - one hour
                    Elevation gain - 500 feet

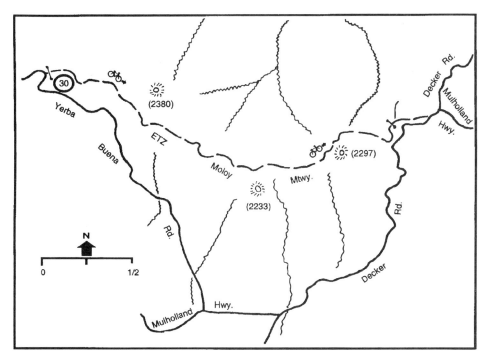

TRIP #30 - ETZ MOLEY MOTORWAY

HIGHLIGHTS: This short, little-known tour on good fire road is long on scenery from beginning to end. The ride is on an elevated ridge which looks down on Carlisle Canyon to the north and the valleys holding Mulholland Hwy. southward. More distant Sandstone Peak, Westlake, Castro Peak and the Pacific shores are viewed at various points. Taken in the opposite direction, the tour is rated moderate to strenuous.

TRAILHEAD: From the San Fernando Valley, take Westlake Blvd. (State Hwy. 23) south seven miles to Mulholland Hwy. (west junction). Turn right (west) and continue 1/2 mile, turning right again at Little Sycamore Canyon Rd. Drive two miles to some roadside residences and a dirt road on the right with a yellow stanchion just beyond the entry. The stanchion, which says "ETZ Moley Mtwy," is difficult to read. From Pacific Coast Hwy., proceed north up Yerba Buena Rd. nine miles (3.6 miles beyond the Circle X Ranch Ranger Station) to the dirt road entry described above.

TRIP DESCRIPTION: Pump uphill on a quality fire road, pass around a large metal blocking gate and grind out a 0.4-mile, average 12 percent upgrade. Take the time on the uphill to enjoy the outstanding views of Sandstone Peak to the northwest, Carlisle Canyon north and directly below and Westlake Lake to the distant northeast. The road levels and the winding route switches over to a southern exposure (0.55). There are coastal views and a look at the valley below, which contains scattered residences and a cluster of three mammoth satellite dishes.

At (0.7) a wide cut across the road berm on the left leads to a lightly overgrown double track. Stay right and continue on the main fire road. Another 1.6 miles of

Near the End of the Initial Upgrade

small ups and downs provides continuous views south, with northern vistas at the sporadic saddles. The area is crusted with chaparral and scattered low trees. In 0.7 mile past the last junction is a road on the left which cuts back and climbs to the ridge above, while other forks beyond lead to dead ends or graded sites. The high-line road shifts back over to the north and begins a steep, sinuous drop with fresh and inspiring views into the Decker Rd. (Westlake Blvd. to the north). Tower-bedecked Castro Peak is clearly evident due east. The 0.6 mile downhill runout outlets at a metal blocking gate where you turn right and coast a few hundred feet to Decker Rd.

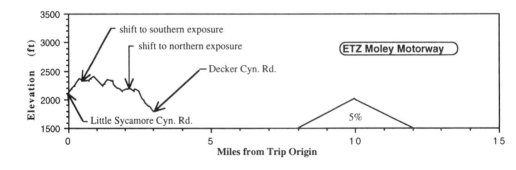

118

TRIP #31 - YELLOW HILL FIRE ROAD

<u>GENERAL LOCATION</u>: Location (Topo) - Trifuno Pass

<u>LEVEL OF DIFFICULTY</u>: Up and back - strenuous
Distance - 5.8 miles ; Time - 2 hours
Elevation gain - 1600 feet

<u>HIGHLIGHTS</u>: Yellow Hill Fire Rd. provides a scenic 2.9 mile, 1600-feet ride (average 10% grade) for dedicated climbers. The route up is on no-nonsense meandering roadway which provides alternating Pacific Ocean and Arroyo Sequit views. As the road nears the upper reaches of this ridgeline climb, the views expand to include the Channel Islands, Santa Monica Bay and the Palos Verdes Peninsula. The downhill return is a payoff for all the uphill legwork.

Overlook Near the Trailhead

<u>TRAILHEAD</u>: From Pacific Coast Hwy. (PCH), turn north on Mulholland Hwy. (1-3/4 miles east of Yerba Buena Rd. and 2-1/2 miles west of Encinal Canyon Rd.) and continue 300-400 yards to a turnout with a metal blocking gate on the road's west side. The gate is marked *Yellow Hill M/W*. Park along the highway nearby or on PCH. Another option is to park in Leo Carillo State Park whose entry is east of Mulholland Hwy. on PCH. This is pay parking, but you can enjoy the picnicking or camping facilities after the ride.

From the San Fernando Valley on U.S. Hwy. 101, turn south on Westlake Blvd. (State Hwy. 23) and proceed seven miles to Mulholland Hwy. Turn right onto that road and continue to off-road parking just north of PCH.

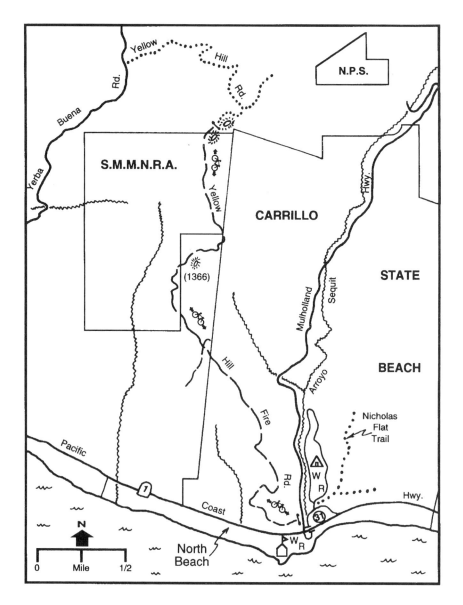

TRIP #31 - YELLOW HILL FIRE ROAD

TRIP DESCRIPTION: Pass around the blocking gate and begin an immediate western traverse up the mountainside on a wide, reasonable-quality fire road. At 0.35 mi. the road shifts northeast, then follows a semi-circular route below a local crest before drifting northwest. Below and to the right (east) is the Arroyo Sequit, Mulholland Hwy. and Carillo State Beach Park. A steady climb along the northwest-tending ridge takes you along continued chaparral-covered slopes, with Mulholland Hwy. falling further away below and to the east. Pass a fire road on the left (1.15) and then cross into Ventura County near a gate noting *State Park Property* (1.4).

120

In 0.15 mile follow the middle fork of a three-way junction and climb to the west side of the main ridge. The Arroyo Sequit is blocked but there are ever-improving coastal views as you continue the no-let-up climb. Enter the marked eastern edge of the Santa Monica Mountains National Recreation Area (SMMNRA), pass under the west slope of peak 1366 (2.0) and swing eastward. After crossing a saddle, swing back northeast and continue upridge. The climb returns you to the SMMNRA (2.4) and in 0.3 mile to the top of the ridgeline where there are superb views, particularly to the south (Channel Islands) and southwest (Santa Monica Bay and the Palos Verdes Peninsula). Pass a *Yellow Hill M/W* sign (2.8), then continue about another 0.1 mile to the trip terminus on a high plateau. Ahead to the north are the (blocked) private residences at the east, upper end of paved Yellow Hill Rd. Your only option at this point is to turn around and enjoy the view-laden 2.9-mile return downhill.

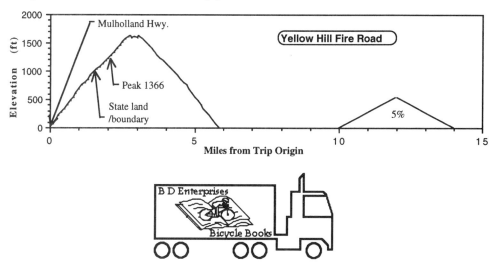

TRIP #32 - SANDSTONE PEAK

GENERAL LOCATION: Location (Topo) - Trifuno Pass

LEVEL OF DIFFICULTY: Up and back - strenuous
Distance - 7.5 miles; Time - 2-1/2 hours
Elevation gain - 1800 feet

HIGHLIGHTS: This ride is actually a marvelous two-part adventure. The initial 1.5-mile climb to Sandstone Peak, the highest point in the Santa Monica Mountains, is a scenic-laden, but lung-busting (average 13% grade) workout. Once there, a short hike up to the summit rewards you with one of the premier Santa Monica Mountain's vista points. The follow-on ride heads west on more modest ups and downs onto Boney Mountain and its treasure peaks. While heading toward the more distant Tri Peaks, you pass Boney Peak, Inspiration Point and Exchange Peak. The drama continues as you bike through a mountain-ringed meadow and dip down into Upper Carlisle Canyon. A turnaround here and route reversal provide a different perspective on the magnificent incoming landmark vistas.

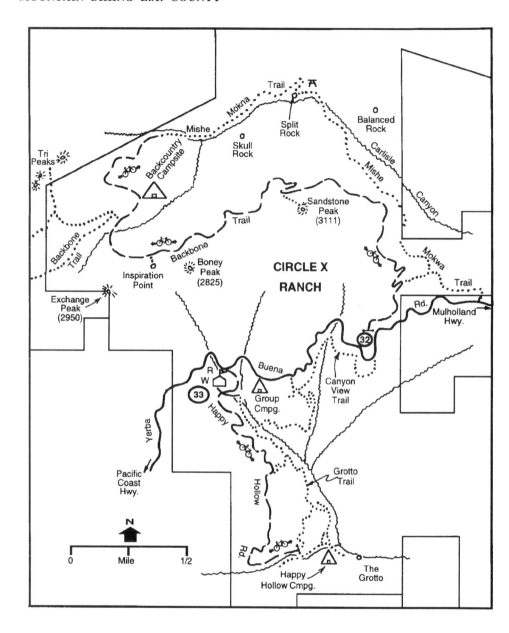

TRIP #32 - SANDSTONE PEAK; TRIP #33 - THE GROTTO

TRAILHEAD: From Pacific Coast Hwy., drive 5-1/4 miles up Yerba Buena Rd., marveling at magnificent Boney Mountain (essentially, the ridgeline of sculptured peaks you see to the north) in the last mile before reaching the Circle X Ranch Ranger Station. Stop here for water, restrooms, maps or advice before driving another mile to the turnoff on the left, marked *Backbone Trail, Parking Area.* Note that across the road is a marker noting *Canyon View Trail* which is for hikers only. From the San Fernando Valley, exit the Ventura Fwy. (State Hwy. 101) at Westlake Blvd. (State Hwy. 23) and drive south seven miles to Mulholland Hwy. (west junction). Turn right (west) and continue 1/2 mile, turning right again at Little Sycamore Canyon Rd. You can drive 4-1/2 miles to the trailhead or add another mile to visit the ranger station.

The Exchange Club, a Los Angeles service organization bought the Crisp Ranch in 1949 and developed the Circle X Ranch foundation as a charitable corporation. The ranch, which grew to include Happy Hollow and other holdings was leased to the Boy Scouts of America (BSA) starting in 1951, then deeded to them in 1979. The Mountains Recreation and Conservation Authority bought the ranch from the BSA and assumed property management in 1987.

**TRIP DESCRIPTION:
To Sandstone Peak.**
Pass around the metal gate at the north end of the parking area and pump steeply uphill on a fire road that requires some navigation to stay on the packed-dirt sections. The road wanders north, then east before switchbacking uphill on the ridgeline leading to Sandstone Peak. The destination peak and Boney Mountain loom above and to the west as you continue past the marked *Mishe Mokwa Trail Connector* (0.4).

Above the Mishe Makwa Trail Connector

The first signs of a previous disastrous fire come into view amid the natural reforestation that you will see on this ride all the way to its terminus. Carlisle Canyon drops further below and to your right (east) as you continue the climb to the road's most northeasterly point (1.0). To the distant east is Lake Sherwood as well as multiple ranges of mountains, including tower-bedecked Castro Peak. Almost due north and across the canyon is Balanced Rock, a seemingly unstable monolith sitting on a carved flat just below the ridgeline. The road turns west and continues switchbacking through mixed rocky, sandy and packed-dirt sections before reaching a crest. The Sandstone Peak summit is above and to the south, while a large plateau is northward and below (1.5).

Continue downhill a short distance where a trail marker notes the entry to the summit trail. This 3111-foot summit is the highest point in the Santa Monica Mountains! Hike up the trail and veer left, ascending to a peak topped with a bronze plaque noting "Mt. Allen." There was an unofficial dedication ceremony in 1969 to rename the peak after W. Herbert Allen, a dedicated Circle X Ranch advocate and financial supporter. The Department of the Interior maintained a long-standing policy of not designating a geographic name which honors a living person. Thus it is Sandstone Peak (not sandstone, but actually volcanic rock!) from which you currently take in the Channel Islands to the south and southwest, Boney Mountain Ridge to the west and the mountains of the Los Padres National Forest to the north.

Plateau Between Sandstone and Boney Peaks

Sandstone Peak to Upper Carlisle Canyon. Follow the improved quality switchbacking fire road as it drops to a flat, then proceeds west toward the dominant Boney Mountain Ridge. You pass to the south of the first of many sculptured sandstone summits, then begin a series of ups and downs (more down than up) passing the Boney Peak spire and the Boney Ridge Trail (currently closed, hiking only) off to the left (south). Next is the marked off-shoot trail up to *Inspiration Point* (2.45). A final uphill pedal leads past a fire road junction to the left in 0.1 mile, which leads to the two water towers above and the trail to magnificent Exchange Peak.

Stay right and drop into a large meadow where there is a signed junction to the left noting *Backbone Trail: Tri-Peaks 0.5 mi.* (no bikes) and your route continuing ahead (north) marked ***Mishe Makwa Trail: Split Rock-1.3 mi., Yerba Buena***

Rd.-3 mi. Cross a seasonal creek bed and pass the Backcountry campsite (check the ranger station to find if piped water is available), then bike on a deteriorating road that passes another trail junction with a marker visible to cyclists heading back in the direction you came noting: *Backbone Trail-0.3 mi. Sandstone Peak-1.5 mi., Yerba Buena Road.-2.8 mi.* Begin a 0.65 mile, 200-foot descent into upper Carlisle Canyon. This segment is on narrowing road with periodic gullied and rocky sections which lead to the canyon creek bed itself. On the way is a cave-lined sandstone monolith north of the trail and a small canyon surrounded by tall sandstone spires to the south (3.75). Past this crossing is a narrow, slightly overgrown single track which is for hikers only. If you want to visit Split Rock, a large volcanic structure split into three separate pieces (wide enough to walk through), you must hike the remaining 1/2 mile down into the creek bed. Otherwise, turn your bike around and revisit all the inspiring natural scenery that you enjoyed on the way in.

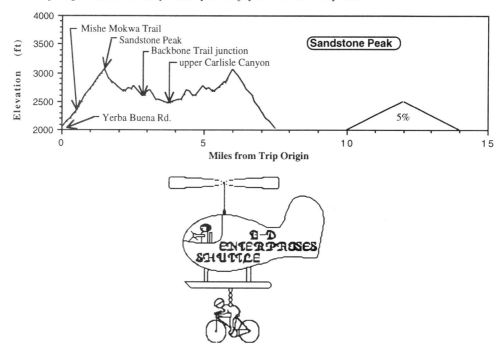

TRIP #33 - THE "GROTTO"

GENERAL LOCATION: Location (Topo) - Trifuno Pass

LEVEL OF DIFFICULTY: Up and back - moderate
Distance - 3.2 miles; Time - 1 hour
Elevation gain - 600 feet

HIGHLIGHTS: This is a down-in, up-out tour from the Circle X Ranch Ranger Station to the Happy Hollow Campground on quality fire road. There are numerous opportunities to take in the mountain and canyon views on the fly. The campground is a great place to park your bikes and hike into the Grotto or to take a breather before tackling the steep, one-mile climb on the way out.

125

Happy Hollow Campground and Gorge Entry to the Grotto

TRAILHEAD: Park at the Circle X Ranch Ranger Station as described in the "Sandstone Peak" trip. There are water, restrooms and maps here.

TRIP DESCRIPTION: From the parking area, follow the dirt road past the gate and bike downhill below the marked junction to the Ranch House. At a tree-shaded low point is an intersection with signs noting *Grotto Trail* (hard left -- hiking only), *Group Camp* (left), and *Happy Hollow Campground* (continue ahead on the road).

Bike past a picnic site, go through a blocking gate and make a moderate climb on continued good quality road. To the left (east) is Peak 2429, while nearer and below is the Grotto Trail and the canyon funneling the headwaters of the Arroyo Sequit. After a road junction to the right (alternate road back to Yerba Buena Rd.) (0.65), the winding, sometimes-rutted road dives toward Happy Hollow Campground.

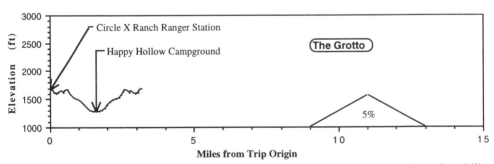

In 1/2 mile, the road cuts sharply west and begins a wide, sweeping downhill curve back to the east. There is a super view to the left (east) of the large meadow

126

and campground on the way down. The campground sports picnic sites, scattered tree cover, restrooms and a mountain-surrounded scenic backdrop. There is also a revered hike to The Grotto through a gorge to the southeast. The hike requires creek crossings and boulder hopping to reach clear rock pools and exotic rock formations.

TRIP #34 - SYCAMORE CANYON

<u>GENERAL LOCATION</u>: Point Mugu State Park
<u>LEVEL OF DIFFICULTY</u>: Canyon plus Overlook Trail Loop - strenuous
[Canyon Loop - moderate]
Distance - 16.7 [13.5] miles; Time - 3 [2] hours
Elevation gain - 1600 [700] feet

HIGHLIGHTS: Any off-roader will enjoy this super-scenic network of paths highlighted by the popular Big Sycamore Canyon and Overlook Trails. Leave the Sycamore Canyon Campground and proceed on a mild uphill in a sylvan setting to the Wood Canyon Trail. Continue a modest climb into lush forest cover to the trail's end at Ranch Center. There are over a dozen spirited, but non-difficult, creek crossings along the way. A short steep upgrade and refreshing 2.1-mile runout on paved Ranch Center Rd. brings bikers to the northern end of the Big Sycamore Canyon Trail, where a spin under overhanging tree cover and through a lovely tree-dotted meadow returns you to the Wood Canyon Trail junction. Less experienced cyclists should retrace the incoming route, staying south on Big Sycamore Canyon Trail.

A rewarding challenge awaits the cyclist who retraces the Wood Canyon Trail westward and tackles the quick-and-dirty "Hell Hill" segment of Overlook Trail. This is a little-used, sheer and exposed upgrade which goes to the Overlook Trail summit area ("the Overlook") from the "backside." From the summit area is a sinuous downhill with scenic exposures, including views of La Jolla Canyon, Sycamore Canyon and the shoreline. Alternates to the "Hell Hill" ascent are to use the Wood Canyon Vista Trail or Guadalasco Trail entry or to follow the most popular approach, which is an up-and-back ride on the Overlook Trail from its southernmost entry.

The area still shows the scars of the disastrous November 1993 fire. However, the affected tree cover is returning and the entire region is bursting with new low-lying vegetation.

TRAILHEAD: **South Entrance.** On State Hwy. 1, drive four miles east of Pt. Mugu or 25 miles west of the Malibu Civic Center to the Sycamore Canyon Campground entrance. Use the camping area parking or hike/bike parking as appropriate (a fee is required and the park is strict on parking rules). Alternatives are to park on

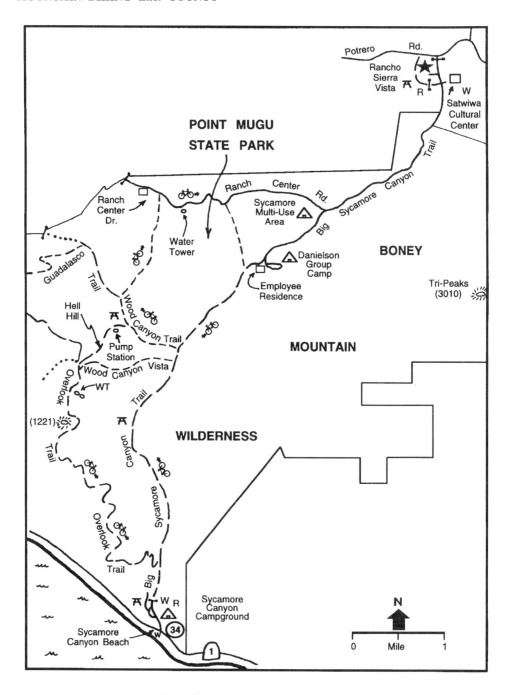

TRIP #34 - SYCAMORE CANYON

either side of Hwy. 1 for a fee or to use the free Caltrans parking lot outside the park west of the Caltrans Big Sycamore Maintenance Station. Observe and respect all parking signs.

North Entrance. On Potrero Rd. in Newbury Park, turn south at Pinehill St., which is 1/4 mile west of Reino Rd. Park at Rancho Sierra Vista or the Satwiwa Cultural Center (restrooms, picnic facilities, and ranger station) that gives out information about Native American Indians and National Park lands.

Bring a couple quarts of water if you tackle the waterless Overlook Trail. In contrast, there are water spigots sprinkled throughout the lower canyon areas.

Point Mugu State Park. This 15,000-acre park has several miles of scenic coastline, and a huge backcountry with lush canyons, chaparral-filled highlands and many scattered peaks.

Near the Big Sycamore Canyon Trail Entry

Its name comes from the Chumash Indian word MUWU, meaning "beach." The Indians lived here for 6000 years before the arrival of the explorer Cabrillo and were one of the most culturally-advanced tribes in California.

TRIP DESCRIPTION: Lower Big Sycamore Canyon Trail. From the south entrance hike/bike area, return to the camp entrance and follow the main road north to its end where a car barrier guards a small bridge over Sycamore Creek. Once on the east side of the creek, follow the graded-dirt path north on Sycamore Canyon Trail, passing hikers, walkers, runners and returning bikers. The first signs of the burned high tree cover appear. After 1/2 mile on a modest grade in a wide canyon with sycamores and oaks, you come to the *Overlook Trail* turnoff; it cuts back almost parallel to this path and is easy to miss, even with the trail marker present. Views west into the hillsides show the lower switchbacks of this scenic "sky-bound" trail.

Pass one of the many water spigots scattered throughout the park. At 0.8 mile is the first of over a dozen shallow creek crossings. (There was typically 6-8 inches of water, and a few deeper, when we passed through in July 1993, but only dry creek beds in January 1996--go figure!) The secret is to bike down to the creek, pick a route between the rocks, dive in and pedal hard past the midway point to master the climb up the bank on the opposite side. The increasingly shaded route passes several hiking trail junctions (no bikes!), a picnic area (2.2) and the easy-to-miss, single track, Wood Canyon Vista Trail junction.

Near "The Overlook"

Wood Canyon Trail. Reach a fork (3.0) with the *Sycamore Canyon Trail/Backbone Trail* to the right and our destination to the left on the **Wood Canyon Trail**. In 0.7 mile of winding mild uphill in shaded canyon is the Deer Camp Junction, another picnic area and the northern terminus of the *Overlook Trail* to the left. Go right (north), pass the *Guadalasco Trail* in a few hundred yards, and bike 1.3 miles on a narrowing trail under scattered tree cover with segments of filtered sunlight. Several more creek crossings bring you to a more exposed area where the canyon widens and into Ranch Center, a small park employee community (5.3).

Ranch Center Road. The next 2.5 miles east on this asphalt ribbon parallels the northern park boundary. First is a no-nonsense, exposed 1/2 mile, 200-foot, climb to a water tower. Beyond is an unnamed, but bikeable, dirt trail that is a short-cut to the upper Big Sycamore Canyon Trail. There are distant views of the Boney Mountain Ridge to the west of this junction. Stay on the paved road and follow a refreshing traverse of the hillsides and "let it out" with a nifty downhill that leads to a "T" intersection at another paved road. To the left (north) is Rancho Sierra Vista/Satwiwa Cultural Center, two miles and a 500-foot climb away.

Upper Big Sycamore Canyon Trail. A turn right leads back to shaded road with scattered sycamore trees and into a large meandering meadow. Follow the road to its end near an employee residence or follow the paralleling dirt trail on the meadow's western edge. In either case, maintain a southern direction and bike past the dirt trail junction which is signed *To Ranch Center Road*. (This is the outlet of the shortcut trail from the water tower previously mentioned.) Follow the steady downhill back to the Wood Canyon Trail Junction (10.3).

Overlook Trail to "Overlook Junction." Non-seasoned bikers should stay on Big Sycamore Canyon Trail and return to the starting point (13.5 total trail miles). Riders looking for a challenge should go right (west) and repeat the short ride to Deer Camp Junction. In contrast to the prior visit, follow the marked *Overlook Trail* on a steep grade that climbs above Wood Canyon and begins a slow turn to the south. What follows is an exposed, sheer uphill which is so steep that it is difficult to get restarted uphill once you have stopped. This is the infamous "Hell Hill." Don half-rode, half-walked this hillside traverse, seeking whatever shade was available at periodic rest stops. The view back down into the canyon and beyond are superb, making the hard work more bearable. A mile of this aerobic challenge leads to what we term "Overlook Junction" (12.0) Ahead is the marked *La Jolla Valley Trail* (hiking only, although its reopening to bikes is being considered) with views across the valley below and the Laguna Mountain Radar Facility at Pt. Mugu. Right is the newly-opened *Guadalasco Trail*. To the left and up is the continuation of the *Overlook Trail*, the destination route. (Note that there are less-steep alternate routes from the canyon. One is the single-track Wood Canyon Vista Trail, twice as long, but a lesser average grade, another the Guadalasco Trail, which is described as a separate trip. However, there are no "free rides" to this area; all entries are strenuous.)

A Second View from "The Overlook"

"Overlook Junction" to the Trailhead. The grade eases and the Overlook Trail meets the outlet of the Wood Canyon Vista Trail. After an uphill 1/2-mile trek, which includes passing a pair of water towers and several saddle crossings, a summit area ("The Overlook") is reached with a great 180-degree panorama of Sycamore Canyon and the Boney Mountain Ridge to the west (12.7). The reward for the uphill effort is a scenic ride across the ridgeline with a nice downhill and a final short upgrade to a second crest. Next is a dandy 3.3-mile, 1100-foot, meandering descent back to the Big Sycamore Canyon Trail. (The most popular route is to use this ascent segment from the campground and return the same way.) The first ocean view is beyond, and the trail winds through a series of hills in a manner that provides many vistas into La Jolla and Sycamore Canyons. In 1.2 miles from the second crest is the *Backbone Trail* entry, which leads south and west down to the Ray Miller Trailhead. In the intervening stretch are scattered shale patches and at least one deep trail rut, which occupied nearly the entire trail--keep your speed in check on the descent.

The path goes by an unnamed trailhead outlet and follows a wide set of sweeps on yet another long hillside traverse which provides views into the campground at the Ray Miller Trailhead. The dirt track turns south, crosses a saddle and works downward off this massive hillside to a point that parallels a hiker's scenic trail. More ocean views appear as the trail works east on a sloping meadow, then reaches a series of steep switchbacks which drop you back into Big Sycamore Canyon. Once back on the main trail, go right (south) and return 1/2 mile to the trip start point (16.7).

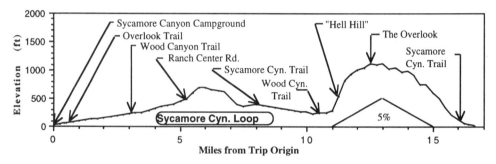

Trip Option. Biking Sycamore Canyon Trail by itself is a treat. The "cheater" option is to start from Rancho Sierra Vista and have a friend pick you up at Sycamore Canyon Campground (it will take your "SAG wagon" longer to get there than you, since this is a lengthy automobile drive). Another easy option is to bike from the campground uphill as far as you want to go, then coast back to the start point.

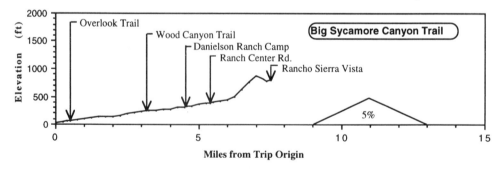

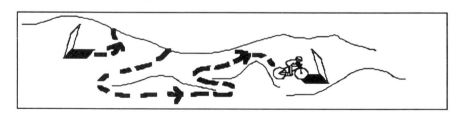

132

TRIP #35 - GUADALASCO TRAIL

<u>GENERAL LOCATION</u>:   Location (Topo) - Point Mugu State Park

<u>LEVEL OF DIFFICULTY</u>: Loop - strenuous
Distance - 12.7 miles; Time - 2-1/2 hours
Elevation gain - 1400 feet

<u>HIGHLIGHTS</u>: Most Sycamore Canyon aficionados bike Big Sycamore Canyon on the Overlook Trail. This newly-opened trail plies the scenic backcountry away from the crowds. From the park's southern entry, a moderate ride up Big Sycamore and Wood Canyons leads to the Guadalasco Trail junction. A steady climb near to the western park boundary leads to a transition south and a scenic-laden, switchbacking climb to Peak 1366. A refreshing downhill, high above the canyons, leads back to the Overlook Trail. A short climb to the Overlook Trail summit area is followed by a downhill runout on that trail with views of Big Sycamore Canyon, the Pacific Ocean and Channel Islands, and distant Boney Mountain.

<u>TRAILHEAD</u>: Same as "Sycamore Canyon" trip.

Coming Down off the Switchbacks

TRIP DESCRIPTION: **Trailhead to Guadalasco Trail Junction.** Bike the Lower Big Sycamore Canyon and Wood Canyon Trails 3.7 miles to the Deer Camp Junction described in the "Sycamore Canyon" trip. A couple of creek crossings and 0.3 mile further is the signed entry to the left (west) to the *Guadalasco Trail* (4.0).

Westward to the "Old Junction." The narrow fire road climbs through the surrounding brush under scattered tree cover alongside and above a creek. The upward push continues westward on a narrowing trail with periodic swings toward the north. A small creek crossing in 0.4 mile leads to an exit from the woodlands to a wide open, hill-surrounded expanse. Left (southwest) in the mountains above are the cutouts that represent your destination switchbacks.

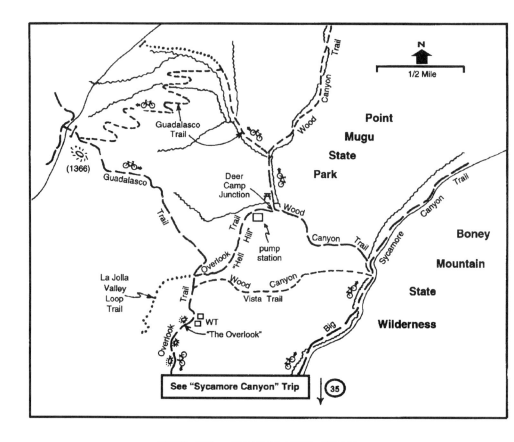

TRIP #35 - GUADALASCO TRAIL

In 0.65 mile along the trail is a junction with a sign to the right stating "Area Closed for Plant Rehabilitation" (this older trail dies further west at a private property line) and left noting *Guadalasco Trail* (4.65).

Up the Switchbacks. Turn left, cross the creek that you have followed on the way in and pass through the last woodland that you will see until you return to Lower Big Sycamore. Your uphill westward and first traverse is an introduction to the first of ten switchbacks that will take you up to Peak 1366. The first switchback sends you east and staring into massive Boney Mountain in the distance. The end of the second switchback takes you across a ravine on wood planking and onto the body of Peak 1366. This peak will be your companion for the remaining and generally shortening tight switchbacks on the way up. The wide hard-packed single track leads you to ever-improving vistas as the incoming route below spreads before you and Boney Peak returns to view with each alternate switchback. The trail climbs to a fire road where there is a sign pointing back the way you came which says *Trail* (6.4).

On to the Overlook Junction. Turn left (right is blocked in about 50 yards), make a short climb on quality surface, and veer south to a crest. A scenic downhill follows the contour of Peak 1366 on its northern flank presenting you with steep canyon views below and further eastward into Wood and Big Sycamore Canyons. In 1.2 miles from the crest is the four-way Overlook Junction (7.9). Pointing back to the way we came is a sign noting *Guadalasco Trail*, while right (west) is a marker with *La Jolla Valley Loop Trail* (no bikes). Left is the northern section of the Overlook Trail ("Hell Hill") and directly ahead is the reference route on *Overlook Trail*.

  "Overlook Junction" to the Trailhead. Follow the section of the same title in the "Sycamore Canyon" trip description 4.8 miles to the start point.

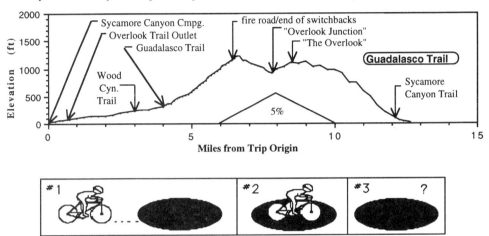

TRIP #36 - RANCHO SIERRA VISTA/SATWIWA

GENERAL LOCATION: Location (Topo) - Newbury Park

LEVEL OF DIFFICULTY: Loop - easy to moderate
                          Distance - 4.9 miles; Time - 1 hour
                          Elevation gain - 400 feet

HIGHLIGHTS: The Wendy Trail is a perfect family ride providing a cruise through hills and meadows from the Satwiwa Cultural Center to the Wendy Walk-in or Potrero Rd. This is a 2.9 mile pleasurable, easy up-and-back from the entry parking area with the Satwiwa Cultural Center added as a bonus. The full tour adds a fun single track up to the Los Robles Trail entry and some short workout uphills on the Rancho Overlook and Pine Hill Trails.

TRAILHEAD: From U.S. Hwy. 101 (Ventura Fwy.) exit south at Newbury Park at Wendy Dr. For westbound travelers, go under the freeway and turn right (west) at the first street which is Old Conejo Rd. Eastbound travelers should motor straight across Wendy Dr. and enter Old Conejo Rd. The street bends south and becomes Reino Rd. Three miles from the freeway exit is Potrero Rd., where you veer right and travel 0.7 mile to Pine Hill Rd. Turn left onto dirt and continue 1/4 mile to a parking area on your left. There is a portable restroom here.

  Rancho Sierra Vista/Satwiwa's western boundary reflects the original Rancho El Conejo land grant by the King of Spain to two of his loyal soldiers. Prior to that time, this area, together with Sycamore Canyon, supported the Chumash Indians. Satwiwa, or "the bluffs," was the name of a nearby Chumash Village, and a Satwiwa Native

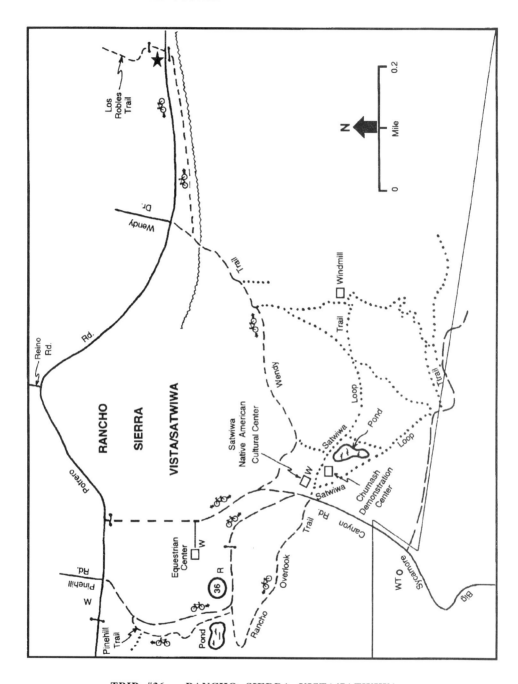

TRIP #36 - RANCHO SIERRA VISTA/SATWIWA

American Indian Natural Area now rests in the general area. Subsequent to the Spanish land grant, the land was subdivided and became ranches for numerous hosts. The property was purchased by the National Park Service in 1980 from the Richard Danielson family, the last private owners of the property.

TRIP   DESCRIPTION: **Wendy Trail to Los Robles Trail Entry.** From the southeast end of the parking lot (the marked entry arch on the northeast end goes to the Equestrian Center), follow a dirt trail to a blocking gate on the main road. The signs note *Satwiwa   Native American   Cultural   Center* and *Pt. Mugu Park Entrance-1/2   mi*. Bike onto the partially paved road to a junction (0.3). The sign points hard left to *Satwiwa Cultural Center* and ahead to *Pt. Mugu State Park*. Also straight ahead and to the right at the base of a small hill is a sign stating *Rancho Overlook Trail*, which you will visit later. Turn hard left, pass the Cultural Center on a wide road and look for the marked *Wendy Trail* entry in 0.2 mile on the right.

Native American Abode near Cultural Center

Immediately after you access the trail, there are gorgeous views across the hills and meadows with the impressive Conejo Peak and the Boney Mountain chain of peaks as a distant backdrop directly ahead (southeast). The wide single track climbs gently south and east, passing a marked hiker's trail (Satwiwa Loop Trail) (0.9). A hill-and-dale ride takes you past a second (unmarked) hikers' trail on the right, then sends you down into a creek which parallels Potrero Rd. (1.5). (For the easy family ride, turn around and retrace your path at this point.)

After a 30-foot ascent, turn right onto a slightly overgrown single track and parallel Potrero Rd. through lush terrain. A 0.6-mile upgrade takes you across a small creek twice just before you reach Potrero Rd. Directly across that paved road is the signed *Los Robles Trail* trailhead and parking lot.

Return to Satwiwa Cultural Center. Backtrack to the Wendy Trail or cruise down Potrero Rd. to the parking area/posting board at the "Wendy Walk-in," where a posting notes *Wendy Trail* (2.55). For the latter route, drop back down and cross the creek and retrace your route to the Satwiwa Cultural Center (3.7).

Rancho Overlook Trail. Bike 100 feet south of the Cultural Center and turn right just below the **Rancho Overlook Trail** marker. A flat stretch, then short but steep climb on a single track takes you to a crest with a great park panorama. North and below is the entry parking area. A 0.2-mile curving downhill leads to the south side of a small reservoir. Proceed almost to the dirt park entry road and look for a sign noting **Pine Hill Trail** (4.3).

Conejo Peak from the Pine Hill Trail Outlet

Pine Hill Trail. Turn left (north) and skirt the reservoir, then hill climb on a single track, roughly paralleling the park entry road. In 0.3 mile of ups and downs (mainly "ups"), you reach a scenic crest where the trail splits. Left passes through a fence opening, however your route is right on a steep return to the park entry road (walk your bike if you have any doubts). A turn right, a short upgrade and a downhill finale on this road returns you to the parking area (4.9).

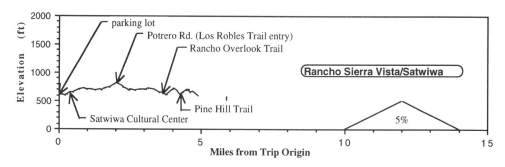

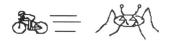

138

TRIP #37 - WEST LOS ROBLES TRAIL

GENERAL LOCATION: Location (Topo) - Newbury Park

LEVEL OF DIFFICULTY: One way - moderate to strenuous
                        Distance - 6.2 miles ; Time - 2 hours
                        Elevation gain - 1000 feet

HIGHLIGHTS: This dynamite single track through the Los Robles Open Space packs a variety of both challenges and spectacular riding in a short distance. An initial easy ridge tour above the developed Conejo Valley gives way to a challenging cyclist's "obstacle course" we designated the "Manic Mile." Beyond is a breathtaking scenic traverse on the steep slopes above Ventu Park and a nearly one-mile downhill blowout on a seemingly never-ending series of steep switchbacks leading to a "catch-your-breath" segment on relatively flat fire road.

TRAILHEAD: From U. S. Hwy. 101 in Newbury Park, exit south at Wendy Dr. (Camino Dos Rios to the north). Follow that road 2-1/2 miles to Potrero Rd. where there is a parking lot for entry to the Wendy Trail of Rancho Sierro Vista. However, you turn left (east), continuing 0.4 mile to a small parking area, marked **Los Robles Trail** on the left. This is the described trip start point. Another option is to extend the trip length by parking at Rancho Sierra Vista proper (see the "Rancho Sierra Vista/Satwiwa" trip). To get there, drive west on Potrero Rd., turn south at Reino Rd. (to stay on Potrero Rd.) and continue 0.6 mile to Pine Hill Ave. Turn left and continue 0.3 mile on a dirt and gravel road until you reach a dirt parking area with a porta-pottie on the left. Consider visiting the Satwiwa Cultural Center and enjoying a post-ride picnic on the nearby grounds if you bike up and back.

Other Entries:

Felton St. - at Lynn Rd. and Felton St. turn south on the latter street and continue to road's end. Enter near the "Los Robles Trail" sign.

Acacia Rd. - at Lynn Rd., turn south on Heavenly Valley Rd., right on Combs Rd., left on McKnight and left on an unmarked road across from 278 McKnight Rd. At road's end is a white blocking gate and a multi-use trail sign (1/2 mile from Lynn Rd.). Parking is very limited -- this is the least preferred entry as a result.

Capitan St. - at Lynn Rd. and Capitan St., turn south and continue 1/2 mile to Lynn Oaks Park (water, grass, trees, playground, picnic facilities). At the upper (south) portion of the park is the entry at a sign reading "Los Robles Open Space and Trail System Access." There is an alternate (but less attractive) entry nearby at the top of the Spruce Hill Ct. cul-de-sac at a white blocking gate.

Acacia Rd., Spruce Hill Ct., Green Meadow Ave., Hillsborough St. (all are entries from the east trail segment) - See "East Los Robles Trail" writeup.

TRIP DESCRIPTION: **Trailhead to Ventu Park Road.** Climb north from the parking area on the single track and cross a paved road which climbs to a nearby water tank. Pass a faint road fork to the right and take in the nearby unobstructed views from the local summit just beyond. Sandstone Peak looms to the southeast while Conejo Mountain and the Mountclef Ridge rise above the valley floor to the northeast and northwest, respectively. Follow the hillside contour around and across the small draws, passing a trail to the left which ducks down into a residential area. More hillside meandering takes you down to a marked trail fork with the sign for the residential access trail to the left noting *slippery surface* (0.8). You continue

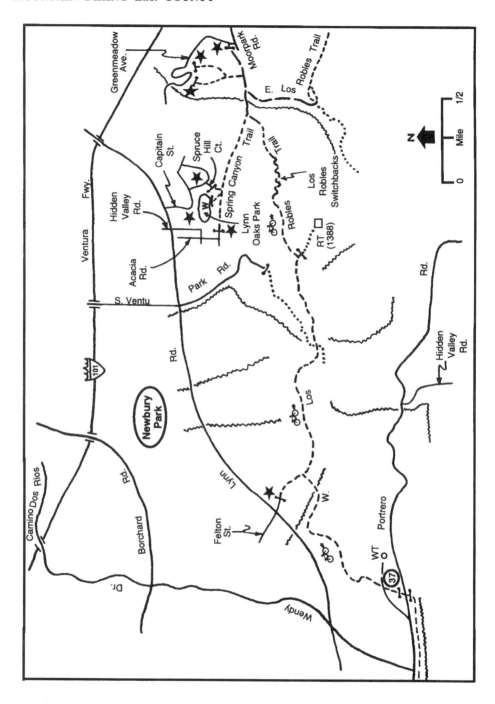

TRIP #37 - WEST LOS ROBLES TRAIL

basically eastward, pulling slowly away from the extensive residential pocket and reach an unmarked junction in another 0.6 mile. Veering left takes you back to development at Felton St. while right and uphill keeps you on the Los Robles Trail.

Los Robles Switchbacks

In the next one-plus mile (we think of this as the "Manic Mile") you tackle a steep upgrade which gives way to a short and steep ramp. (As you approach it, you will feel sure that this can't be part of the trail!) Next is a steep roller-coaster section on a right-of-way between adjoining private properties, followed by a winding ramble on rutted, sandy and sometimes rocky track through a bumpy plateau. On the way is a sign noting *Trail* with an arrow pointing left at a junction which diverts you from private property (2.2). There is a view of a complex of towers on a peak ahead which is near your destination route. A climb above the plateau takes you out of the Manic Mile onto a short stretch of road past another division sign which ways, *Stay on Trail*, and a nearby marker noting *Lake Sherwood*. In a short distance you reach Ventu Park Rd. (2.8). Above and just off the road is the tower complex you saw earlier.

Ventu Rd. to Moorpark Road. Cross Ventu Rd. following a marker that says, *Los Robles Trail East, Please stay on Trail*. Climb a couple of switchbacks through tree cover, then begin a 0.7-mile, single-track, treed, flat traverse below a ridge with a sharp drop and great San Fernando Valley views to the left (north). You cross the ridge, shifting over to the southeast (4.0), then wind northward around the ridge. Nearby you reach a viewpoint with the tower complex now well above, a canyon to the right and the canyon floor well ahead and below connected to your path by a wild 0.9-mile series of switchbacks.

The switchback trail is steep and surface quality varying -- the sharp switchbacks are sandy and somewhat torn up and require you pay close attention to your smooth, non-skidding turns. You let out of this segment and bike a short straight-line patch (the first in a while) and cross a seasonal creek at canyon's bottom. A short climb and then gradual drop in the wide canyon brings you to a four-way intersection (5.7). Ahead and over a small rise is a spur trail leading to a scenic crest, left (northwest) is the marked *Spring Canyon Trail* (ends in one mile at Acacia Rd., Capitan St. or Spruce Hill Ct.), and right (east) is a sign noting *Moorpark Rd. 0.5 mi*. A nearby sign notes the *Los Robles Trail East/Los Robles Trail West* split with our current direction eastward. Finally there is a sign pointing back the way you came which says *Rancho Sierra Vista Natural Park - 7.4 miles*. In 0.1 mile, reach a sign which notes that *Los Robles Trail East* is a hard right (south) and the outlet *Moorpark Rd. Entrance* is straight ahead. A 0.4-mile flat traverse through some vegetation brings you to a trail use information board and a large yellow metal gate at the Moorpark Rd. exit. On the entrance side of the gate is a sign noting *Los Robles Trail* and a smaller sign with an arrow pointing west noting *West Conejo Crest* (6.2).

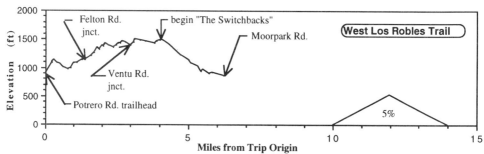

Trip Option: Start the ride from the parking lot in Rancho Sierra Vista/Satwiwa as described in the trip of the same name. The 2.1-mile extension deposits you at the Los Robles Trail entry.

TRIP #38 - LOS ROBLES TRAIL (East and West)

GENERAL LOCATION: Location (Topo) - Newbury Park

LEVEL OF DIFFICULTY: One-way - strenuous
                            Distance - 10.1 miles; Time - 3 hours
                            Elevation gain - 2200 feet

HIGHLIGHTS: The combined west and east Los Robles Trail segments make for an excellent physical challenge. The trip is generally on the Conejo Crest ridge spine, sandwiched between the housing developments along Potrero Rd. and the Ventura Fwy. The tour leaves the Potrero Rd. trailhead, meanders above the developed Conejo Valley, then drops and climbs to a perch above Ventu Park. A mile-long set of switchbacks drops to the junction of west and east trail segments. Next a gradual roller-coaster ride takes you just below the Conejo Crest where you join an exciting single track.

TRAILHEAD: Same as "Los Robles Trail" for the trip described below. See "East Los Robles Trail" for eastside entries.

TRIP DESCRIPTION: **West Los Robles Trail. This** section follows the trip of the same name to the four-way intersection (5.7). Just beyond is a sign noting the *Los Robles Trail East/Los Robles Trail*, where you continue eastward. In another 0.1 mile, make a hard right, following the *Los Robles Trail East* sign.

East Los Robles Trail. The marker just noted is at about 0.35 miles from the Moorpark Rd. trailhead described in the "East Los Robles Trail" Trip. Use the eastside trip description for the trip continuation.

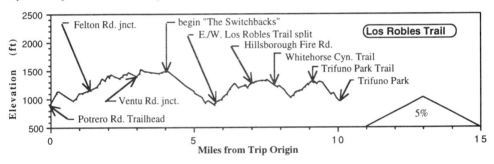

Trip Option: The trip can be extended 2.1 miles by starting from the west side at Rancho Sierra Vista. The trailhead is described in the trip of the same name. Follow the route which takes you by the Satwiwa Cultural Center, then parallels Potrero Rd., dumping you across the street from the marked *Los Robles Trail* entry.

143

MOUNTCLEF RIDGE/SIMI HILLS

TRIP #39 - MOUNTCLEF RIDGE

<u>GENERAL LOCATION</u>:   Location (Topo) - Newbury Park

<u>LEVEL OF DIFFICULTY</u>: Loop - moderate to strenuous [technical section]
Distance - 5.1 miles; Time - 2 hours
Elevation gain - 750 feet

<u>HIGHLIGHTS</u>: Though short on miles and elevation change, this is a dandy exercise for bikers looking for a good, mildly technical ride. The Lower Butte trail leads over a side ridge and around to the north side of Mountclef Ridge. The trip continuation on the Santa Rosa Trail provides a great 1.5-mile traverse below Mountclef Ridge, high above Santa Rosa Valley. You cross over the crest and navigate down the extremely technical Santa Rosa switchbacks, then ride on a mesa back to civilization. This completes the circuit around the north segment of the volcanic ridge. The off-road portion of the route is almost entirely single track and requires periodic rock dodging throughout the tour.

Just Above Santa Rosa Trail/Santa Rosa Valley Backdrop

<u>TRAILHEAD</u>: From U.S. Hwy 101 in Newbury Park, exit north at Lynn Rd. and proceed 3-3/4 miles to Wildwood Cyn. Ave. Turn left, drive 3/4 mile to the intersection with Big Sky Dr. and find parking.

The 1700-acre Wildwood Park lies in an area of significant volcanic activity millions of years ago, as witnessed by the rugged Mountclef Ridge. The Wildwood and Arroyo Canyons were formed by headwater erosion emanating from a high lake basin that used to exist here. The park is home to many animals ranging from mule deer and less-frequently sighted mountain lions to raccoons, squirrels and hawks. A wide variety of plant life attracts sightseers and botanists.

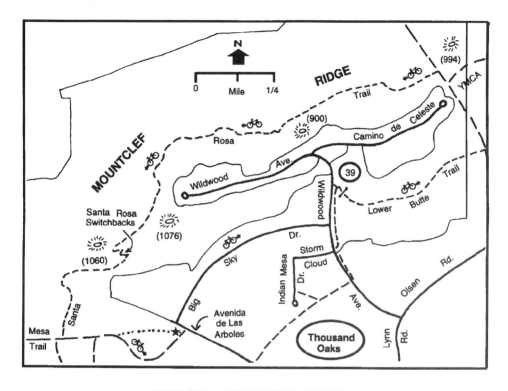

TRIP #39 - MOUNTCLEF RIDGE

Native Americans occupied hunting camps and permanent villages in the area as early as 600 B.C. The Spanish colonization of California saw the area granted to Ignacio Rodriguez in 1803 as part of "Rancho El Conejo." The last of the Chumash Indians were relocated north to the San Buenaventura Mission shortly after the area became cattle grazing land. In the 1930's through 1960's, numerous films and television series were shot in this locale. The land was acquired by the Conejo Recreation and Park District in 1966 and expanded to include Wildwood Mesa in 1987.

TRIP DESCRIPTION: **Lower Butte Trail.** Bike about 200 yards north up Wildwood Ave. and look for the sign to the right (east) announcing the trail rules. Follow the immediately ascending single track back south, paralleling Wildwood Ave. A 0.5-mile, 200-foot climb on surface that is rocky and rutted leads you to a crest with good views of the nearby volcanic formations on your right (now south) and the Mountclef Ridge to the north. (Ignore the numerous, less prominent single tracks on the way up.) A 0.3-mile downgrade takes you onto a small flat to a three-way intersection. Straight ahead leads you further into the flat, right (south) goes to nearby Mountclef Village, and left takes you on the fabulous Mountclef Ridge loop.

A left here and another left in 0.1 mile at the next fork takes you below residences on Camino de Celeste. Just beyond, a trail which comes down from that area meets your route at a brown metal gate. Here, signs announce *Lower Butte Trail* (where you came from) and ***Santa Rosa Trail*** (where you are headed) (1.15).

Santa Rosa Trail. Climb to a scenic crest where the road to the right wanders

145

northwest toward Mountclef Ridge and the YMCA near N. Moorpark Rd. However, your fate is to navigate the steep and slightly rocky route directly ahead which rockets down toward the Santa Rosa Valley sprawled 900 feet below. In 0.15 mile, you leave that steep downhill route and turn left (west) at a Conejo Open Space guidelines marker. This begins a 1.5-mile southwesterly traverse which follows below the Mountclef ridgetop. First a short downhill lulls you before offering a variable grade, rock-dodging upgrade which passes a hiking trail spur to the left (and a Wildwood Park guideline sign) (1.9). This leads to a continuing stair-step climb with continuous Santa Rosa Valley views and a passage above several northerly-and-westerly-tending canyons. You gain the trip summit (2.6), then cross a saddle with *Trail* markers clearly showing the prescribed route in both directions.

Santa Rosa Swithbacks

Beyond the saddle, a keep-your-eyes-on-the-trail single track clearly shifts over to a southerly exposure and the southwestern Mountclef Ridge segment comes clearly into view. Below is the first look at one of the technical expert's greatest challenges, the Santa Rosa Switchbacks! Nurse your two-wheeler down the steep rock-strewn, railroad-tie-crossed, knife-like switchbacks (we dismounted for most of this section) for a few hundred yards, then follow a westerly traverse on a more bikeable segment. Continue tracking below and through some of the volcanic formations, passing a marked **Trail Closed** sign at a northbound foot trail junction. In a short distance, the trail turns south, drops off the face of the ridge on an invigorating downhill and dies at a "T" intersection with a dirt road (Mesa Trail) (3.4). Here trail markers note *Santa Rosa Trail*, pointing back the way you came.

The Wind-Down Segment. Turn left (east) and pedal to a second intersection where the postings note *Ave. de las Arboles* straight ahead and **Parking Lot #1** to the right. You may want to take a 0.5-mile up-and-back diversion to the parking lot for a great overlook of Wildwood Canyon. (We included this diversion in the reference trip mileage.) Continuing straight ahead takes you along a wide, quality-surfaced dirt road around a bluff and past the outside parking lot at Avd. de las

Arboles. A left turn on this street leads to Big Sky Dr. (4.4) where you climb on the paved residential street and then coast back to Wildwood Ave. and your car (5.1).

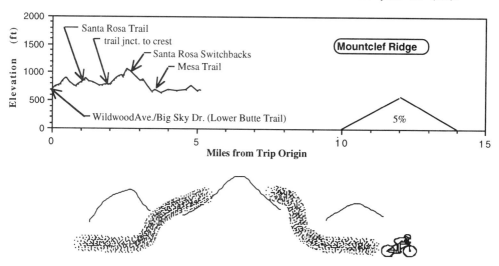

TRIP #40 - LIZARD ROCK/WILDWOOD CANYON

GENERAL LOCATION: Location (Topo) - Newbury Park

LEVEL OF DIFFICULTY: Loop - moderate to strenuous [technical section]
Distance - 6.1 miles; Time - 1-1/2 hours
Elevation gain - 850 feet

HIGHLIGHTS: The loop described provides an excellent sampling of the variety of trails offered in Wildwood Park. An easy 0.9 mile segment on wide-open Wildwood Mesa gives way to a short workout climb to Lizard Rock, a local favorite scenic viewpoint. A screaming, rock-strewn downhill on the south segment of Lizard Rock Trail (for advanced riders only) drops you 500 feet in 1/2 mile to Lower Wildwood Canyon. A serene ride through lush vegetation takes you by several picnic areas, Paradise Falls and the Nature Center. A final creek-side run takes you to an outlet ridge climb which returns you to paved streets and closure of the loop.

TRAILHEAD: From U.S. Hwy 101 in Newbury Park, exit north at Lynn Rd. and proceed 3.1 miles to Avd. de los Arboles and turn left (west). Continue to road's end at Big Sky Dr. and find parking in the nearby dirt lot.

TRIP DESCRIPTION: **Mesa Trail.** Follow the rolling dirt road at the south end of the parking lot onto a wide mesa, heading west. The volcanic Mountclef Ridge dominates the landscape to the north while hidden-from-view Wildwood Canyon parallels the road to the south. Pass the marked *Santa Rosa Trail* (0.3) and the *North Tepee Trail* entry just beyond. Continued unobstructed views include a look at distant Lizard Rock in your direction of travel. A nearby marked fork (0.9) leads left for the most easily accessible entry to *Lizard Rock*, while the reference route veers right to *Box Canyon*.

147

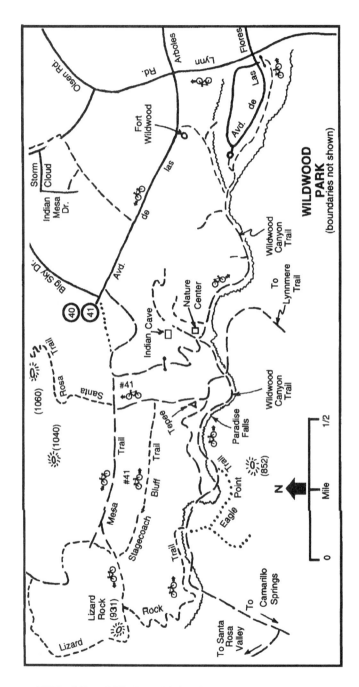

TRIP #40 - LIZARD ROCK/WILDWOOD CANYON
TRIP #41 - STAGECOACH BLUFF TRAIL

148

To Lizard Rock. A short dip and climb leads to a "T" intersection where there is a grand view of Box Canyon below. Right leads to ridge's end and a brushy trail down into the canyon. (From the canyon, there is a steep, narrow back-door entry to Lizard Rock which is a challenging hiker's trail and a major push-a-bike for most riders.) Left is the prescribed route which skinnies down to a single track, climbs a small ridge and dumps back down to the main Lizard Rock access trail. A sign across the trails points southbound for *Stagecoach Bluff Trail*, while you turn west (right) and pump a steep grade with loose dirt. Far below you to the left is a massive sewage treatment plant and a sign on the trail noting *To Lower Wildwood Canyon,* your destination (1.3). Take a short diversion and enjoy the view from atop Lizard Rock (a hundred yards or so further up the trail) before heading downhill.

Climbing to Lizard Rock

Lizard Rock Trail. This southern part of Lizard Rock Trail starts on a steep, rocky single track which is typical of the entire downgrade. This is very technical biking! There are inspiring views across Hill Canyon and the seasonal Arroyo Conejo to the west, though hard to enjoy unless you stop. You rocket down the scrub-filled mountainside, switchback to the east in 0.25 mile, barrel down a steep-to-sheer ridgeline, then follow a series of steep and sharp switchbacks for 0.2 mile before reaching a more easily rideable portion just above the sewage plant. You outlet at a signed "T" intersection (1.9). Right is *Hill Canyon* on a trail which skirts the plant's end, and left (east) is your route into **Wildwood Canyon.**

Wildwood Canyon Trail. You immediately transition to "another world" amongst bushes and tree cover with a creek below and to your right. A nearby junction fork is marked *Skunk Hollow Picnic Area* to the right (also the west side entry to *Eagle Point Trail* and *Lynnmere Trail*) and **Paradise Falls** to the left. Towering above and south is the massive monolith topped by Eagle Point. Stay left, then cross and recross the creek, taking time to stare up at the north and south walls that confine the canyon. Continue upstream on a packed dirt road and stay right at the next fork (left climbs steeply to Tepee Out Look -- a large modern Tepee-like structure) (2.3). You pass through Wildwood Canyon Picnic Area complete with restrooms, water fountains, a large barbecue spit, a water hole and generous tree cover. Sycamores dot the area and there is even some bamboo.

Paradise Falls

An *Eagle Point Trail* sign notes its eastern entry point just before another creek crossing. Pass Sycamore Flats Picnic Area and reach a trail junction just west of picturesque Paradise Falls. Right is to the falls, straight ahead dead ends beside the falls and left (below the ridge) leads up some railroad-tie steps to a fork. The immediate junction left cuts back northwest and climbs to the previously-mentioned Tepee access road. Stay right on the smaller trail and climb above the creek, closed in on a narrowing path between the canyon wall and a chain-link fence. The canyon opens, pass Little Falls Picnic Area and then reach a four-way junction with enough signs to make you think of the old Bob Hope movies, like "The Road to Zanzibar" (3.0).

A left takes you up on an eastern access to *Tepee*, while right leads to the *Lynnmere Trail* (Lynnmere Connector). Straight ahead (and back the way you came) is the **Wildwood Canyon Trail** which you follow. In 0.2 mile is another major dirt road junction. (Left and uphill in a couple hundred feed is a further split, with the unmarked road left heading up to Parking Lot #1 and the marked right trail leading to *Indian Cave*.) However, you go right on a rustic bridge over a creek, following the markers noting **Wildwood Canyon Trail/Nature Center/Wildwood Fork**. Immediately beyond, you pass the marked *Indian Creek Trail* to the left, then the Nature Center to the left (water fountain and Meadows Cafe) and follow a sign straight ahead noting **Fort Wildwood-1 mi.**

Next pass the marked steep *San Miguel Trail* which is again to the left and bike a quality dirt road on a generally modest climb above Mission Canyon Creek. Follow the now more shallow, tree-shrouded canyon 0.7 mile westward, crossing the creek twice and passing the small, unmarked Gold Canyon Trail on the left, and making a final creek crossing. A short upgrade leads to a final trail fork (4.0).

Wildwood Canyon Near the Multi-signed Junction

Return Leg. Left is the *Wildwood Fort Trail* which climbs steeply up a set of railroad-tie steps. We avoided the steps and followed the ***Avd. de las Flores*** outlet (Los Flores Trail) trail right on a very steep 100-foot ridge climb to a crest behind a line of residences. The trail splits just beyond, with the left fork heading up to the cul-de-sac at the end of Flaming Star Ave. The reference route follows the single track straight ahead and outlets at the south end of Avd. de las Flores (4.4). All that remains is to follow that paved road 0.3 mile east to Lynn Rd., turn left and bike 0.4 mile to Avd. de los Arboles, turn left again, biking another mile to the trailhead (6.1).

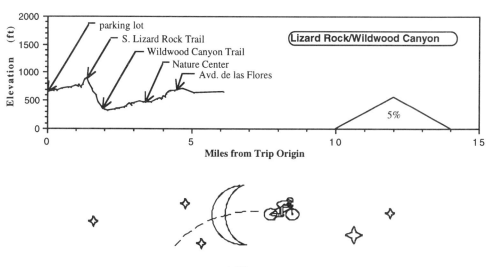

151

TRIP #41 - STAGECOACH BLUFF TRAIL

<u>GENERAL LOCATION</u>:   Location (Topo) - Thousand Oaks

<u>LEVEL OF DIFFICULTY</u>: Loop - moderate
Distance - 2.5 miles; Time - 1 hour
Elevation gain - 150 feet

<u>HIGHLIGHTS</u>: Next to doing an up-and-back Mesa Trail ride, this is the least painful way to see Wildwood Canyon. A 1.2-mile ride on Mesa Trail leads to the Stagecoach Bluff Trail turnoff. On this bluff-side segment, you are treated to many captivating views of the canyon below and the trails leading up the south canyon wall. There is one short, steep climb and some rock-dodging sections which bump the trail rating from "easy" to "moderate."

<u>TRAILHEAD</u>: Same as "Lizard Rock/Wildwood Canyon" trip.

Lookout on Stagecoach Bluff Trail

<u>TRIP   DESCRIPTION</u>: **Mesa   Trail.** Follow the rolling dirt road at the south end of the parking lot onto a wide mesa heading west. The volcanic Mountclef Ridge dominates the landscape to the north while hidden-from-view Wildwood Canyon parallels the road to the south. Pass the marked *Santa Rosa Trail* (0.3) and the *North Tepee Trail* entry just beyond. The latter will be your exit trail. Continued unobstructed views include a look at distant Lizard Rock in your direction of travel. A nearby marked fork (0.8) leads right to *Box Canyon*, while the reference route veers left toward the most easily accessible entry to ***Lizard Rock***. Another 0.3 mile leads to a left-pointing marker stating ***Stage   Coach Bluff Trail***.

152

Stagecoach Bluff Trail. A left turn (south) takes you on a quality packed-dirt single track towards Wildwood Canyon. This quality path bends east and follows the northern bluff above the canyon -- stop periodically and enjoy the many overlooks. Cross a small revine (1.5) and begin a climb which becomes rocky and steep near the crest. A short, bumpy ridge scramble takes you to a second crest where there is a particularly grabbing view of Paradise Falls in the canyon and Tepee Outlook on the bluffs below. Pass the numerous small off-shoot trails and dodge the rocks on your descent back to the mesa. The path smoothes in the final segment before you reach N. Tepee Trail. (There is a sign at the junction noting that you have just exited *Stagecoach Bluff Trail*) (2.0).

The Return Segment. Right (south) takes you down past Moonridge Trail (no bikes) to Tepee Outlook in 0.3 mile. However, turn left and cycle 0.2 easy miles back to Mesa Trail on good-quality fire road. Turn right (east) onto the Mesa Trail and retrace your incoming route (2.5).

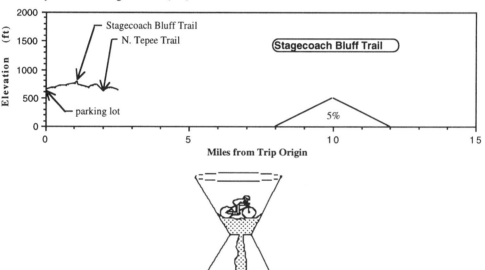

TRIP #42 - LYNNMERE TRAIL

GENERAL LOCATION: Location (Topo) - Thousand Oaks

LEVEL OF DIFFICULTY: Loop - strenuous
Distance - 6.2 miles; Time - 2 hours
Elevation gain - 1400 feet

HIGHLIGHTS: Far less used than the canyon trails, this single-track "sleeper" competes with the best rides in Wildwood Canyon. From the Lynn Rd. entry, you are treated to 1.1 miles of fun riding and challenging ravine hopping before working your way over to the 1.7-mile ride along the south wall of Wildwood Canyon. This scenic, woodsy section leads to a climb to an unblocked vista at Eagle Point and is the classic Lynnmere Trail. From Eagle Point is a drop into a small, lush canyon followed by a rigorous climb to the trip's crest at Peak 981, the second 360-degree view point

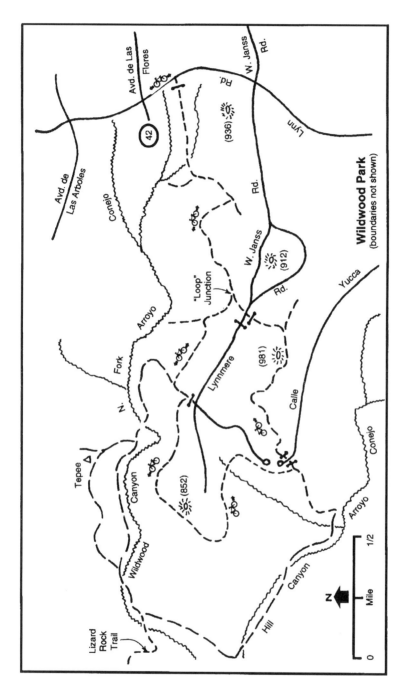

TRIP #42 - LYNNMERE TRAIL

on the tour. A descent to, and crossing of, Lynnmere Rd. leads to a connector with the 1.1-mile incoming ravine roller-coaster segment.

TRAILHEAD: From U.S. Hwy 101 in Newbury Park, exit north at Lynn Rd., and proceed 2-3/4 miles to Avd. de las Flores and turn left (west). Park on this street near Lynn Rd.

TRIP DESCRIPTION: **Lynn Road to "Loop Junction."** Set your odometer to 0.0 at the parking spot. Return to Lynn Rd. and bike south 0.1 mile to the south side of the canyon. The trail is just beyond the metal auto barrier. Bike uphill past the *Conejo Open Space Rules* marker and follow the wide, smooth, single-track west. Before you is a chaparral-packed series of little ridges with a dirt ribbon route winding through the terrain. A mild 0.3 mile traverse with Peak 936 to your left leads to a steep downhill into the first of many ravines, this one with a running creek. Stay to the main trail on the left, cross the creek and climb past a spur trail on the right. Another ravine and a smaller spur trail greet you as you climb to a major trail junction. Both trails rejoin further up the route; however, the left fork is sheer and rutted, leading you to wisely head right. A less-strenuous up-and-down trek leads to another junction before reaching a fenced-in residential community. This is what we call "loop junction" and the trail left and up is your future outlet (1.1).

East of Loop Junction

Loop Junction to Eagle Point. Turn right and prepare to enjoy a 1.7-mile ride high on the south bluffs above Wildwood Canyon. The first mile is on a continued single track that climbs and drops, generally skirting above the ravines that dive down the canyon wall. You catch sight of the Lynnmere Connector coming up from the canyon on your right before meeting that steep fire road (2.2). There is a *C O S C A* (Conejo Open Space Conservation) marker near the junction.

Turn left (south) and climb 20-30 yards to another *C O S C A* marker on the right, following that single track uphill. The trail works westward, dives downhill on a series of railroad-tie water bars for 30-40 yards (bike carry required), and continues traversing through heavy overgrowth on the southern run. Another set of heavy water bars greet you as you get great glimpses of Tepee Outlook across the canyon. A continued sinuous course takes you alongside and below a gated community on W. Lynnmere Rd., then south on a climb directly above Wildwood Canyon. You are now on the massif leading to Eagle Point, which is intimidating when viewed from the canyon floor. The single track becomes steeper and the trail quality deteriorates as you crank past several small spurs to a crest at Eagle Point (Peak 852) (2.75). A 360-

degree view greets you, with the Santa Monicas in the distant south, Hill Canyon (including a sewage treatment plant) below and to the south and west, Wildwood Canyon and Mountclef Ridge to the north, and the gated community you are circumnavigating below and to the east.

Conejo Crest as Seen from Peak 981 Area

Eagle Point to Loop Junction. Cross a saddle and bike steeply down the stark ridgeline (a trail down to Eagle Point Trail and Skunk Hollow Picnic Area in Wildwood Canyon is touted to drop southwest off the saddle, but we may have overlooked it). The now wider trail winds south and west, leaving you looking at impressive Hill Canyon to the right (south) and a smaller canyon to the left below residences. Continue dropping into the lush smaller canyon on a narrowing trail and take the right fork downhill at the first major junction (left goes a short distance towards the residences and dies) (3.4). Cross a creek, then climb to a trail which follows below the fenced residences to an outlet 0.3 mile beyond the creek crossing. Turn left (right goes down to Hill Canyon) and bike a short way to the paved Calle Yucca cul-de-sac.

Cross the street and follow the dirt trail north along the brick wall, starting a 0.8-mile, 380-foot ascent that is the trip's most difficult segment. Follow the single track as it winds up north and east, skirting the residential complex and climbing to the mostly-undeveloped upper section of Peak 981. Reaching the crest requires some serious climbing and bike carries over short sections which have both wood and rock water bars. Once gaining the summit, however, you are rewarded with another superb 360-degree vista (4.6). Head east along a scenic ridge, ignore smaller off-shoot trails, and reach a major junction in 0.15 mile. The right fork continues southeast along the ridgeline, while the left (the reference route) takes you down steeply to paved Lynnmere Rd. above the electronic gated entrance to Lynnmere Estates (4.8).

Across the street is a *Conejo Open Space Rules* sign and the entry to the now northbound single-track. A short climb takes you above the gated estates to the left,

156

then drops you to a "T" junction in 0.3 mile from the electronic gate. You have now returned to "loop junction."

Retrace your incoming route from this point, returning to Lynn Rd. and your waiting auto on Avd. de Las Flores (6.2).

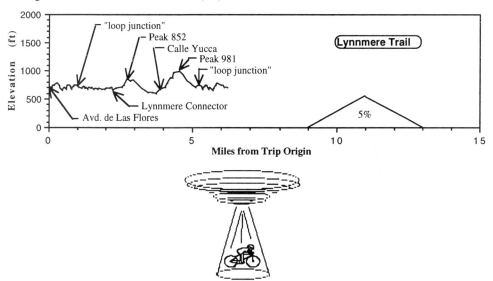

TRIP #43 - CHEESEBORO CANYON

<u>GENERAL LOCATION</u>:   Location (Topo) - Calabasas

<u>LEVEL OF DIFFICULTY</u>: Up and back - moderate
Distance - 9.6 miles; Time - 1-1/2 hours
Elevation gain - 600 feet

HIGHLIGHTS: Exploring Cheeseboro Canyon is essentially three trips in one. The lower Cheeseboro Canyon Trail segment plies the mouth and takes you on quality, packed dirt road through the narrowing canyon with a mix of open scenes and sheltered areas of tree cover. The Sulphur Springs Trail portion passes under more extensive cover of Valley Oaks and sycamore trees on narrowing roadway, depositing you near Sulphur Springs and an odorous, milky-white creek segment. The cycle traffic thins beyond as you transit a much rougher and sometimes slightly-overgrown single track at the canyon's upper reaches. Trip's end is at Sheep Corral in the chaparral-filled open spaces below the canyon's northern back wall. Throughout the entire venture, you share the canyon floor with a small sporadic creek which runs freely during the rainy season.

TRAILHEAD: From State Hwy. 101 (Ventura Fwy.) exit at Chesebro Canyon Rd. (Note the difference in spelling as you will be cycling in Cheeseboro Canyon.) Turn north on Palo Camado Cyn. Dr. and turn right (north again) on Chesebro Cyn. Rd. In 0.7 mile is a well-marked parking area to the right, noting *Cheeseboro Canyon, Santa Monica Mountains Conservancy*. If the lot is full, continue about 1/4 mile further, now on gravel, and park in the second lot.

157

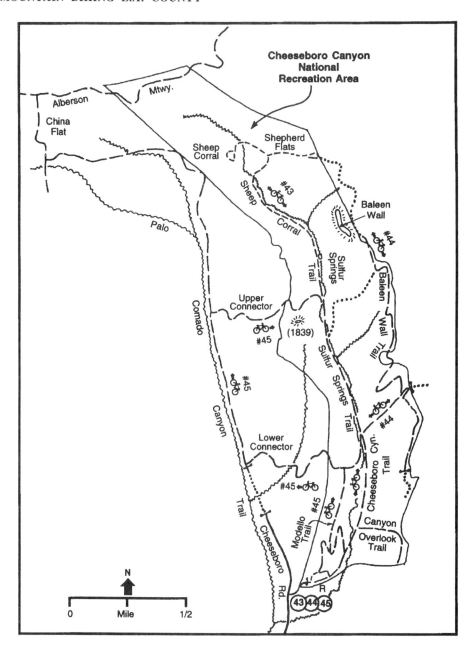

TRIP #43 - CHEESEBORO CANYON; TRIP #44 - BALEEN WALL TRAIL
TRIP #45 - PALO CAMADO CANYON

Cheeseboro Canyon is a natural wildlife area between the Santa Monica Mountains and the Santa Susana Mountains to the north. It was heavily grazed by

158

cattle for over 150 years, but the cattle were removed when the canyon became public park land. Both natural and active means have started to restore the canyon to its pregrazing state for the enjoyment of hikers, equestrians and cyclists.

TRIP DESCRIPTION: Cheeseboro Canyon Trail. From the parking area alongside Cheeseboro Canyon Rd., bike 0.3 mile on packed dirt surface to the National Park Service (NPS) information board. General area information and a trail map are posted here and there is a porta-pottie nearby. Signs at this trailhead note that *Modello Trail* is left and our destination, *Cheeseboro Canyon Trail*, is straight ahead. Another 0.5 mile through an open meadow and into the tree-peppered canyon mouth leads to the first *Modello Trail* junction (0.8) below the recently-burned western ridgeline (junctions are marked all the way to Sheep Corral in the canyon). In 0.2 mile and a creek crossing is the *Canyon Overlook Trail* junction east. Proceed through the mostly open canyon on packed-dirt road and reach a fork marked *Sulphur Springs Trail* and *Palo Comado Trail* to the left and *Baleen Wall* Trail to the right (1.6).

Cheeseboro Canyon Trail

Sulphur Springs Trail. Just beyond a creek crossing is the junction left (west) with the second *Modello Trail* junction, which also leads to Palo Comado Canyon. You continue north on the Sulphur Springs Trail starting a 1.8-mile spin through overhanging tree cover, pass a shaded picnic area (the road spur nearby on the right leads to the Baleen Trail), and continue up canyon past another *Palo Comado Trail* marker (1.8). Just beyond is a hiker's-only trail exit east marked *Baleen Wall Trail*. The trail narrows and the surface roughens as you work through the trees -- the increasing odor tells you that you are near Sulphur Springs. At (3.4) you cross the milky creek at the closest approach to the springs. Take time to look upward and east to view the Baleen Wall rock formation through the tree cover. The massive rock outcrop resembles the baleen in a whale's mouth and was so named.

Sheep Corral Trail. The trail narrows more and gives way to rocky sections with several easy-to-technical creek crossings. The canyon openes up significantly and chaparral replace the prior abundant tree cover. In 1.4 miles of snaking through the sometimes overgrown trail, you reach trail's end and an open flat with a marker noting *Shepherd Flats* (4.8). 159

Shepherd Flats

From here you can explore the single-track trails to the west which lead in a few hundred yards to the overgrown Sheep Corral (see "Palo Comado Canyon" trip) or simply watch the hawks circling for prey in the open grasslands. The single track to the east leads 0.3 mile to a "T" fire road intersection with the turn left switchbacking up to Alberson Fire Rd. and a right leading south and up steeply to the Baleen Wall -- these are not NPS-maintained roads and you are not encouraged to use them as part of the NPS Cheeseboro Canyon Site.

Trip Options. 1) **Modello Trail** - At the NPS information board at (0.3), take the (moderate) marked trail and meander up the ridgeline above a burned out section of grassland that gives you an excellent view into Cheeseboro Canyon. You can take the first fork right (east) (0.75) or continue north another mile on a spur trail before coasting down to the canyon floor. The options are to continue either up the canyon (left) or return to the parking area (right). This is also one means of access from the east to the marked Palo Comado Canyon Trail; 2) **Canyon Overlook Trail** - continue 0.7 mile past the NPS information board and turn east at the marked (moderate to strenuous) trail and climb steeply 0.75 mile to the eastern ridge above the canyon. From the knoll at trails end is a vista of the entire canyon, from the mouth below to the headwall above Shepherd Flats. You must return the way you came.

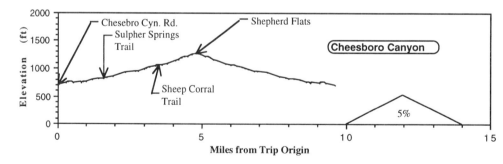

TRIP #44 - BALEEN WALL TRAIL

GENERAL LOCATION: Location (Topo) - Calabasas

LEVEL OF DIFFICULTY: Up and back - strenuous
Distance - 9.2 miles ; Time - 2-1/2 hours
Elevation gain - 1400 feet

HIGHLIGHTS: The Baleen Wall tour extends off the Cheeseboro Canyon Trail and travels 0.7 easy mile through a small, shaded canyon to a depression among the surrounding hills. A robust 2.3-mile series of ups and downs puts you at a scenic overlook of Las Virgenes Canyon and mountain ranges to the east. A short hike west from here takes you to the top of the rock croppings of the Baleen Wall. The cycling workout continues as you return the way you came and enjoy a blowout 300-foot, 0.6-mile sinuous downgrade before returning to Cheeseboro Canyon and your car.

TRAILHEAD: See "Cheeseboro Canyon" trip.

Biker Heading for the Switchbacks

TRIP DESCRIPTION: **Cheeseboro Canyon.** The canyon entry and first 1.6 miles is as described in the "Cheeseboro Canyon" trip. Here you fork right (northeast) at the *Baleen Wall Trail* marker.

Baleen Wall Trail. Bike up a packed dirt fire road and pass the spur road to the left in 0.3 mile which crosses the creek and reconnects with the Sulphur Springs Trail. Your route swings more eastward and continues on a mild upgrade through a modest narrow canyon with a shaded section and small paralleling creek. In 0.7 mile from the Baleen Wall Trail fork, you sit at a junction where you look at two road options, both uphill. Straight ahead is a power line service road that is described as an option below. You turn left (north), stare up at the series of impending switchbacks that you will climb, and throttle onward and upward.

Pump on a 300-foot, 0.6-mile climb (average 10% grade) with nary a tree, following various compass points on the way up. Pass above a huge white water tank and declare a temporary victory shortly beyond near one of the many transmission

161

towers (2.9). Two more serious dips and climbs take you above many smaller canyons on the ridge's west side. The latter rugged climb takes you by a small post noting, *No established NPS trails beyond this point*, to a tremendous overlook. This point is 0.3 mile from the post amongst a group of rock outcroppings which provides views of upper Las Virgenes Canyon and the mountains to the east. This is the high point of the fire road (4.3). (On the way is the *Baleen Wall Trail* to the west, a hikers-only trail back to Cheeseboro Canyon.) After enjoying the rest break and view from the overlook, rotate your bike and return to Cheeseboro Canyon the way you came (8.6).

Viewpoint At the Rock Outcroppings

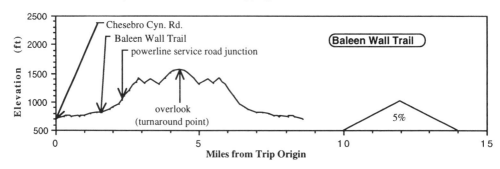

The Beyond. Beyond the NPS marker post previously mentioned, the NPS discourages travel since it is outside the Cheeseboro Canyon Site boundary. We ask that you honor restrictions on further travel. We are also concerned that many bikers continue on since there are no prohibitive markers on the northbound segment. The fire road does continue on one last workout up and down, then drops

162

steeply to a flat with a single-track junction to the left (west) in 1.1 mile. All spurs along the way are roads leading to transmission towers. The road continues north and switchbacks up to a crest on the south edge above Simi Valley (Alberson Fire Rd.) The single track left takes you through a meadow 0.2 mile then drops 0.1 mile on a rocky, rutted technical path to Shepherd Flats -- ignore the single-track trail junction to the right in the meadow, which heads back to Alberson Fire Rd. From the flats is an easy coast back to Chesebro Canyon Rd. as described in the "Cheeseboro Canyon" trip.

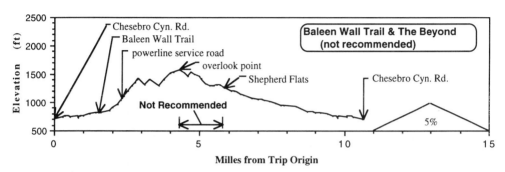

Trip Option - Power line Service Road. At the junction at (2.3) you can also explore south on a road that provides service entry to the transmission lines. This is an excellent route for achieving a bird's eye view of lower Cheeseboro Canyon. An initial 0.8-mile, 150-foot climb and a following set of ups and downs leads you to a metal gate noting private property beyond (1.2). Ignore spur roads on this segment as they all deadend at the transmission poles. There is a "triangle" junction at 0.5 mile from the start point (the road west and downhill is one of the spurs) with a single shade tree that is very inviting on a hot day!

TRIP #45 - PALO COMADO CANYON

GENERAL LOCATION: Location (Topo) - Calabasas

LEVEL OF DIFFICULTY: Loop - moderate to strenuous
Distance - 9.0 miles; Time - 2 hours
Elevation gain - 1300 feet

HIGHLIGHTS: Recently-opened Palo Comado Canyon offers a lesser-used route than Cheeseboro Canyon though it provides equally pleasant and scenic surroundings. To get to the canyon requires the use of one of two connectors, both which offer some hearty climbing. The described route follows the Modello Trail onto a scenic ridgeline above and west of Cheeseboro Canyon, then uses a roller-coaster connector route to Palo Comado Canyon. The easy and idyllic canyon route continues to the northern connector which takes bikers to a super-scenic crest before dumping back into the upper end of the Sulphur Springs Trail in Cheeseboro Canyon. Beyond, cyclists enjoy an easy, generally downhill return through the canyon to the start point.

TRAILHEAD: See "Cheeseboro Canyon" trip.

Palo Comado Canyon is a natural wildlife corridor between the Santa Monica Mountains and Santa Susana Mountains. It had been used most recently as a cattle ranch. To halt its planned development into a luxury-home community and PGA golf course, this former Jordan Ranch property was accrued by the state in a land swap arranged with comedian Bob Hope. It is now open for public use by hikers, equestrians and bikers.

South End of the Modello Trail

TRIP DESCRIPTION: **Modello Trail.** From the parking area beside Cheeseboro Canyon Rd., bike 0.3 mile on packed dirt to the National Park Service (NPS) information board. Signs at the trailhead note *Cheeseboro Canyon Trail* straight ahead and our path, *Modello Trail*, on the left. Follow the exposed, steep, single track up a small canyon to a "U" bend above the head of the canyon, reverse direction southward and climb to a ridge at a "T" intersection (0.8). Signs show *Modello Connector* back the way you came and *Modello Trail* along the ridge (north). Right goes down into Cheeseboro Canyon, but you head straight ahead for a spirited 0.7-mile roller-roaster ride on the burned-out ridge above and parallel to the canyon. On this packed dirt road is an unobstructed vantage point of the surrounding local canyon areas; spread out to the west is the San Fernando Valley.

Palo Comado Canyon. At (1.5) a post notes *Modello Trail* back the way you came and right (alternate return to Cheeseboro Canyon) and lightly-used *Palo Comado Canyon* to the left (west). A turn west and another 1.1 miles of moderate-to-steep hill climbs and drops on a narrowing road leads to a downhill let-out alongside horse stables and a barn. The wide trail reaches a "T" intersection with a sign noting that *Palo Comado Canyon Trail* is to the right or north (left through a metal gate leads into private property -- stay out). The next 1.25 miles sends you through an oak woodland with the canyon creek evident on the packed-dirt road's west side. The slightly wandering road is relatively flat and provides the type of idyllic surroundings that city dwellers dream of.

Looking North Along Modello Trail

The Upper Connector. At (3.85) you reach the junction road on the right which takes you back to the Sulphur Springs Trail and the road is marked *Cheeseboro Canyon*. A series of fun alternatives are available by continuing up Palo Comado Canyon (see "Trip Option" below), however, our route turns right (east) onto the connector. You tackle a steep winding upgrade on a good quality surface which takes you up to a series of perches from which to view Palo Comado Canyon below, the Baleen Wall Trail ridgeline to the east and the Simi Hills to the north. In 0.3 mile the grade lets up some and you climb on a ridge below the dominant Peak 1839, then reach a false crest before dipping and climbing to the actual summit (4.55). Here you get a dead-on view of the Baleen Wall across Cheeseboro Canyon.

Pass through an open metal gate and stay on the main (middle) road. The steep trail to the right climbs toward Peak 1839 and the trail left follows a plateau for about 100 yards then dives down steeply on hazardous surface northbound. The sinuous middle road works its way steeply downhill, passes a lone ample shade tree, then dumps into shaded Cheeseboro Canyon at the marked *Sulphur Springs Trail* (5.1).

Cheeseboro Canyon Return. You turn right (south) and cruise the canyon on a general downgrade with a few short ups and downs and a couple of creek crossings. In order, you pass the marked *Modello Trail/Palo Comado Canyon* junction (7.2), *Baleen Wall Trail* (7.3), *Canyon View Trail* (7.9), south *Modello Trail* outlet (8.1) and return to your car at Chesebro Rd. in 9.0 miles from the start.

Trip Option. Past the Upper Connector (3.85), continue up Palo Comado Canyon to the Simi Hills crest at Alberson Fire Rd., about two miles and 500-feet elevation gain. We understand that the fire road works west over to China Flats or east to connect with Cheeseboro Canyon from its northern wall. There is a question as to whether public access is allowed, thus we did not further explore this trip extension.

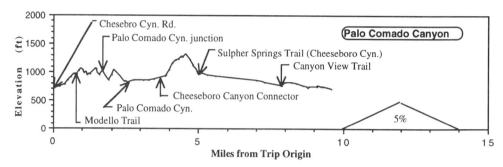

SANTA SUSANA MOUNTAINS

TRIP #46 - ROCKY PEAK

GENERAL LOCATION: Location (Topo) - Simi Valley East

LEVEL OF DIFFICULTY: Loop - strenuous [technical section]
Distance - 11.4 miles (loop); time - 2-1/2 hours
Elevation gain - 2000 feet

HIGHLIGHTS: The 2.5-mile Rocky Peak Trail is a neat mountain bike trip providing excellent vistas from the trailhead to the ridgeline below Rocky Peak. The trail is surrounded by interesting and varied rock formations. A mile extension along the scenic ridgeline puts the biker at the Chumash Trail junction. This 2.4-mile serpentine, single-track downhill is very steep, in poor condition in some areas and has other sections with steep drops along the narrow trail. Riders could arrange for a car shuttle at trail's end at Chumash Park, or bike 5.4 more miles into Simi Valley and up Santa Susanna Pass Rd. to complete the loop.

TRAILHEAD: From Interstate Hwy. 405, turn west onto the Ronald Reagan Fwy. (State Hwy. 118), proceed ten miles and turn off just beyond Santa Susanna Pass. At the end of the short exit road is the parking area at the signed entrance to Rocky Peak Park. From the Simi Valley area, take Santa Susana Pass Rd. two miles from the Kuehner Dr./Katherine Rd. intersection and go left (north) on the bridge over the

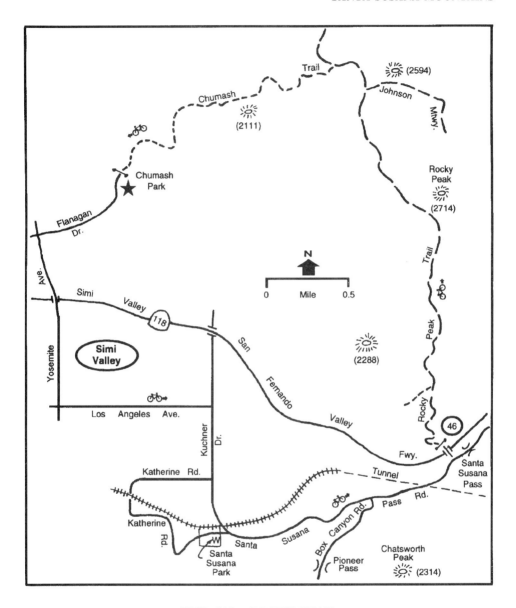

TRIP #46 - ROCKY PEAK

Ronald Reagan Fwy. Continue to the parking area.

The Santa Susana Pass was used by Chumash Indian hunting and trading parties for centuries as a preferred route from Simi Valley to the inland mountain areas.

TRIP DESCRIPTION: **Rocky Peak Trailhead to Chumash Park.** Wheel your bike around the barrier and climb steeply uphill on the rocky, rutted fire road that

167

is shared by hikers, bikers and equestrians. This workout, winding uphill provides mixed views of Simi Valley and the crusty peaks of Big Mountain to the west and has spectacular rock formations scattered about the trail. The rugged climb is shared by passages along several rock-strewn plateaus on either side of the road. In two miles of steady uphill, reach a lengthy plateau from where the steep, switchbacked final push on the western flank of Rocky Peak comes into view. This very steep 1/2-mile transit takes you to the top of a ridge. On the right is an unsigned, 1/2-mile, single track trail leading to Rocky Peak, with 360-degree vistas (on a clear day) of Anacapa Island, Simi Valley, the Santa Monica Mountains and San Fernando Valley.

Lone Rider with Rocky Peak Backdrop

Keep north along the ridge, where more beautiful views await. About one ridgeline-mile after the Rocky Peak summit trail junction, and after passing the Johnson Motorway (fire road) junction, is the signed **Chumash Trail** to the left (3.5). Route options are: 1) return to the Rocky Peak trailhead; 2) stay north along the ridgeline for two miles to the park boundary (we understand there is a large, inspiring oak savanna there); or 3) take the 2.4-mile Chumash Trail south and west down to Chumash Park. This route follows the latter option. A word of warning -- this trail has some extremely steep parts with dramatic drop-offs and should only be attempted by patient and experienced riders. Conditions of the trail are best explained by noting that the existing, narrow-foot trail was "hacked out" over a period of several days. Highlights of this winding 1150-foot (average 9% grade) downhill are a mostly flat 0.6-mile ride past a forest of massive "rock piles," and a 0.8-mile downhill, that includes a journey 150-feet above an unnamed canyon. Climb to a saddle and follow a super-steep, 400-foot drop in less than 1/2 mile. The undeveloped grassy knolls of Chumash Park are seen on the last and flatter 0.2 mile of the trail (6.0).

Rocky Peak Loop Option. If you did not arrange a car shuttle, close the loop by cycling on the asphalt roadways into Simi Valley and up Santa Susana Pass Rd. The 5.4-mile segment involves a fast downhill on Flanagan Dr., a more shallow downgrade on Yosemite Ave. and a flat cruise east on Los Angeles St., the trip's lowest point. Simi Valley proper has many eateries, service stations and markets. Follow a wide curve right (south) on Kuehner Dr. on Class II bikeway and pass Katherine Rd., the entrance to Santa Susana Park (restrooms, water, picnic tables) just beyond the railroad tracks (9.5). Swing east and pedal by picturesque Hideout Willies and several other interesting, venerable establishments.

The road narrows to two lanes and begins a serious uphill on what is now Santa Susana Pass Rd. The winding road ascends past Box Canyon Rd. and works its way near to, and at the elevation of, the Simi Valley Fwy. There is a train tunnel in the canyon between the freeway and Santa Susana Pass Rd. Locals say the sound of trains leaving the tunnel and entering Simi Valley is downright eerie. In 1.5 miles from Hideout Willies is the freeway overpass which returns you to the trailhead (11.4).

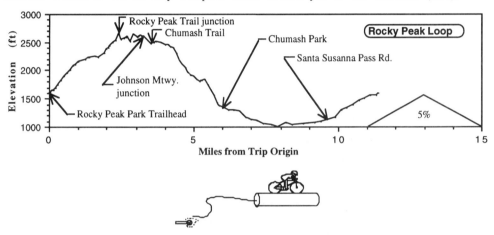

TRIP #47 - LIMEKILN CANYON

GENERAL LOCATION: Location (Topo) - Oat Mountain

LEVEL OF DIFFICULTY: Up and back - moderate
Distance - 7.0 miles; Time - 1-1/2 hours
Elevation gain - 700 feet

HIGHLIGHTS: Lower Limekiln Canyon below Rinaldi St. is recommended for all cyclists, including children and beginners. North of Rinaldi St. requires modestly improved skills. You are treated to creek crossings, a creek-side cavort under plentiful tree cover and a roller-coaster spree well above Limekiln Canyon on the panoramic upper trail stretches. The final trip segment is on a serene trail stretch below tree cover.

TRAILHEAD: From the Ronald Reagan Fwy. (State Hwy. 118) near Porter Ranch, exit south at Tampa Ave. and continue 3/4 mile to Tunney Ave. Turn right and then left immediately at the first street which is Calvin Ave. Park near the intersection. The trail entry is across Tunney Ave. and a few hundred feet south where a sign proclaims *Limekiln Canyon: Lower Trail*.

For bikers wishing to skirt the less challenging lower trip section, exit as before but turn north on Tampa Ave., then west on Rinaldi St. and park near the marked entry to Limekiln Canyon just before the bridge and on the north side of the road.

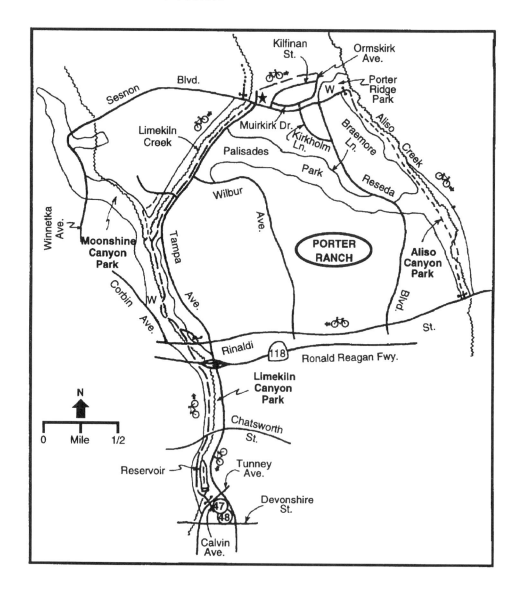

TRIP #47 - LIMEKILN CANYON
TRIP #48 - LIMEKILN/ALISO CANYONS LOOP

TRIP DESCRIPTION: **Trailhead to Rinaldi Street.** Climb the asphalt road to a vantage point above the reservoir with Limekiln Canyon Creek to the right (east) and residences in the hills to the left and above. In 0.6 mile on the flat, you do a short, steep climb and cross Chatsworth St. where there are signs on both sides of the road that note trail entries. Across the street is poorer quality asphalt, but the "funner" option is to take the small paralleling single track to the west of the road for 0.3 mile until it returns to the road near a sign along your route stating *Old Mission Trail*.

170

You pass under a set of highly elevated bridges (Ronald Reagan Fwy.), pass a road fork to the left which leads up to residential environs and continue on gravel/packed dirt path. You continue to a tunnel under Rinaldi St. and bike through midstream in Limekiln Canyon Creek! Don's experience says to take off your sunglasses when navigating this reasonable quality, but rock-strewn passage. On the north side exit of the tunnel you reach another trail fork, right taking you to an exit at Rinaldi St. and left to the trail continuation (1.5).

Rinaldi Street. to Trail's End. You take the left fork and follow any one of several paths which wander through a beautifully shaded picnic area and rejoin near the creek Cross Limekiln Canyon Creek and follow the wide packed-dirt trail under tree shade to a shaded overhang/ picnic area with a tree growing through the structure and a water fountain (1.8). Pass a sign noting *Rattlesnakes*, cross the creek and pedal on a mild upgrade which takes you further above the canyon bottom. A feeder-creek crossing and a short upgrade are followed by your arrival at a trail fork 0.4 mile from the shaded overhang/picnic area. on the south side of the fork is a stately oak near to and on the creek side of the trail. The trail markers were torn down when we passed through, however, left is the Moonshine Canyon diversion. You go right and uphill, passing below some residences.

North of Hollow Springs Road

The grade lessens as you stare down at the canyon bottom far below. Next you pass under the Hollow Springs Rd. bridge and work your way up to one of several street entries along Tampa Ave. (2.4). A series of short, steep ups and downs on the packed-dirt trail takes you further from, but roughly parallel to, Tampa Ave. You return to a point near that road in 0.4 mile where a sign greets you: *Limekiln Trail: Rinaldi-1.0* (back the way you came); *Sesnon-0.6* (the direction you are going).

You follow another roller-coaster segment in more dense tree surroundings alternately working toward and away from Tampa Ave. remaining well above the canyon. You reach another marked junction with a sign noting *Aliso Canyon* and pointing to the trail to the right which takes you back south and directly up to Tampa Ave. in a short distance. A broken sign points left and probably would say *Moonshine Canyon*. You continue directly ahead and reach Sesnon Blvd. near Tampa Ave. in 0.2 mile (3.5). The sign at the Sesnon Blvd. entry points back the way you came and notes *Wilbur-0.6, Rinaldi-1.6.* All that remains is to meet up with your car shuttle or enjoy the delightful coast most of the way back to the start point.

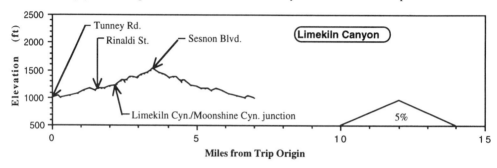

Trip Option. If you take the fork into Moonshine Canyon (2.2), all options we tried were strenuous and required hearty biking/physical skills. A good option for the adventurous is to follow a single track down to Moonshine Canyon Creek, cross it and work your way a short distance to the slightly overgrown trail. At the second set of trail intersections, take the east fork which leads to a steep uphill. This takes you onto a ridge between Moonshine and Limekiln Canyons and, after a final steep climb alongside some tennis courts, deposits you at Hollow Springs Dr. near a bridge over Limekiln Canyon. Just across the bridge is Tampa Ave.

TRIP #48 - LIMEKILN/ALISO CANYONS LOOP

GENERAL LOCATION: Location (Topo) - Oat Mountain

LEVEL OF DIFFICULTY: Loop - moderate
                         Distance - 9.3 miles; Time - 2 hours
                         Elevation gain - 800 feet

HIGHLIGHTS: The pleasant 3.5-mile climb on the "Limekiln Canyon" tour is followed by a short stint on a multi-use trail below the foothills, a 0.6-mile spin through a residential neighborhood and a breezy downhill into Aliso Canyon. The

1.4-mile canyon transit is free form with many options that all lead to the canyon outlet at Rinaldi St. The canyon ride winds through low foliage with many small ups and downs and several stream bed crossings. The loop is closed using paved streets to return to the trip origin.

TRAILHEAD: See the "Limekiln Canyon" trip. To just do the Aliso Canyon tour, exit north at Tampa Ave. and drive 2-1/4 miles to road's end. The Aliso Canyon trip in this direction is rated easy and the up and back tour is moderate. There is horse and foot traffic in both canyons that deserve the right of way.

TRIP DESCRIPTION: **Limekiln Canyon.** Take the 3.5-mile "Limekiln Canyon" tour to its end at Sesnon Blvd.

Upper Aliso Canyon

To Aliso Canyon. Enter the multi-use trail at the end of Tampa Ave. and bike east and uphill behind a fenced residential development. The trail crosses a cul-de-sac and continues on a flat section ending at unmarked Ormskirk Ave. (4.0). A sequence on paved road is to follow Omskirk Ave. (which becomes Muirkirk Dr.) 1/3 mile, left (south) on Kirkholm Ln. and immediately left on Sesnon Blvd., continuing to its terminus (4.6). On this transit you circuit the pleasant grass-carpeted, shady Porter Ridge Park, which also has a water fountain and restrooms.

Aliso Canyon. Pass through the gate on the north side of Sesnon Blvd. and enjoy a 150-foot drop into the canyon, following a "U" bend at the canyon floor and head south. You drop 250-feet from Sesnon Blvd. to Rinaldi St., however, you get a mini-workout on the ups and downs and in the sand patches scattered throughout the canyon floor. At 0.3 mile from the end of Sesnon Blvd., you reach a major trail junction with the trail left heading uphill to the end of the eastern segment of Sesnon Blvd. and the right trail (your route) dropping down along the creek. From here you continue through low foliage and scrub, picking the trail that suits your fancy, staying in the canyon. Our preferred option is to work over to the east side of

173

the canyon, return west and cross the creek over a small wooden bridge, pass under a tree stand behind some nearby stables and exit the canyon at Rinaldi St. (6.3).

Return to the Trailhead. Bike right (west) 1.8 miles which includes some mild uphill to Tampa Ave., where there are gas stations and a small shopping center on the southwest corner. Turn left, coast one mile down to Tunney Ave., turn right and return to your car at Calvin Ave. (9.3).

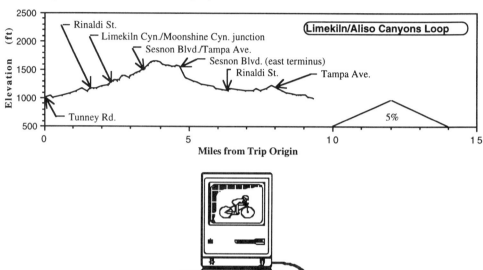

TRIP #49 - MISSION PEAK

GENERAL LOCATION: Location (Topo) - Oat Mountain

LEVEL OF DIFFICULTY: Loop - strenuous [technical section]
Distance - 6.3 miles; Time - 2 hours
Elevation gain - 1400 feet

HIGHLIGHTS: A real surprise, this is a "must-do" tour for in-shape cyclists looking for a good workout climb to a scenic summit (Mission Peak) and experienced single trackers looking for an outback, challenging downhill (Bee Canyon). The 2.25-mile, 1200-foot summit climb provides you with some of the best 360-degree views outside the San Gabriel Mountains and, why not, since this is the second highest peak in the City of Los Angeles! The single-track ride into Bee Canyon is a completely different beast. This little-used route is lightly overgrown near the entry, but a reasonable-quality single track with few surprises other than a couple of steep-to-sheer downgrades that demand good brakes and established (not expert) riding skills. Views of the east Bee Canyon Wall are awe-inspiring. The drop down into the canyon will bring a smile to your face. The outlet ride in Bee Canyon and through O'Melveney Park proper is the perfect scenic warm down for the end of a beautiful trip.

174

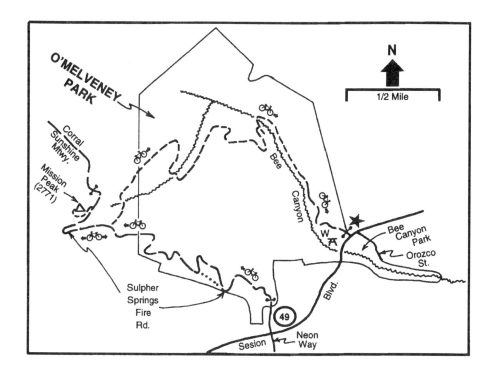

TRIP #49 - MISSION PEAK

TRAILHEAD: From State Hwy. 118 (Ronald Reagan Fwy.) exit north at Balboa Blvd. and drive 2.4 miles to Sesnon Blvd. Turn left and continue 3/4 mile, passing your O'Melveney Park outlet near Orozco St. and arrive at Neon Wy. Turn right (north) and continue to the end of the cul-de-sac where there are a posted set of trail use rules and a mountain lion warning sign. From San Fernando Rd. in the one-mile stretch south of Interstate Hwy. 5, turn south at Balboa Blvd. and drive 3/4 mile to Senson Blvd. Turn right (west) and proceed 3/4 mile to Neon Wy. Trip note: There are water fountains on the Bee Canyon segment -- in our usual conservative fashion, we suggest that you not rely on them to work.

O'Melveney Park, the second largest park in the City of Los Angeles, takes its name from a family of lawyers who bought the property in 1941 and maintained a "gentlemen's ranch." Though the cattle are no longer present, the orchards, ranch house and barn still remain. The O'Melveney's deeded a part of their ranch to Los Angeles and the city purchased the remainder, opening the multi-use park in 1981.

TRIP DESCRIPTION: Climb to Mission Peak. Beyond the gate you are immediately treated to a testy uphill. The winding packed-dirt road works past a scattered tree or two providing periodic shade on the way up the otherwise mostly barren slopes. The views back to the trailhead, the Los Angeles Dam area and the spread-forever San Fernando Valley improve with altitude. You pass a road fork near (0.7) (the only true decision point below the peak itself), staying right on the better-quality, less-steep road. The route works generally northwest and climbs to a cross-roadway fence with an open segment that you pass through (1.5). To the right (east) of the road is a hard-to-see single track that will be your return exit.

175

Just Below the Summit

A lengthy westbound traverse takes you past a couple of isolated shade trees, then switches back east to a flat with a full clump of trees. The road circuits the summit on the east side, then continues on an arc to a road junction just north of Mission Peak. The road ahead (north) continues to a metal gate at a private property boundary; you make a sharp left and climb in an ascending circle to the peak (2.25). At the summit is an unobstructed view of the San Gabriel Mountains to the east, the Santa Monica Mountains to the south and the surrounding Santa Susanas. Also here is a raised stone memorial to Dr. Mario De Campos, a hiking enthusiast who cherished the peak.

Mission Peak Summit

Descent into Bee Canyon. Coast back down the peak 0.7 mile to the open fence and single track noted on the inbound ride. Turn northeast and follow this slightly overgrown trail across a flower-bedecked meadow, then on a winding traverse which gives way to a screaming beeline directly down a short ridgeline. You then

176

follow a series of turns, first directly toward the imposing eastern wall of Bee Canyon, then switching direction to parallel the canyon itself. A periodic look back up the rolling hills and scattered peaks that you are navigating is impressive.

Just Before the Plunge into Bee Canyon

A very steep downgrade north toward the canyon gives way to an equally steep southbound segment that dumps down to a graded bench above the canyon complete with a slab holding an aluminum water fountain (4.3). Bike back north about 100 feet (continuing south here takes you a short distance to a mountain wall with a steep foot trail) and follow the short, steep traverse to the canyon floor. A "U" bend at the bottom takes you across a low wooden bridge over the creek and sends you southbound on a varied-width trail with some dirt sections. Looping up in either direction from the narrow canyon provides some awesome scenery. Continue mostly on the east side of the canyon winding through the clumps of low foliage and scattered trees and passing additional water fountains. Continue mostly on the east side of the canyon, winding through the clumps of low foliage and scattered trees, passing additional water fountains.

Completing the Loop. Past the canyon mouth the area transitions to the developed part of O'Melveney Park with white fencing, mowed lawns and tree cover. At the first junction at the fence, turn right (left goes in the same general direction) and follow the trail along the fence towards a metal shed and the O'Melveney family ranch house. On the south side of the house, transition over to a wide road and follow it a short distance to the parking area along Sesnon Blvd. All that remains is to pedal 0.7 mile up Sesnon Blvd. to Neon Wy. to complete the tour (6.3).

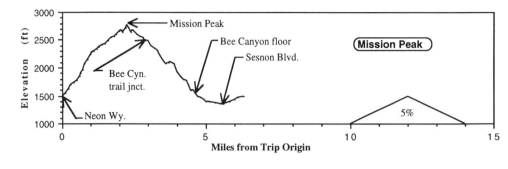

UERDUGO MOUNTAINS/SAN RAFAEL HILLS

TRIP #50 - BRAND MOTORWAY

GENERAL LOCATION: Location (Topo) - Burbank, Pasadena

LEVEL OF DIFFICULTY: Up and back - strenuous
Distance - 7.0 miles; Time - 2-1/2 hours
Elevation gain - 1800 feet

HIGHLIGHTS: Brand Motorway is a stressing workout, no more no less! You start from the manicured lawns and tree shade of the lower park, proceed past the landmark Brand Library and Doctor's House, pass by the shaded remnants of Brand's exotic nature display and then begin a steady, no-nonsense (10%+ average grade), three-plus mile climb to the Verdugo Overlook. The route takes you up Pomeroy Canyon then over to Brand Canyon. You work your way above the head of Brand Canyon and gain the ridgeline near a well-placed bench at the overlook. Rest your tired body on the bench, enjoy the best of the many west-facing views on the way up, and prepare for the rewarding downhill dash back to the park.

TRAILHEAD: From State Hwy. 5 in Glendale, exit northwest at Western Ave. toward the Verdugo Mountains and continue 1-1/2 miles to road's end at Mountain St. Turn right and then immediately left into the marked Brand Park entrance. Park across from the Brand Library.

Brand Park's namesake was a wealthy insurance businessman who built El Mirador. This 5000 square-foot mansion with its Taj Mahal exterior of massive arches

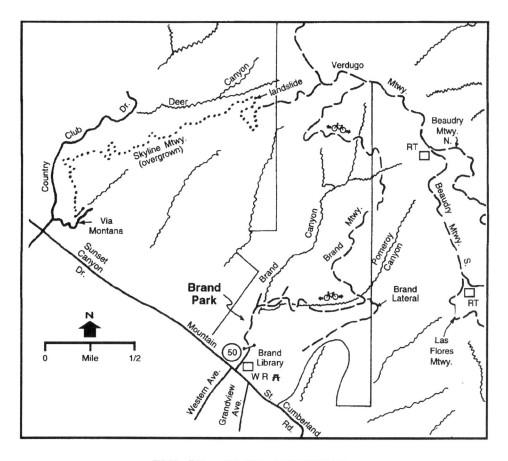

TRIP #50 - BRAND MOTORWAY

and domes is now the Brand Library. The well-manicured estate was also stocked with exotic flora, water falls, fountains and even a private club whose foundation you pass early in the trip. Per Brand's will, the nearly 500-acre property was deeded to the City of Glendale upon the death of his wife in 1945, 20 years after Mr. Brand's death.

TRIP DESCRIPTION: **Entrance Point to Brand Lateral Junction.** Bike to the northwestern corner of the parking area and pass through the open fence where markers note *Brand Park Landfill* and *Doctor's House*. Follow this asphalt road past the Doctor's House, a lovely Victorian structure once occupied by four doctors which was transported to this site. Climb above a debris basin, then lift your bike over a metal blocking gate (0.2). The first of many ever-improving views of Burbank and across the valley to Griffith Park appear back over your shoulder. Continued uphill takes you past an out-of-the-place cluster of tropical vegetation (Brand's grounds were once covered with mixed flora, waterfalls and fountains) to a multi-way junction in 0.35 mile. Left leads to the Brand Cemetery, while the rightmost paved (one way) surface is your route up Pomeroy Canyon. You leave the shaded environs and climb, biking on dirt road after 0.6 mile. Near the head of Pomeroy Canyon is a street sign announcing *Brand Lateral* -- no outlet, to the right and *Brand Mtwy.* left, which is the prescribed route (1.05).

179

Just Above the Brand Lateral

Brand Lateral Junction to Verdugo Overlook. The road steepens and works over to Brand Canyon and you follow the mountain contour above the canyon, gazing upward at your destination route and ridgetop. This "no-nonsense" climb passes next to a power pole (a bank of transmission lines follows the canyon) (2.6) and crosses under the lines in another 0.15 mile as you cross above the head of the eastern Brand Canyon split. The generally northbound route bends west, continues relentlessly upward (providing many great opportunities to stop and view the populated valley floor well below), then passes above the west canyon split (3.0).

Further climbing takes you around a west-facing outcropping and then sends you northeast toward the ridgetop. The road flattens, then leads to a "T" intersection at Verdugo Mtwy. (3.5). Nearby is a rest bench, which indicates that you have attained the Verdugo Overlook. Before returning to Brand Park, plop your tired fanny on the bench and take in the views of Burbank, Glendale and Griffith Park.

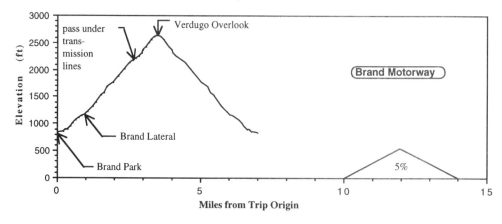

Trip Options. There are many options off the Verdugo Mtwy., particularly if you have the good fortune to have a car shuttle. The options are best identified by reviewing the "Verdugo Motorway (Summit Ride)" trip map. If you have no shuttle, the loop can be closed using the surface streets. All trips in the Verdugo Mountains can be closed in this fashion, without adding a lot of extra mileage or elevation gain.

Glendale Backdrop Near the Climb's Half-way Point

TRIP #51 - BEAUDRY LOOP

GENERAL LOCATION: Location (Topo) - Pasadena, Burbank

LEVEL OF DIFFICULTY: Loop - Strenuous [technical sections]
                        Distance - 6.0 miles; Time - 2 hours
                        Elevation gain - 1600 feet

HIGHLIGHTS: This bite-sized loop is a fine workout with scenic vistas from the trip onset that just get better. At the lower Beaudry Mtwy. junction the route turns west onto Beaudry Mtwy. S. (the north branch is a gut-buster climb) onto a 2.2-mile winding upgrade above the canyon enveloping Deer Creek. At the upper Beaudry Mtwy. junction and Verdugo Mtwy., you switch over and climb Beaudry Mtwy. N. to the trip summit at an array of radio towers. A scenic southerly traverse leads to the Las Flores Mtwy. junction and a swing east takes you through a two-mile arc that provides successive focused views of the Glendale/Burbank area, L.A. Civic Center, the San Rafael Hills and the La Canada/La Cresenta environs. The ever-present San

181

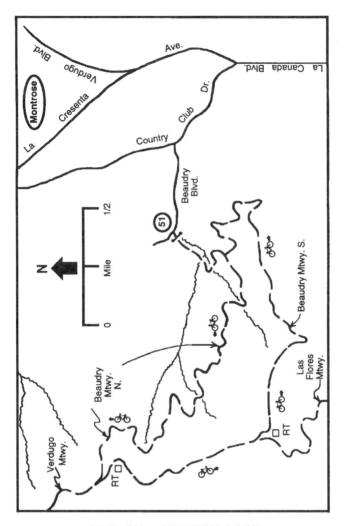

TRIP #51 - BEAUDRY LOOP

Gabriel Mountains in the distance are an additional treat. Sections of Beaudry Mtwy. S. beyond the Las Flores Mtwy. junction are steep to sheer and rutted, demanding at least moderate riding skills and your complete attention.

TRAILHEAD: From State Hwy. 2 (Glendale Fwy.), exit west at Mountain St., travel 1/2 mile to Verdugo Rd. and turn right. In 1/4 mile veer left on La Canada Blvd. and drive 1/2 mile to Country Club Dr. and turn left. Follow that road 1/2 mile to Beaudry Blvd., turn left, and find parking near the Beaudry Terrace intersection.

TRIP DESCRIPTION: **Road Entry to the Lower Beaudry Motorway Split.** Follow the paved road south alongside the debris basin to a metal blocking gate. The road turns to dirt, pulls away from the debris basin and passes under tree cover. Cross over Deer Creek and a second northerly feeder and climb a steepening, winding road to a "street-signed" junction. *Beaudry S.* is to the left and your route, **Beaudry N.**, is to right (0.45). (Beaudry Mtwy. S. is a super-challenging climb only recommended for bikers with "thunder thighs.")

Montrose and San Gabriel Mountains from Beaudry Motorway North

Beaudry Road North to the Upper Beaudry Road Junction. The road breaks into the open and begins a 1.6-mile, 900-foot climb alongside and to the head of the canyon holding Deer Creek. We saw a charcoal gray fox on the way up. The winding route follows the contour of the southern slopes on the twisting climb. The destination summit and cluster of KBLA radio towers is visible for much of the climb, and a little roadside water tank offers a greeting at the 1.1-mile point.

Once above the canyon head, the route swings from north to west and reaches a viewpoint at a fire break. Tujunga, La Cresenta and La Canada are spread below with the stately San Gabriel Mountains as a distant backdrop. Due north is the Mt. Lukens massif with its own radio tower array. In another 1.2 miles is a junction (2.6). Verdugo Mtwy. starts at this point and veers to the northwest (right), while the entry to Beaudry Mtwy. S. is a sharp left and uphill.

Beaudry Motorway South. A 0.4-mile variable upgrade takes you onto a saddle with the first of the grandiose views to the south and more to the north. The climb terminates on the fenced east side of the KBLA tower cluster. From here you can view the cities below, greater Los Angeles, and both the Pacific Ocean coastline and Catalina on clear days. The downhill southbound takes you across another lower, but equally scenic saddle, and then to a concrete foundation sitting above and to the right of the dirt road. On the slopes behind is yet another radio tower. Just beyond is a three-way junction with Las Flores Mtwy. to the right, a steep uphill to the radio facility in the middle and the Beaudry Mtwy. S. continuation to the left. (3.6).

A steep, sometimes rutted, downhill that has you braking and dodging ruts, (an interesting combination) leads you to a small turnout with a peek down to the Las Flores Mtwy. and the first of many views into Glendale, the L.A. Civic Center and beyond (4.0). Just after, take the right fork at the junction below another concrete structure. You reach the trip's southernmost point and make a hairpin turn back north below Peak 2112. The Glendale Fwy. and San Rafael Hills dominate your view as you navigate a sheer, rutted downhill while heading northeast. A saddle crossing a flat provides an initial view down into your entry area near the debris basin and another look at Beaudry Mtwy. N. You pass to the south below Peak 1753, climb to a crest, then wind past a concrete structure with a spur entry (4.9).

Beyond the easternmost trip point the road turns north and then west, circumnavigating Peak 1753 while dropping down toward the entry canyon. A sweeping upward vista lets you see your entire circuit, Beaudry Mtwy. N. climbing to the KBLA towers, the tower above the Las Flores Mtwy. junction and your future route down to the debris basin. A steep and sinuous downgrade returns through scattered tree cover to the Beaudry Mtwy. junction (5.55). Repeat the incoming route and return to the trailhead (6.0).

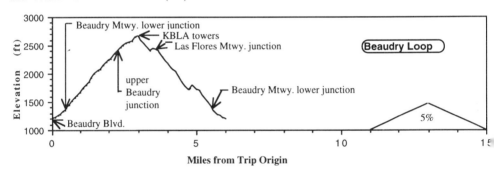

TRIP #52 - VERDUGO MOTORWAY (SUMMIT RIDE)

GENERAL LOCATION: Location (Topo) - Burbank, Pasadena

LEVEL OF DIFFICULTY: One-way - strenuous
Distance - 11.4 miles; Time - 3 hours
Elevation gain - 2000 feet

HIGHLIGHTS: We did this one on a foggy day -- the temperature was right, but we missed many of the scenic view points. The dandy tour climbs through Stough Canyon and onto Verdugo Mtwy. 2.2 miles to a refreshing 0.4-mile flat ridgeline traverse. (Stough Canyon is the most direct access to Verdugo Mtwy.) A series of variable-grade climbs and some flats leads past the Verdugo Lateral, Hosteller Mtwy. and Whiting Woods Mtwy. junctions to a point below Verdugo Peak, the high point of the 13-mile long range. A mostly downhill ride continuation southbound takes you past the Brand Mtwy. and a genuine park bench and then diverts you southwest to the end of Verdugo Mtwy. at the Beaudry Mtwy. North/South junction. A climb to the

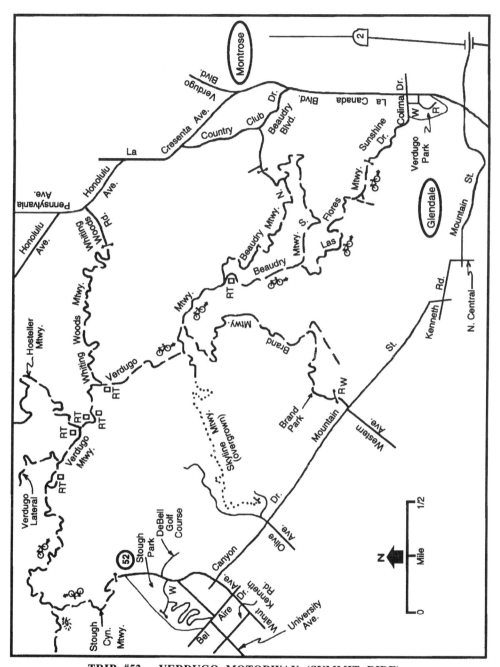

TRIP #52 - VERDUGO MOTORWAY (SUMMIT RIDE)

ridgeline summit on Beaudry Mtwy. S. leads past the largest radio tower array in the range. At the final dirt junction of the tour, rocket down the canyons containing Las Flores Mtwy. to paved Sunshine Dr. and outlet at terrific Verdugo Park.

185

TRAILHEAD: From Interstate Hwy. 5, exit north at Burbank Blvd., continue 1/4 mile to N. 3rd. St and turn left (northwest). Turn right at the next two streets (Delaware Rd. and Glenoaks Blvd.), then left (this circumnavigates Burbank High School) and proceed toward the Verdugo Mountains 1-1/2 miles, passing the DeBell Municipal Golf Course. Park at the far end of the lot near the fire gate entry to Stough Canyon Mtwy. (This is a two-way road, even though all parking is slanted downhill.) (Note that above Sunset Canyon Dr., you pass Lockheed View Dr. and the Stough Park entry. Stough Park is an excellent alternate starting point.)

On the Short Climb Just Below Verdugo Peak

TRIP   DESCRIPTION: **Stough Canyon Motorway to Verdugo Motorway.** Pass through the metal blocking gate and climb 0.15 mile where the pavement turns to dirt. Parallel a channel to your right and begin a very rigorous 0.4-mile switchbacking climb, passing a road junction to the left which leads to water tanks. Pass above a canyon head on your right, then meet another road junction, again staying to the right (0.8). Pedal up the scrub-filled mountainsides on exposed, good quality road (typical of most of the ride), bearing north and climbing to another junction. This is the Verdugo Mtwy. (1.35). A spur trail cuts back south and above your incoming route, while the westbound fire road (to your left) leads to Chandler and Wildwood Fire Rds.

Verdugo Motorway Eastbound to Hosteller Motorway. Turn right and gain a northern exposure with views of the Tujunga/La Canada area and the more distant slopes of the San Gabriel Mountains. Make a winding swing below the peaks on your right, eventually heading south, and start a 0.4-mile, relatively flat southwesterly traverse to the next climb (2.6). Pump northbound, reverse direction sharply, then swing east again, climbing above the heads of more of the northerly canyons and reach a junction in 0.9 mile. A 0.15-mile diversion right, which we took, leads up to a radio tower and an outstanding view site. A return to the junction and turn eastbound leads below a lined cluster of pine trees, the first and only tree cover on

186

the tour. The road climbs below a tower-bedecked summit on the right and meets a wide road junction beyond (4.2). The road to the left, with a yellow stanchion marked *C.1* is the Verdugo Lateral -- a 1/2-mile ride to a dead end. You go right and traverse below the ridge on your right, enjoying the view which opens southbound and eastbound to the tower on Verdugo Peak. The 0.4-mile flat leads to another junction above the head of a northern canyon at Hosteller Mtwy. (4.6).

Near the Head of Dead Horse Canyon

Verdugo Motorway Eastbound to Whiting Woods Motorway. Cross a saddle and shift from a northern to southern exposure, then climb to a scenic south-facing outcropping. A swing north takes you past a narrow asphalt road which climbs in a couple of hundred yards to Verdugo Peak and a radio tower. Stay left on the main road (or divert to the peak), make a short climb, then swing east and start downhill, Across the valley to the north is the ever-present and distant Mt. Lukens with its bevy of radio towers. Continue the eastbound traverse to a point where Whiting Woods Mtwy. snakes up from the north and meets Verdugo Mtwy. (5.3). That motorway is to the left (on the canyon side) and a radio tower access road is to the right and uphill.

Verdugo Motorway Southbound to Brand Motorway. Continue the downhill traverse on the middle road, heading southbound with excellent views into La Canada. You pass a water tower and continue mostly downhill to a junction with the Skyline Mtwy. which heads to the right (See "Trip Option" below.) (6.55). Stay left and pass the very steep middle road which climbs to the nearby ridge. Off to the east and below is steep, massive Henderson Canyon. A swing east brings you to the Brand Mtwy. junction and a park bench in another 0.15 mile. At this scenic site on the mountain spine is a pole with a cluster of unreadable road signs.

Verdugo Motorway Southeast to Las Flores Motorway. Stay to the left and continue downhill on Verdugo Mtwy. You pass below some transmission lines and reach the upper Beaudry Mtwy. junction. This is the terminus of the Verdugo Mtwy. Beaudry Mtwy. N. comes up on the left (7.3). Turn right and climb Beaudry Mtwy. S. toward an array of KBLA radio towers on the ridge above. Traverse below the towers, climbing east, then south and gain the ridge top directly on the east side of the fenced-in tower group. A southbound downhill takes you past a flat concrete structure on your right (east) to a junction. Beaudry Mtwy. S. veers off to the left, a sheer upgrade in the middle leads to a radio tower, and you hang a right to Las Flores Mtwy. (8.25).

187

Las Flores Motorway to Verdugo Park. You start a 1.3-mile steep dirt downhill which passes below the last of a series of power poles in 0.15 mile. The exposed and winding route slithers downward above the head of Dead Horse Canyon, turns east, then continues to drop through another smaller canyon. In about a mile, as you continue a long sinuous drop southeast, you hear the first road noise in a spell and spot residences to the east. The road crosses a paved uphill offshoot which goes left to a water tower (10.0), then passes a dirt path to the right in another 0.2 mile. Las Flores Mtwy. ends at a paved (but otherwise uninhabited) cul-de-sac (10.5).

Another 0.2 mile leads to a metal blocking gate which forces you to lift your bike over or squeeze it through the narrow openings. You are now at the head of Sunshine Dr. (where you can park your car if taking the trip in the opposite direction). A 0.8 mile, 300-foot drop down Sunshine Dr., which becomes Colina Dr. near the bottom, leads to an entry to Verdugo Park. The park has abundant tree shade, grass, restrooms, barbecue facilities, children's playground and baseball and soccer fields (11.4). Might we offer the suggestion to celebrate your Verdugo Mountains adventure with a well deserved picnic?

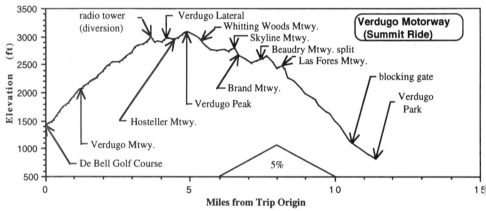

Upper Skyline Motorway

Trip Option: Skyline Motorway. We did the 3.0-mile, 1500-foot elevation loss in April '96 (or it did us!). It is not recommended unless you and your partner(s) have excellent bicycle skills, are well prepared for mechanical and medical emergencies, and have a desire for the truly out-of-the-ordinary adventure. A short climb off of Verdugo Mtwy. is followed by a downhill, rutted and rocky road to an "intersection" in 1/4 mile.

Right is a path to an overlook, while left takes you onto an overgrown road with a "game trail" winding through the brush. If you don't like the first 100-200 yards, turn back! In another mile of ride and push, you reach the head of Deer Canyon where a "road" cave-in forces you to portage your bike down a very steep and slippery slope. Another mile of bike and body stress while traversing the south side of Deer Canyon leads to a saddle and a short uphill. Beyond is a sinuous downhill and increasing, but still distant, development until you outlet at Via Montana near Camino de Villas road (near street address 1713). Amongst the other extended preparations for the ride, wear long pants and top to minimize "brush bite" and hitchhiking ticks.

TRIP #53 - CHANDLER AND STOUGH CANYONS

GENERAL LOCATION: Location (Topo) - Burbank

LEVEL OF DIFFICULTY: One way - moderate to strenuous (Stough Canyon exit)
Distance - 4.7 miles; Time - 1-1/2 hours
Elevation gain - 800 feet

Burbank Airport as Seen on the Initial Climb

HIGHLIGHTS: This is the least-strenuous ride onto the Verdugo Mountains spine. The entry is via Chandler Canyon on a short, but generally-steep two-mile climb past

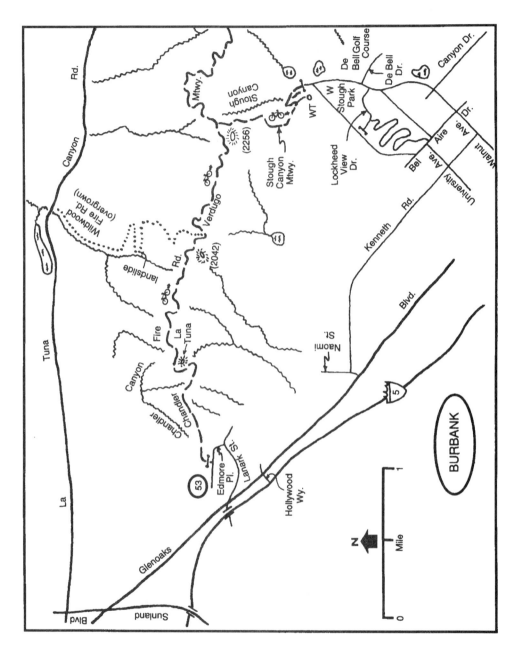

TRIP #53 - CHANDLER AND STOUGH CANYONS

La Tuna and Peak 2042. The Burbank views are fabulous! A short climb leads to a sweeping turn and runout to the head of Stough Canyon Mtwy. Then a steep, tight winding downhill takes you to an outlet near the DeBell Golf Course

TRAILHEAD: Exit north on the Golden State Fwy. (Interstate Hwy. 5) at Hollywood Wy. and turn left at the first street, Glenoaks Blvd. In 1-3/4 mile turn right at Lanark St. and climb 2/3 mile to Edmore Pl. In a couple of hundred yards on the right is a yellow gate with a "Restricted Entry" sign. Park on the opposite side of the street and below the gate.

TRIP DESCRIPTION: **Chandler Fire Road.** A difficult initial uphill north provides the first of many upcoming views of the Burbank airport and the city environs back over your shoulder. In 0.2 mile the route flattens, turns northeast and leads upwards toward carved-out La Tuna. A shift to the south over a small ridge (0.5) steers you across a couple of scenic saddles on a welcome flat. A winding climb to the western face of La Tuna (0.95) is followed by a downhill and a series of winding ups and downs (mostly "ups") near the ridgeline. Canyon views greet you on both sides on this segment. At the two-mile point is a great northern exposure and an opportunity to look back to your incoming route. Follow a curving, flat arc below Peak 2042, which is to your right with a pole imbedded at the summit (2.0). As you swing south and downhill in 0.2 mile, there is an easy-to-miss single track to your left with a sign noting *Road Closed*. This is the non-recommended Wildwood Fire Rd. (The overgrown road caved in a mile below this junction and the path skinnies down to a game trail. We did not explore the outlet.) Past this junction, the Chandler Fire Rd. becomes the Verdugo Mtwy.

Wildwood Fire Road Entry

Verdugo Motorway. Continue past the Wildwood Fire Rd. exit and follow on and below the ridgeline on a roughly eastbound sinuous road which climbs and dips to a scenic overview of a large canyon which is the northern companion of Stough Canyon (2.95). To the distant east is Peak 2646, and well below its summit, is the continuation of the Verdugo Mtwy. northeast bound. From this scenic overlook, drop down and pass a small side trail to the right in 0.2 mile. A steep descent takes you onto a deeply-rutted section of roadway and guides you to the Stough Canyon Mtwy.

191

junction (3.4). Trip options from here are to drop down Stough Canyon to the De Bell Golf Course (1.3 miles downhill) or to continue climbing northeast along the Verdugo Mtwy. (See "Verdugo Motorway (Summit Ride)" trip for both options.) The elevation contour below shows the former option.

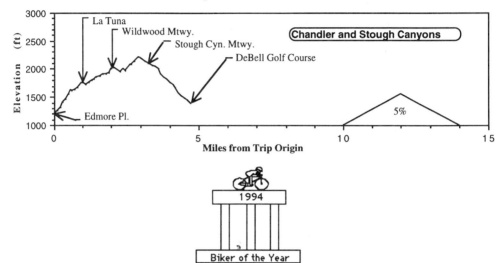

TRIP #54 - HOSTELLER/WHITING WOODS MTWYS.

GENERAL LOCATION: Location (Topo) - Burbank

LEVEL OF DIFFICULTY: One way - moderate to strenuous [technical sections]
Distance - 7.1 miles; Time - 2-1/2 hours
Elevation gain - 1400 feet

HIGHLIGHTS: Hosteller Mtwy. is the easiest and most popular access to Verdugo Peak, with about 1400 feet of climb in 3.8 miles. From La Tuna Canyon Rd, a 0.4-mile warm-up stretch gives way to a stair-step winding climb which takes you to a superb vista at the motorway's most easterly point. Soon after bending south, you see the radio tower on destination Verdugo Peak and scale the ridge to Verdugo Mtwy. An uphill to a point just below the peak is followed by a short downhill traverse over to Whiting Woods Mtwy. The Whiting Woods Mtwy. segment is a 2.8-mile steep (somewhat technical) downhill which will have you braking through the myriad of both sweeping and horseshoe turns. There are continuous sweeping vistas of La Cresenta and La Canada below, Henderson Canyon and great over-the-shoulder views of the Verdugo Mountain crest. The exposed motorway terminates near a shaded glen at the Henderson Canyon outlet creek.

TRAILHEAD: From State Hwy. 210 in La Canada, exit at La Tuna Canyon Rd., pass under the freeway and find a parking turnout on the left just beyond the eastbound on-ramp. If you want to tackle one of the toughest extended climbs in the Verdugo Mountains, start from the Whiting Woods Rd. trailhead. Exit the Foothill Fwy. south at Pennsylvania Ave., continue 1/4 mile to a point where the road bends to the left, then turn right at Whiting Woods Rd. At road's end in 1/4 mile at a metal blocking gate is the trailhead. The ride in this direction is rated strenuous to very strenuous.

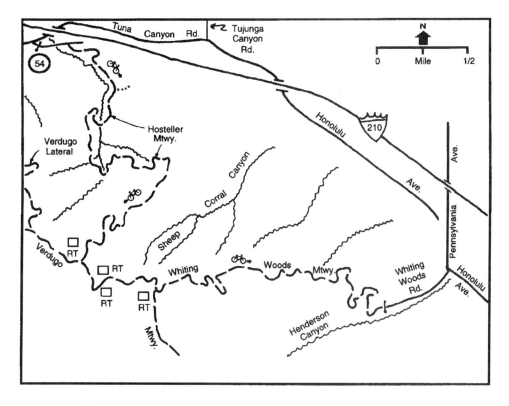

TRIP #54 - HOSTELLER/WHITING WOODS MOTORWAYS

TRIP DESCRIPTION: **Hosteller Motorway to Verdugo Motorway.** From the parking area, pass around the metal blocking gate and bike south on a paved, 0.4-mile, nearly flat warm-up stretch. A short, steep upgrade takes you in the direction of, and well above, the freeway. At a fork, turn right, staying on pavement and continue climbing past the transition to dirt road (0.7). A gradual turn west and a shallow traverse give way to a steep horseshoe-bend ascent that eventually points you south for 0.4 mile. A winding uphill north and east leads around the base of a peak to the easternmost point on the Hosteller Mtwy., where there are superb views of La Canada, La Cresenta and the San Gabriel Mountains (2.4).

Swinging south, the motorway transits above impressive Sheep Corral Canyon. In this area the radio towers at the Verdugo Mountain crest (south) become visible for the first time. Across the canyon to the east is the Whiting Woods Mtwy., your outlet route. You pass above the head of Sheep Corral Canyon's western branch, then execute a sinuous climb southwest which brings you to Verdugo Mtwy. just east and below the tower-bedecked zenith. At the junction is spread before you the Los Angeles Civic Center (distant southwest), Burbank and its namesake airport (southwest) and Glendale (due south). The Pacific Coast and Catalina are visible on clear days! At the junction is a yellow stanchion labeled *C4* (pointing west).

193

Hosteller Motorway (Forest Service Vehicle Above)

Verdugo Motorway to Whiting Woods Motorway. Turn east and climb toward the radio tower on Verdugo Peak. In 0.2 mile is a southerly outcropping with another sweeping vista point. A turn north sends you directly toward Verdugo Peak where you have an option to veer right on asphalt and climb to the radio tower or stay left and take a short climb on Verdugo Mtwy. to a crest below and west of the tower. The dirt road swings north and east, providing great La Canada/Tujunga views, passes above the southernmost reaches of Sheep Corral Canyon and meets a three-way junction (4.3). To the right is a paved access to a radio tower complex and straight ahead is the Verdugo Mtwy. extension. To the left is an unmarked yellow stanchion and the steeply descending Whiting Woods Mtwy.

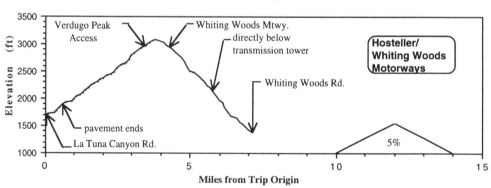

Whiting Woods Motorway. Turn a hard left and steer south and steeply downhill. Put those brakes on as you begin a 2.8-mile, 1600-foot descent (over a 12% average grade). Below and to the west is the tortuous ridgeline descent, a feeder branch of Henderson Canyon dead ahead and the La Cresenta/La Canada areas spread out in the distant valley to the north and east. While dodging the scattered, lightly-

194

rutted road sections you look down to a water tower and pass the locked cistern box below it (4.8).

Whiting Woods Motorway

In 0.2 mile is a mostly flat saddle (one of the few level segments on this downhill) with a view down to a major northern branch of massive Henderson Canyon. Pass below a power transmission tower (5.3), a second cistern box (5.5) and reach a superb overlook of the La Cresenta area and the Foothill Fwy. The wide road starts snaking (literally, as we saw a rattlesnake on the road) southwest and traverses above the main Henderson Canyon branch, passes under some power lines (6.2) and dives toward the canyon's outlet creek. Once along the creek, head into lush, treed bottom land and meet the trailhead gate at the shaded end of Whiting Woods Rd.

Road Companion

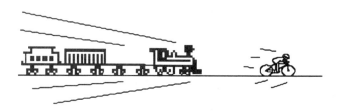

TRIP #55 - SAN RAFAEL HILLS

<u>GENERAL LOCATION</u>:   Location (Topo) - Pasadena

<u>LEVEL OF DIFFICULTY</u>: Up and back - moderate
Distance - 5.1 miles; Time - 1-1/2 hours
Elevation gain - 1050 feet

Initial Climb

HIGHLIGHTS: The described trip climbs from the Forest Hill Dr. entry gate to the San Rafael Hills crest. From the start and throughout the trip, you are treated to views ranging from the stately San Gabriel Mountains to the metropolises of La Canada, La Cresenta and Glendale, the Verdugo Mountains, and even the towering greater Los Angeles skyscrapers. The ascent peaks at the Old Cerro Negro Lookout and drops down on Gladys Mtwy. to a turnaround point at Camino San Rafael.

TRAILHEAD: From State Hwy. 2 (Glendale Fwy.), exit east at Verdugo Blvd. and proceed 1/2 mile to Descanso Dr. and turn right. In 0.2 mile, turn right at Padres Trail and left at the next street, Forest Hills Dr. Continue uphill to road's end, parking well clear of the metal entry gate.

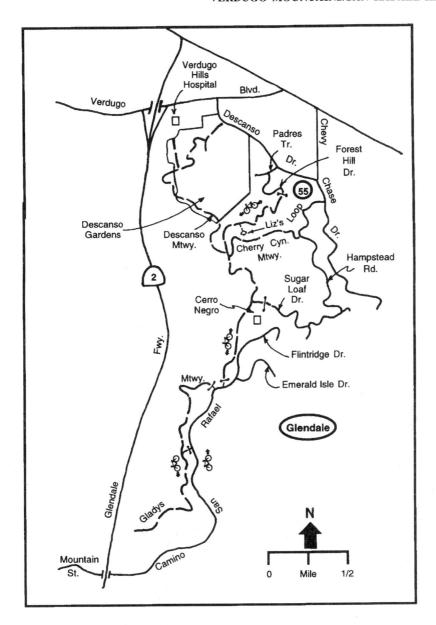

TRIP # 55 - SAN RAFAEL HILLS

TRIP DESCRIPTION: **Trailhead to Cerro Negro.** Pass around the blocking gate and climb the winding fire road, enjoying the views north of La Canada/La Cresenta and the more distant San Gabriel Mountains. In about 0.3 mile, pass the exit to the left which is marked *Liz's Loop* (lookout point). Also noted is the *Cherry Canyon Fire Rd.-0.4 mi.* (outlet at Hampstead Rd.), and, pointing back the way you entered, *Forest Hills Fire Rd. Gate-0.3 mi.*

197

Continue south on the main road another 0.2 mile to a multi-way junction. Left is a power line access circle while right is a circuitous west and then northbound route to Descanso Gardens and the Verdugo Hills Hospital Overlook Continue ahead and downhill on the wide fire road toward the old Lookout Tower atop Cerro Negro in the distance. A drop and then a rise takes you past the marked *Range Lateral Mtwy.* on the right to a paralleling asphalt road with a yellow blocking gate.

Critter Tracks Below Cerro Negro

To the left (east) is a wide trail that comes up to the main road with a sign noting: *1.1 mi. to Verdugo Hills Hospital Overlook*; *0.9 mi. to Descanso Gardens Fire Rd.* (trailhead); and *0.7 mi. to Forest Hill Dr. Fire Rd.* (trailhead). This wide trail is the Cherry Canyon Mtwy. In the direction you are headed is the marker **Cerro Negro Loop Trail**. The dirt road to the right that cuts directly back north and uphill is for transmission pole access. Nice views west display the Verdugo Mountains and the Glendale Fwy. below. Follow the San Rafael Hills ridgeline and reach a plateau with the signed single track **Owl Trail** (1.0). In 0.3 mile, after a 100-foot stair step climb, pass a fire road to the left that outlets at Sugar Loaf Dr. A short uphill leads to the trip's high point below the old Cerro Negro fire lookout tower site (now a repeater station) (1.45).

Cerro Negro to Trip's End. What is now Gladys Mtwy. drops down steeply behind a line of residences, climbs up to a crest below the transmission lines, then dives down to paved Camino San Rafael at a metal gate (1.95). Continue 100-feet south and turn right onto a dirt road with another metal gate that you circumvent. The road follows the hill contour below the summit and works generally downhill, passing below a point where the transmission lines take an abrupt course change to the west (2.5). Across the freeway are the Verdugo Mountains with Beaudry Mtwy. North and South (see "Beaudry Loop" trip) clearly slashing their way up the mountainside.

A 0.1-mile climb takes you to a plateau where a fire road cuts back north and uphill. The tops of the highest greater Los Angeles skyscrapers are evident from this perch peeking above the hills of Elysian Park. You can continue about 1/2 mile south on Gladys Mtwy. as it parallels above Camino San Rafael and, as we understand, dead ends in the hills above the Glendale Fwy. Options are to take the full tour, reverse the incoming route, or to take the fire road down to Camino San Rafael and return to Gladys Mtwy. at the metal gate (1.95-mile point on the incoming ride) after a 0.5-mile, 200-foot climb. We did the latter and retraced our route back to the Forest Hill Dr. entry (5.1).

Trip Option. Take the Cherry Canyon Fire Rd. or Descanso Gardens Fire Rd. off the route described, then make your way back to the trailhead via the hilly surface streets. Bring a street map as the road system is very confusing in this general area.

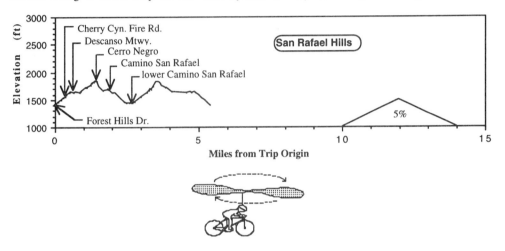

PUENTE HILLS

TRIP #56 - SKYLINE TRAIL - WEST

GENERAL LOCATION: Location (Topo) - El Monte, Whittier

LEVEL OF DIFFICULTY: One way - moderate to strenuous
Distance - 5.8 miles; Time - 2 hours
Elevation gain - 1250 feet

HIGHLIGHTS: You start near Rio Hondo College on a series of single-track switchbacks and climb a paved road with an overlook of the Police Academy firing range, the Rio Hondo College campus and Rose Hills Cemetery. The route reverses direction on paved road, then transitions onto dirt and climbs a ridge to the northern trip summit. A downhill takes you south where a 1.1-mile easy climb leads to a second summit. A switchbacking downhill on single track leads to Turnbull Canyon proper and the final 1.3-mile easy coast passes through lush woodlands to an outlet at Turnbull Canyon Rd.

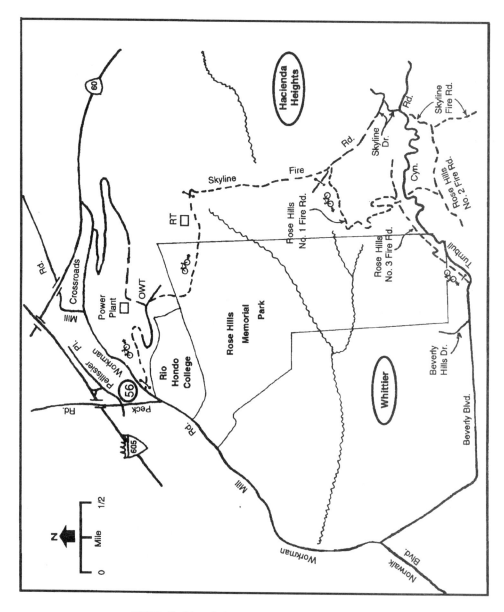

TRIP # 56 - SKYLINE TRAIL - WEST

TRAILHEAD: From the San Gabriel Fwy. (U.S. Hwy. 605), exit south at Peck Rd. Northbound traffic is directed to Pellissier Pl. where a right turn leads to Peck Rd. Take the first turnoff to the left off of Peck Rd. which is Workman Mill Rd. A couple of hundred yards beyond to the right is a metal gate (just beyond a small blockhouse) with a dirt road beyond and an *Equestrian Trail* sign. Park off of Pellissier Pl. if you are doing an out-and-back ride.

200

View from North Summit

TRIP   DESCRIPTION: **Workman   Mill   Road   to   the   North   Summit.** Almost immediately, the road skinnies down to a single track which switchbacks upward, roughly paralleling Workman Mill Rd. At the first junction, right leads to a turnaround, so turn left and continue the undulating climb, taking in the views north to Mt. Wilson in the distance. In about 0.5 mile the trail flattens and you enjoy a look down into the Police Academy Firing Range. After crossing a saddle bike onto pavement (0.6) and climb west to an overlook of Rio Hondo College, noting the small domed observatory in the hills above the school. Rose Hills Cemetery is in the hills beyond. The paved road then bends back east and climbs further to a four-way intersection near a water tower (1.2). Turn right on paved road, then exit right almost immediately onto dirt at the *Equestrian* marker. (The roads left and ahead lead to the nearby power plant and an access road for dump trunks to climb to the Puente Hills Landfill, respectively.)

The dirt road climbs steeply on a ridge which provides views of the massive landfill to the left (east) and Rose Hills ahead and off to the right. A rigorous 0.7-mile climb takes you up to a summit lined with radio towers where you return to pavement for the last 0.1 mile of the uphill. Just beyond the summit on a well-deserved flat is a small grove of trees and a picnic table (no water). Take a break and enjoy the views north to the San Gabriel Mountains and south for the first look into Whittier (2.1). Unfortunately the massive Puente Hills Landfill occupies your view northwest and directly below.

North Summit to Turnbull Canyon Road. A short ride beyond the trail-side rest area, you pass through a metal gate with a sign noting *Skyline Hiking and Riding Trail* and return to dirt road for the remainder of this trip. A steep downhill east and then south takes you on a road between fences. (The fence to your right

201

encloses Rose Hills and private property while the paralleling trail to the east of the road merges later.) At 2.7 miles you see a *Skyline Trail* marker on the trail to the east (across the fence) pointing in your current direction and back in the direction you came -- a small equestrian trail heads east from that marker. Pedal south between the fences, pass through a gate and bike past a small junction trail that cuts in hard left. Continue with the fence line to your right, passing the heads of several small canyons to your left.

You hit a junction with two trails to the left, an equestrian trail which drops east toward the canyon and an uphill power-line access trail (3.55). Stay right along the fence, climb to the trip summit and enjoy the first view of Turnbull Canyon and the like-named road to your left. You reach another junction in 0.15 mile with the Skyline Trail continuing on the dirt road to the left (it drops to Skyline Dr. and Turnbull Canyon Rd. further east of our described outlet) and a hard right leading through a metal gate into privately-owned Rose Hills. Veer right, again staying along the fence. This is Rose Hills #1 Fire Rd. Follow a steep switchbacking downhill for 0.4 mile before executing a final short climb and reaching a sign along the trail noting *Trail: Closed Area*.

Below the North Summit

A short drop brings you into Turnbull Canyon and you reach a junction with an uphill road to the left and your outlet road to the right (4.5). Cross the mostly dry creek and head southwest to a metal gate and start a 1.3-mile gentle coast on Rose Hills #3 Fire Rd. along the lush, tree-shaded canyon bottom. The route roughly parallels Turnbull Canyon Rd. above and meets a "T" junction at (5.0) where you turn left and eventually pass through two metal blocking gates before reaching Turnbull Canyon Rd. (5.8).

Trip Option. To do the trip in reverse, drive up Turnbull Canyon Rd. about 1/4 mile above (east of) Beverly Hills Dr. Look for the metal blocking gate on the left. There is parking beyond Beverly Hills Dr. on the south side of Turnbull Canyon Rd.

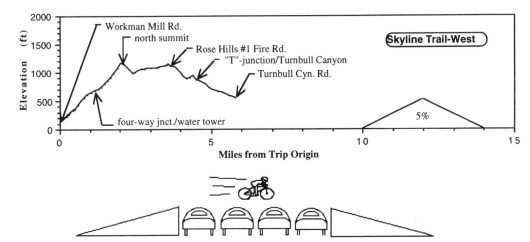

TRIP #57 - SKYLINE TRAIL - EAST

GENERAL LOCATION: Location (Topo) - Whittier, La Habra

LEVEL OF DIFFICULTY: One-way - moderate to strenuous
                               Distance - 8.0 miles; Time - 2-1/2 hours
                               Elevation gain - 1200 feet

HIGHLIGHTS: This hilly adventure uses a collection of fire roads and equestrian trails to explore the eastern Puente Hills. From the hillside perches, cyclists are treated to many views of the Hacienda Heights, Whittier and La Habra Heights areas. The route starts from Turnbull Canyon and plies both natural and developed areas as it extends east across (actually under) Colima Rd. and Hacienda Blvd. Bring a topo map, a street map and this guide for what can be a navigational challenge.

TRAILHEAD: From the Interstate 605 Fwy. (San Gabriel River Fwy.), exit east at Whittier Blvd., turn left (northeast) at Norwalk Blvd., and proceed 1/2 mile to Beverly Blvd. Turn right onto Beverly Blvd. Near Painter Ave. in 1-3/4 miles, the road changes name to Turnbull Canyon Rd. In 1-1/2 miles beyond Painter Rd., on a winding curve, is a small metal gate and trail entry on the right. A hard-to-read stanchion says *ROSEHILL2*. This is the Rose Hills #2 Fire Rd. entry.

TRIP DESCRIPTION: **Trailhead to Colima Rd.** Bike uphill as the trail widens into a fire road and pass through a spring-loaded gate on the right of a larger gate. In 0.3 mile at a "T" intersection, turn left onto Skyline Fire Rd. and climb along a ridge which leads atop Peak 1312, noting the extensive housing developments on either side of you on the ascent. Cross a saddle and climb eastward to Workman Hill, staying to the right at the junction below the hill (1.0). You begin following below the transmission lines as you will do for much of the trip. Now southbound and downhill, pass a corral, staying on the main road, then follow a single track to the right at the next fork (1.8). Pass through a gate and follow the trail sign right in 0.2 mile. In another 0.2 mile, cross paved Frame Ave, staying on the equestrian trail, and make a short steep climb. Following is a descent to Holmes Circle (2.6) and then a continued 0.4-mile drop to Colima Rd.

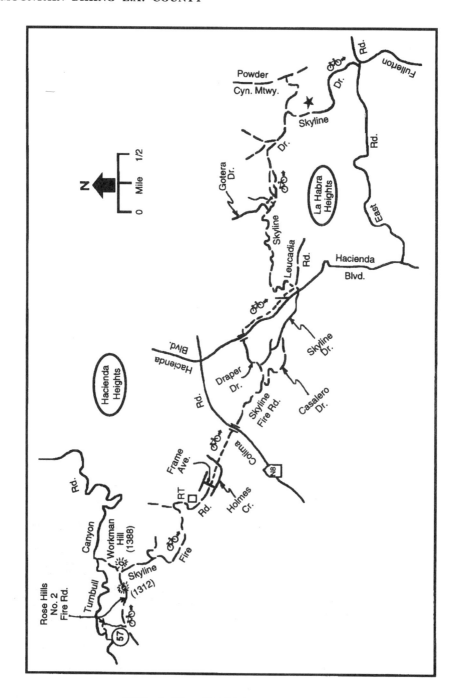

TRIP # 57 - SKYLINE TRAIL - EAST

Colima Rd. to Hacienda Blvd. Cross Colima Rd. using the underpass and begin climbing. In 0.4 mile, bear left to rejoin Skyline Fire Rd., continuing to parallel the powerlines. Cycle between and through the Puente Hills proper in this exposed stretch with mixed glimpses of Hacienda Heights to the north and La Habra Heights to the south. At (3.6) bear left at the transmission line tower with the *Equestrian Trail* sign and descend 0.4 mile on paved road to Hacienda Blvd. (4.1). Observe the massive golden-roofed Hsi Lai Buddhist Temple directly in front of you, the largest of its type in the Western Hemisphere.

Hacienda Blvd. to East Rd. To your right near the *Curved Road, Next 3 Miles* sign is the destination Hacienda Blvd. underpass. Once on the street's east side, follow the paralleling equestrian trail south 0.7 miles, crossing a paved driveway before reaching Skyline Dr. Here you turn left. Follow the signed bridal path to the left (north) and climb 0.2 mile, continuing straight past a gate with a post noting *Skyline 4*. This places you on dirt Skyline Dr. (4.8).

Pedal through scattered patches of greenery as you continue climbing. Bike straight ahead at a junction 0.4 mile further. Bear right at the transmission tower near a residential development (6.0). In about 0.1 mile and just before reaching a paved road, take the trail to the left, cross the paved road and continue on dirt Skyline Dr. Turn right shortly at the first gate and climb steeply to a scenic local summit (6.3). Continue east on the fire road staying to the right at the forks (6.6) and (6.9). At the latter junction we understand that the road left leads east and north to Schabarum Regional Park via Powder Canyon. (Check with the park to confirm that this is legal public access if you intend to take this approximately 1-1/2-mile alternative.)

In less than 0.1 mile is a gate at the head of paved Skyline Dr. Descend on that street one mile through a residential area to East Rd. (8.0). Meet your loyal car shuttler near this intersection or work your way back west via surface streets (high-speed autos in sections and heavy traffic in Whittier).

Hsi Lai Buddhist Temple

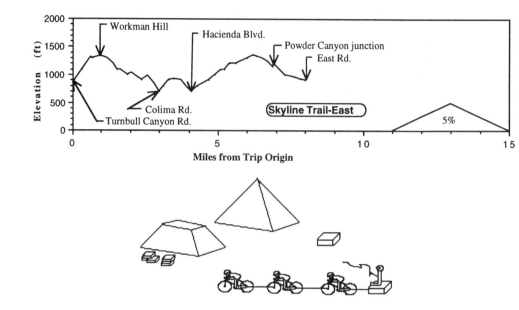

POTPOURRI

TRIP #58 - WALNUT CANYON

GENERAL LOCATION: Location (Topo) - San Dimas

LEVEL OF DIFFICULTY: One way - moderate
Distance - 3.7 miles; Time - 1 hour
Elevation gain - 200 feet

HIGHLIGHTS: This is a two-segment trip along year-round Walnut Creek. In the first 2.6 miles, you drop onto Walnut Canyon and navigate upward fifteen creek crossings amid walnut and oak forest and lush meadow land. On the way you pass several picnic areas and, more likely, will encounter equestrians. At the S. Reeder Ave. bridge, you can exit and return south (left) to Via Verde and work your way back on surface streets to the start point. If you continue on the lower segment, you cross below the S. Reeder Ave. bridge, make several creek fords and are treated to a 0.2-mile cycling adventure in the creek proper. The outlet is near the point where the natural creek turns into a concrete channel. You return on a frontage trail to Covina Hills Rd. Options are to meet your trusty "SAG wagon" or to close the loop on surface streets.

TRAILHEAD: From the Interstate 210 Fwy. exit west at Via Verde Ave. and drive another 300 yards to San Dimas Ave. Turn right (north) and parallel the freeway. In 3/4 mile on the left (just before San Dimas Ave. ducks below the freeway) is a dirt parking area. Here is a multi-use trail marker as well as a sign noting *Walnut Creek County Park*.

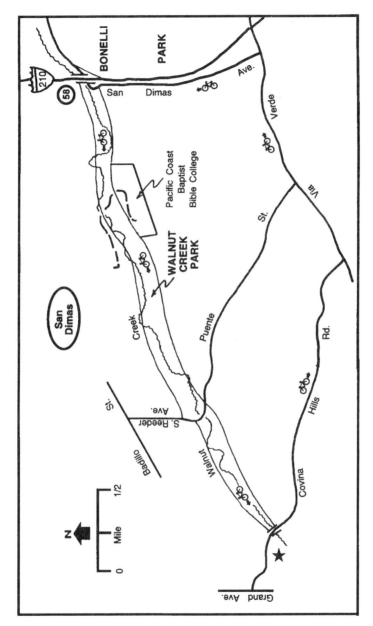

TRIP #58 - WALNUT CANYON

TRIP DESCRIPTION: **Trailhead to South Reeder Avenue.** Drop south steeply from the trailhead, then switchback north through dense tree cover. In 0.25 mile you reach the canyon bottom and track Walnut Creek on your left. In a short distance, make the first of over 20 creek crossings (including several over bridges) on the oak and walnut tree-dotted canyon floor. At 0.7 mile is an asphalt road

207

heading left and marked *Pacific Coast Baptist Bible College/Private*, while you travel right on the bridge over Walnut Creek. Just past, drop down off the road left on a single track to the trail continuation. This trail parallels the road for a short distance.

East of Pacific Coast Bible College

More creek fords lead into a narrowing park section. The fence line announces that residences line both sides of the small canyon. The route passes an equestrian staging area and crosses Walnut Creek before reaching the first of several trail forks (1.4). Bear right (most of the upcoming forks rejoin the main trail downstream). Pass two nearby picnic areas in the next 0.3 mile, continue taking the right forks at major junctions and cross into and out of tree cover. At about the 2.5-mile point is a trail split with a "Poison Ivy Warning" sign. The left fork leads you down into the creek where you bike/ford right to the trail continuation. After climbing a small rise, you look left and see a bridge (S. Reeder Ave. overpass) and a nearby trail fork (2.6). Right takes you up to the paved road, while left takes you beneath the bridge.

South Reeder Avenue to Covina Hills Road. Dive into and ride down the middle of Walnut Creek, looking for an outlet to the right. Bike nearly parallel to the road, cross a bridge over the creek and pass an overgrown picnic area (2.9). A couple more creek crossings leave you in a narrow, wooded, fenced-in trail section where you now have no option other than to navigate the creek proper. The winding, wet 0.2-mile section that follows is a real challenge. We're sure the spectators in nearby homes get a few chuckles watching bikers' attempts to stay on the pedals. You leave the creek just short of where it bears right and becomes a concrete channel (3.3). Climb the dirt/crushed asphalt mound ahead and bike to the left of the fence above the channel. To your left (south) are fenced residences where every dog in the county will bark as you pass by on your way to the outlet at Covina Hills Rd. (3.7).

Trip Option. To close the loop on surface streets, turn left on Covina Hills Rd., bike two miles to Via Verde and turn left. Via Verde is mostly flat, then climbs briskly (about 350 feet in 1-1/2 miles) to San Dimas Ave. near the 210 Fwy. Turn left (north) and descend a mile until you reach the turnout parking lot at the trip origin.

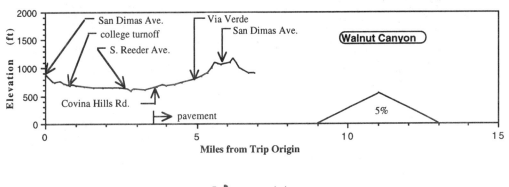

TRIP #59 - BONELLI PARK

GENERAL LOCATION: Location (Topo) - San Dimas

LEVEL OF DIFFICULTY: Loop - moderate to strenuous
Distance - 9.7 miles; Time - 2-1/2 hours
Elevation gain - 1100 feet

HIGHLIGHTS: The described route is only one of many options for exploring Bonelli Park. There are no lengthy gut-busting climbs, but the large number of smaller climbs will wear you down on a hot day. The trip described explores the western park edge, then works its way over to grand vista points above Raging Waters and atop the Puddingstone Spillway. A level tour through the picnic areas on the northern shore and marshlands to the east continues along the reservoir's eastern edge. Once back on Via Verde, a diversion returns the cyclist to the hilly environs of the southern edge of the park. The hilly tour loops the biker back to the park's western entry.

TRAILHEAD: From U.S. Hwy. 210 in the San Dimas area, exit west at Via Verde, cross over the freeway and turn right into the marked Park and Ride area (prior to reaching San Dimas Ave.).

TRIP DESCRIPTION: **Trailhead to the Puddingstone Spillway.** Bike back across the freeway on Via Verde 0.15 mile and turn right on a dirt equestrian trail before reaching the park entry gate. Follow it down to a "T" intersection and turn right, passing through a tunnel below Via Verde in another 0.1 mile. The next 1.4 miles on dirt is on a series of ups and downs through trees and thick, high chaparral. At 0.4 and 0.5 mile, pass two trail spurs which lead left and uphill toward the freeway. First views of the Puddingstone Reservoir open up in this area. At 0.85 at a "T" junction, turn left and climb, then veer right at the next junction in 0.1 mile and descend. You cross a creek on a small bridge and bike your way over to the west end

209

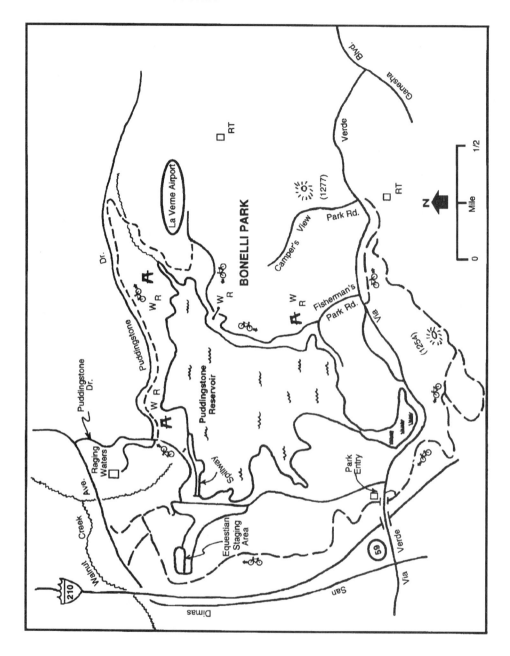

TRIP #59 - BONELLI PARK

of an equestrian staging area, passing a wide road to the right (1.6). The route becomes exposed in this area.

The road climbs, then begins to veer east and you bike along a fence to an opening and a junction. Left goes 0.3 mile to an outlet near San Dimas Ave. Instead turn right and climb 0.1 mile to the next junction where a right takes you to the top of the spillway. A left turn takes you 0.25 mile steeply uphill and north to a dead end plateau with an excellent unobstructed view of the San Gabriel Mountains, the more distant Los Angeles Civic Center and a look down into the Raging Waters Theme Park. (We could feel that cool water on the 90-degree day that we did this ride.) Returning from the plateau, take the first junction left and climb the short, steep switchbacks to the spillway where you are again rewarded with views of Raging Waters (ride out onto the flat area to the left) and the Puddingstone Reservoir (2.9).

Raging Waters Overlook

Puddingstone Spillway to Fisherman's Park Road. Follow the paved road atop the spillway east and pass a dirt road to the left (it drops near the spillway outlet and climbs back to the paved road you're following). Just short of the paved road "T" junction with a *Raging Waters* sign pointing left, turn right onto a fenced-in equestrian trail and follow it 0.1 mile through the gates. Continue downhill toward the reservoir (picnic areas, snack bar, restrooms) and then work your way east over to a wide dirt trail which is below and paralleling the park's automobile access road (Raging Waters Dr.) (3.4). (An "ugly" alternate is to bike through the parking lot.) This tree-shaded trail crosses several parking lot entry roads on a relatively flat 1.2-mile cruise to the fenced western perimeter of the La Verne Airport.

Bike the dirt path along the fence south to a creek, turn right (west) and parallel the creek before crossing it on a small bridge (4.9). Pedal 0.4 mile through marshland before returning to the reservoir edge and reach the end of a wooden fence (5.4). A "U" turn on pavement leads to a recreational vehicle area. (The paved road heading east goes to Norm's Hanger, the airport restaurant, in about 1/2 mile.)

Eastern Edge of Puddingstone Reservoir

Continue west (toward the reservoir), pass a restroom and bike to a chain link fence marked **Road Closed** which has a biker/walker entry on the left (5.8). A mild, rippling paved road follows the contour of the eastern reservoir edge where you have a chance to race the water skiers. The road leads to a shaded picnic area with restrooms, then reaches a "T" junction with unsigned Fisherman's Park Rd. (6.5).

Fisherman's Park Road to Park and Ride. Turn left on paved street and climb gently 0.3 mile to marked Via Verde. Turn right and proceed about 100 yards while looking for a dirt parking area to the left with a sign noting *Mounted Assistance Unit Staging Area*. Bike through the staging area, then climb about 100 yards and turn left (east) onto a dirt road. The road climbs, drops and parallels eastbound on Via Verde before turning back hard right (west) (7.2) and continuing to climb. You reach a panorama-laden summit with views of Puddingstone Reservoir below and the San Gabriel Mountains in the distance. A descent leads past a four-way junction (continue straight), then you are presented with a dedicated climb to the trip's apex. Enjoy the southern exposure of Pomona and the San Bernardino Fwy. below and the Chino Hills in the distance.

Follow the *Equestrian Trail* signs, generally facing the opposite direction, as you drop and execute turns at consecutive junctions: left at (8.1), right at (8.3) and left at (8.6). Continue mostly west for another 0.4 mile until reaching a point directly above the Foothill Fwy., where instead of tracking the steep climb ahead, turn right at the junction. On a downhill just before reaching Via Verde (9.1), turn left, then climb 0.1 mile to a junction. Turn right and continue 0.3 mile on a northwest track where you meet the incoming trail. The tunnel under Via Verde is ahead, but you veer right toward the *Raging Waters/Bonelli Park* sign, returning to Via Verde (9.4). Turn left and climb to the start point at the Park and Ride area (9.7).

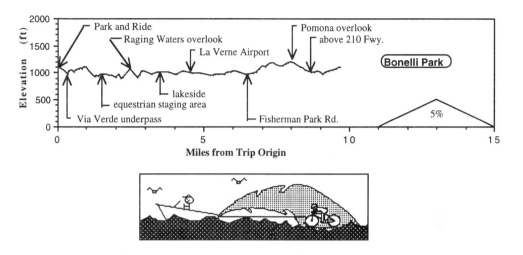

TRIP #60 - PORTUGUESE BEND

GENERAL LOCATION: Location (Topo) - Torrance, San Pedro, Redondo Beach

LEVEL OF DIFFICULTY: Major Loop - moderate to strenuous
[Minor Loop - moderate; technical sections]
Distance - 5.3 [2.3] miles; Time - 1-1/2 [1] hours
Elevation gain - 1100 [600] feet

HIGHLIGHTS: Major and minor loop trips from Del Cerro Park into Portuguese Bend are described below. The **Major Loop** works all the way from the ridgeline near the start point down to Palos Verdes Dr. S. on the bluffs above the ocean. The return route is a gutsy climb back through Portguese Canyon. Both tours visit the rustic heights of Eagles Nest, a premier vista point and picnic spot. The **Minor Loop** burrows down Altamira Canyon, traverses to the main fire road (Crenshaw Blvd.) and returns via a very scenic southerly-exposed uphill that is common to both tours.

TRAILHEAD: Follow Crenshaw Blvd. south to Park Pl. just short of the road's terminus. Turn right and park in super-scenic Del Cerro Park (open dawn to dusk). There are no restrooms or water at the park. Take in the views of the Palos Verdes Peninsula and Portuguese Bend below (your ultimate destination) from the park's southern bluff before or after the ride. This is also a dandy site for a post-ride picnic.

Why is this magnificent canyon in the middle of paradise so underdeveloped? Because there has been constant land movement and attempts to stabilize the land have not been entirely successful. Most homes in Portuguese Bend sit atop pneumatic jacks which are adjusted periodically to keep the homes level. The "official" Portuguese Bend cocktail is served in a glass with a gnarled stem. The above-ground piping with expansion joints scattered along the length and the open aluminum drainage pipes that you will see along the roads and trails are remainders that this is not your most stable territory -- you get the idea!! The rides described are for reference only. With a spirit of adventure you could spend all day roaming this super territory. The region is so open and landmarks so plentiful that it is impossible to get lost (not to say that you will always find the most convenient routes!).

213

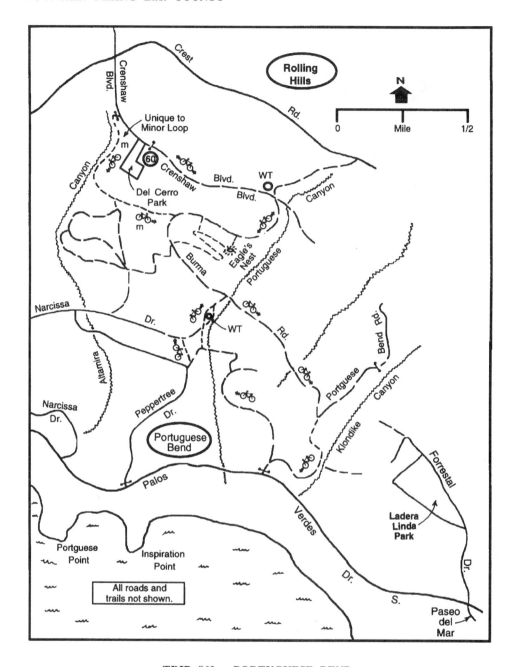

TRIP #60 - PORTUGUESE BEND

TRIP DESCRIPTION: Major Loop - Del Cerro Park to Palos Verdes Drive South. Cruise east from the park on Crenshaw Blvd. to its end at a large metal gate. What follows is a beeline, 1/2-mile, light-rocky surfaced-downhill with eye-opening

214

views of the canyons below. Just past a water tower is a four-way intersection; the junction left climbs steeply uphill to residential Rolling Hills, while the straight-ahead continuation route steers you steeply downhill to upper Portuguese Canyon.

Cruising Eagle's Nest

Your reference route takes the right fork on the main fire road and follows a sweeping curve on a mild downgrade which swings south and then bends to the west. Take the next major trail junction (0.7) which heads left on a short, steep uphill to Eagle's Nest, one of the best view points on the ride. Below tree shelter, you have a sweeping view of the road and trail maze that you are heading for, as well as the rugged peninsula shoreline.

Bike west and downhill along the ridge about 50 yards (don't return to the fire road) and look for a clear trail that branches left and immediately funnels you back east. This is the start of a sinuous, steep, singletrack runout which dumps out back at the main fire road. Locals note that this (unsigned) main road has officially changed names from Crenshaw Blvd. to Burma Rd. at this four-way intersection.

Turn left (1.3) (turning right will take you toward Altamira Canyon) and follow the power lines and above-ground piping. Make a subtle Portuguese Canyon crossing, meeting a steep fire road to the right with heavy surrounding greenery which leads to a water tank below. This is the return route junction. A right turn here takes you steeply into lower Portuguese Canyon, from which their is no painless return. If in doubt, return via the main road.

The described route stays on the dirt Burma Rd. "freeway" below the power lines. You carve a rising traverse below the bluffs, then tackle a steep southbound segment leading to a grand overlook point on what is now (unmarked) Portuguese Bend Rd. (2.3). The road continuation heads northeast to Rolling Hills Estates while the reference route dives south down the very steep ridgeline (you may want to walk your bike on the upper steepest section). At the first flat ledge below, follow the fire road left (east) and work your way east and south, staying above Klondike Canyon.

215

(The trails into the canyon lead over to Ladera Linda Park, a neat mountain biking area in itself.) The outlet fire road passes alongside some trailers, then transforms into a winding, graded-dirt road which abruptly ends and deposits you at a fire road entry from nearby Palos Verdes Dr. S. (2.7).

Major Loop Return. Turn right, pump north, and follow an arc westward on loose dirt, passing up all fire roads and trails heading west toward the community of Portuguese Bend. You pick up and follow the galvanized water drainage pipes. In this segment, you can look directly ahead and up to Del Cerro Park. The power lines on your inbound trip are visible above and to the right.

You pull away from the drainage piping, head for the backside of Portuguese Bend, subtly cross Portuguese Canyon, and continue to the second of two small fire roads heading right (3.45). A 100-yard workout climb leads to a telephone pole-lined ridge, where you turn right and follow an ever-steepening ridgeline. Ahead and above is another (perpendicular) set of power lines, which is in the area of your destination. Push/pump your bike up a sheer grade, looking down on the water tank that you saw on your way in. Keep heading for the power poles above, gasping your way up the final stretch to the main fire road (Crenshaw Blvd.) (3.75).

Turn left and follow the main road moderately uphill under the power poles, passing several off-shoot trails and roads as the packed-dirt road bends northeast and then east. The junction with the *Minor Loop* is at the 4.15-mile mark while the westernmost trail from Eagle's Nest is crossed at 4.35 miles Continue another 0.1 mile past the Eagle's Nest turnoff you followed on the incoming route, then backtrack uphill and tackle the 170-ft. traverse back to the gate at paved Crenshaw Blvd. A brief level spin returns you to Del Cerro Park (5.3).

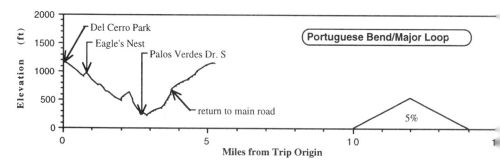

Minor Loop. (Odometer reset to zero.) Don't let the moderate rating and 2.3-mile distance of this loop fool you. Though short on distance, it is long on variety and technical challenge in a couple of segments! From Del Cerro Park, turn left on Crenshaw Blvd. Cross to the south side of the street and follow a metal fence set into brickwork pylons on a downhill dirt trail which leads to an ornate portal. Squeeze around the blocking post and stare down into the funnel of Altamira Canyon. Follow a very steep and rocky single-track as it snakes its way down the canyon on the east canyon flank -- you may want to walk your trusty bike on parts of the upper section. In 0.3 mile, views down to Portuguese Bend on the rugged coast open up. The surface improves and the downgrade moderates as your route bends east and traverses a ridge, then drops very steeply into a smaller canyon where you pass through a narrow funnel to the canyon bottom. (This section is difficult to walk, much less attempt to ride.)

Upper Altimira Canyon

You are challenged with a steep ascent through brush on the single track's outlet and a short, rocky, shallow traverse before reaching the main fire road (unmarked Crenshaw Blvd. no less) (0.85). Turn left and follow the main road steadily uphill, transiting between a large hill to the north and a smaller knoll south. At a small trail junction (1.05), turn right and follow a low-gear, single track uphill to the ridgeline of the knoll, continuing several hundred yards to the top of Eagle's Nest. Enjoy the spectacular peninsula view before pointing your wheels north and directly downhill on a short trail which ends back at the main fire road. Follow the road as it takes you on a wide semi-circle uphill to a four-way junction near a seeming oasis (1.5). Turn left, pass a water tank, then climb dirt Crenshaw Blvd. on a 0.6-mile, 170-ft. steady uphill traverse (with super views of the canyon below) to a blocking gate. Pass around the gate and pedal on a short, paved road stretch back to Del Cerro Park (2.3).

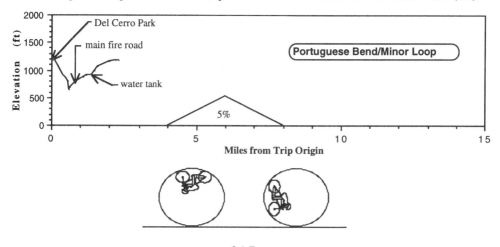

TRIP #61 - PALOS VERDES BLUFFS

GENERAL LOCATION: Location (Topo) - San Pedro

LEVEL OF DIFFICULTY: Loop - moderate [short, technical sections]
Distance - 4.0 miles; Time - 1 hour
Elevation gain - 400 feet

HIGHLIGHTS: This super ride is an explorer's special in terms of the variety of trails, coastal scenery and vegetation. There are fire roads and a myriad of crossing trails and single-track paths. The next hundred yards may bring you a climb or a drop through a gully, through high brush or to an overwhelming coastal vista beside a palm tree or dense coastal chaparral. You start from undeveloped Palos Verdes Shoreline Park, climb beside a canyon, traverse a small coastal ridge, then wander on the coastal edge of an expansive coastal bluff, looping back on a more inland route on the return. If you are able to follow this route exactly, you get the Marco Polo Award. But not to worry, the landmarks are many and evident throughout. One warning -- stay away from the edges of precipitous cliffs on the spur trails!

TRAILHEAD: From the Harbor Fwy. (Interstate 110) at its terminus in San Pedro, turn left (south) onto Gaffey St., drive 1-3/4 miles to 25th St., turn right and proceed 1-1/4 miles to Western Ave. Turn left (toward the ocean), right in 1/2 mile at S. Paseo Del Mar and left in 1/2 mile at Stargazer Ave. After another right turn on Warmouth St., proceed a short distance and park near the street's end at a concrete wall.

Palos Verdes Peninsula Park

TRIP DESCRIPTION: Palos Verdes Shoreline Park - Outbound. At street's end, follow the trail along the wall toward the ocean. The wall turns to fence and, at the

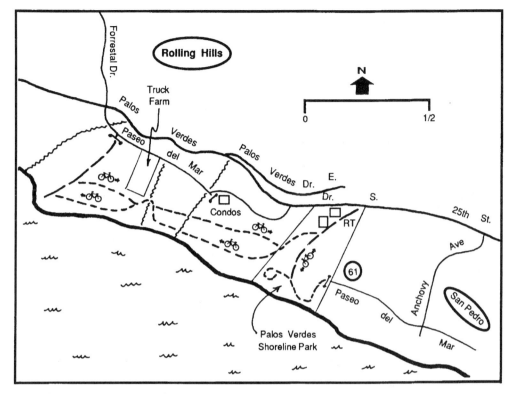

TRIP #61 - PALOS VERDES BLUFFS

bluffs, turn right and follow the precipitous single track along the bluffs several hundred yards to the end of the fenced trailer park. A downhill dash takes you to a trail junction to the right (left goes several hundred yards to a cliff mound with a superb coastline overlook) (0.3). Take the right fork and climb steeply 0.25 mile on a small, sometimes rutted trail adjacent to a canyon on the left. A junction comes up with the right fork heading up sharply to Palos Verdes Dr. S. and our route veering left and climbing to a fenced, flat traverse with one of many upcoming coastal views.

At the end of the fence, you leave the park and drop down into the "bluff of many trails." Our route was to take each junction to the left (ignoring, of course, those obviously leading to cliff edges). The mixed packed dirt, rocky and mildly-rutted trailway follows many ups and downs past chaparral- and low brush-covered terrain, passing through a small gully or two. At 1.4 miles, you reach a steep gully with a fenced-in truck farm. Take the path into the gully to the backside of the farm.

Follow the trail 0.15 mile, passing the first junction left and taking the next path heading toward the cliffs. You pass through a "mini-jungle" on a single track that leads you to a scenic cliff-side route. In the 0.2 mile of keep-your-eyes-on-the-path cycling that follows, you pass a spur switchback trail that drops downward sharply to a beach access and reach one of the main fire road entries from Paseo Del Mar. Straight ahead is one of the favorite Palos Verdes hang-glider take-off points. However, you turn right (north) and look for a path to the right which takes you back in the direction you came (2.2).

219

Along the "Bluff of Many Trails"

Return Route. Bike the single track back north and east through brush of varying heights, enjoying little ups and downs and head towards a truck farm and large condominium complex. In 0.7 mile return to the gully behind the truck farm. Drop down into the gully and join a single track that works back up behind the condominium complex and, in 0.2 mile, meets one of many four-way junctions below a high knoll. A steep diversionary ride/hike up to the knoll (pushing your bike up is a real challenge) leads to a bench with a great view of your entire area ingress and egress. Pedal south and east, picking the higher trails if you are looking for the greatest challenges. Return to the fenced lateral trail that you came in on (3.4), tretrace your incoming route, returning to the trailhead in 2.95 total miles.

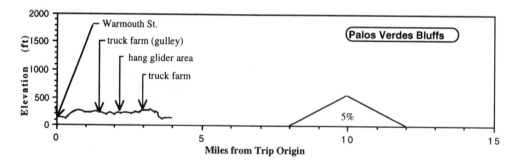

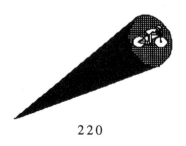

TRIP #62 - POINT VICENTE PARK

GENERAL LOCATION: Location (Topo) - Redondo Beach

LEVEL OF DIFFICULTY: Loop - moderate [technical sections (optional)]
Distance - 3.3 miles; Time - 1 hour
Elevation gain - 300 feet

HIGHLIGHTS: This general area is a delight for cycling explorers, jumpers and sightseers. The single tracks and wider bike trails criss-cross the entire, mostly flat, coastal plateau. You can select your route as you go. We have described a sample counterclockwise loop that starts at the parking lot's northwest edge, skirts "jumper's paradise," then parallels Palos Verdes Dr. S., heading west into successively less-traveled terrain. The route turns south and navigates around a series of small washes before reaching the coastal bluffs. The super-scenic, one-mile ride along the bluffs, the perfect finish for an already delightful ride, returns you to the Interpretive Center near your start point.

Keep an eye open for bikers in blind turn and jump areas. Stay alert along the bluffs and keep your bike under control. There have been many injuries and a few deaths (cyclists going over the bluffs) in this area. Given these qualifiers, cyclists of modest technical ability can enjoy these environs as much as the "high-techers."

Point Vicente Park/Point Vicente Lighthouse

TRAILHEAD: From the Harbor Fwy. (State Hwy. 110) at freeway's end, turn left (south) and proceed two miles to 25th. St. Turn right and continue 7-1/4 miles on what becomes Palos Verdes Dr. S. to the marked ocean-side turnoff (look for the Pt.

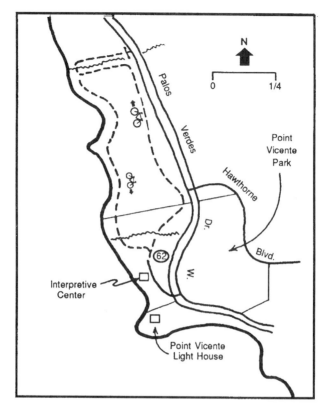

TRIP #62 - POINT VICENTE PARK

Vicente Lighthouse) to the *Point Vicente Park and Interpretive Center*. Turn left and drive to the second parking area. If you miss the park's turnoff, do a "U" turn at Hawthorne Blvd. and return 1/2 mile. From the San Diego Fwy. (Interstate Hwy. 405), exit south at Hawthorne Blvd. and drive roughly thirteen miles to road's end at Palos Verdes Dr. S. Turn left (east) and continue 1/2 mile to the park's turnoff. There are restrooms and water at the Interpretive Center.

There is also an entry through the metal fence to the northwest end of the biking area which you pass near at (1.4) on the described bike trip. It is about 3/4 mile west of Hawthorne Blvd. on Palos Verdes Dr. S. just before reaching the first developed home sites on the south side of the street.

Plan a picnic after your ride and explore the park's facilities. The park sports numerous picnic sites with benches, scattered tree cover, water and restrooms and some spectacular ocean and Santa Catalina views. The Point Vicente Interpretive Center has exhibits on the Palos Verdes Peninsula geology, cultural history, and coastal life and serves as a whale watch location from December through April. The Point Vicente Lighthouse, which is open to tours only under special circumstances, is located at the southern end of the site.

TRIP DESCRIPTION: **To the Western Boundary.** Look for the sign at the northwest corner of the parking lot that notes the park hours. This is the main trail entry. Keep making right-hand turns to stay on the ride area periphery while heading for the Admiral Risty Restaurant (one of our old favorites!) across Palos Verdes Dr. S. While following the sometime short, steep ups and downs in this modestly-vegetated coastal plateau, keep an eye left for "jumper's paradise," an area particularly blessed with some excellent hills for doing airborne jumps. In 0.35 mile you bear left (west) just before reaching the fence along Palos Verdes Dr. S., drop into a wash, then climb to a small plateau on the opposite side. You are now at the beginning of the explorer's segment (0.5).

Cycling the Bluffs

Head west following any one of a number of single tracks, wider dirt trails, and remnants of old asphalt road sections as you work your way roughly parallel to Palos Verdes Dr. S. At the "next" junction, choose the flat or the hill climb, the open section or that which visits an overgrown section of path, the technical or the better quality path, all the while staying in a general westerly direction toward a residential pocket. When you reach a large (unpassable) north-south gully just short of the residences, it is time to turn left (south) (1.4)

The Scenic Bluffs Ride. We took the 0.4-mile trek to the bluffs by staying right at each junction, except when interrupted by a steep wash. (Note: in 0.1 mile after turning south is a safe transit across the gully which cuts back north to Palos Verdes Dr. S. -- this is the only other "legal" exit from the park that we know of.) The secret here is to follow the trail which stays near the wash, then either skirts above at or crosses it at a low section. At the bluffs, you turn left (east) and view the Pt. Vicente Lighthouse in the distance, then follow the bluffs 10-15 feet from its scenic, but deadly edge 100-200 feet above the shoreline (1.8).

The next 0.9 mile is a sightseer's delight. Travel alongside two separate coves with many opportunities to view the long line of coastal bluffs and the activities of swimmers, shell hunters and fisherman below. Again skirt the deep washes across your path (and think about trying the smaller ones) as you bike toward Point Vicente Park. Follow a path along the chain-link fence on the park's west and north border, then take the return path right (south) at the four-way intersection you came in on (2.8). Soon is another junction with the left path taking you back to the parking area and the right following a path to the enclosed park's southwest edge. Turn right and carefully cycle the shared walkway/bikeway along the bluffs and enjoy yet more ocean views and a crew of happy locals and tourists. Pass the Interpretive Center and turn left (north), returning to the parking lot (3.3).

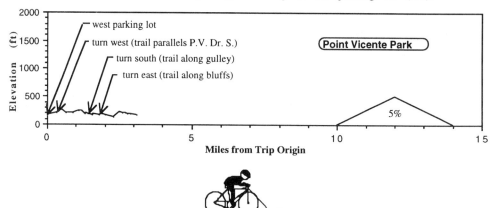

TRIPS #63-66 - SANTA CATALINA ISLAND

Visitor Information

A grand and different experience is to mountain bike the back roads of Santa Catalina Island. (Biking in Avalon is covered in our *Bicycle Rides: Los Angeles County* book.) The backcountry is dry and mountainous, but the scenery and general flavor of the territory is unique and rewarding. There are two ways to bicycle at least parts of the island: 1) buy a one-person permit ($50.00), or family permit (spouses and minor-aged children) ($75.00) (good from May 1 to April 30); or 2) sign up for the "Catalina Clean Air Challenge" in late April or early May (advertised in bicycle magazines or register at designated bicycle shops or sporting goods stores). In the former case, contact the Santa Catalina Conservancy (310-510-1421) and the latter, the American Heart Association (213-935-5864). For more information, contact the Catalina Visitors Bureau, Box 217, Avalon, Ca. 90704 (800-428-2566) or the Avalon Visitor, Information and Services Center, 423 Crescent Ave., Avalon, Ca. 90704 (213-510-2000).

Mountain bikes and helmets are required in the backcountry (beyond Hogsback Gate, which is northwest of and above Avalon). Mountain biking is restricted to the roads noted in the maps provided. Overnight camping is permitted at designated campsites. Contact Two Harbors Visitor Services at (310) 510-0303 or 510-2800 for reservations and information. Permits and the latest detailed maps are available at the Conservancy Office, 125 Claressa in Avalon or at the Airport-in-the-Sky (Catalina Airport) (310-510-0143). The map is a must in order to track changes in route status or closures. Bring a healthy water supply -- we carry three quarts as a precaution. Water can be found at Two Harbors, Little Fisherman's Cove Campground, Little Harbor Campground, Haypress Picnic Area near Toyon Junction, Airport-in-the-Sky, the Buffalo Corral area on the road to Two Harbors and El Rancho Escondido. Confirm which sources have water before you depart on your adventure.

Ferries to Catalina can be found under "Cruises" in telephone books. Avalon can be reached from either Long Beach, San Pedro or Newport Beach on the mainland. Two Harbors can be accessed from Long Beach or Avalon. The ferries allow you to bring your bike and backpacks or other luggage.

Hiking trails are also noted on the maps provided. Hiking permits (free) can be obtained during working hours from the Catalina Island Conservancy, 125 Claressa Ave., Airport-in-the-Sky, Two Harbors Visitor Services, Los Angeles County Interpretive Center, Hermit's Gulch Campground, and Wrigley Memorial & Botanical Gardens.

The authors have provided general notes on the Santa Catalina rides primarily based on participation in the Catalina Clean Air Challenge. The notes are terse because the authors succumbed to the fun and excitement of the three day bike-riding bash, as opposed to operating in the normal "slow-as-you-go" mode using compass, altimeter, voice recorder and cameras. Bring this biking guide and also obtain the information and maps noted. You will have sufficient information to tour and enjoy all the island has to offer.

History

The island "26-miles across the sea" was inhabited by different groups of Native Americans over 7000 years and "discovered" by European explorer Cabrillo in 1542. Sixty years later, Viscaino of Spain visited the island and named it "Santa Catalina" after St. Catherine of Alexandria. In the 1790's sea otter hunters poached on the Spanish domain and Yankee smugglers used the island as a haven during the Mexican era. Under American rule came squatters with sheep and cattle, Union soldiers (their barracks still stand at two Harbors) and vacationers in the 1880's. Ownership changed hands many times. When William Wrigley Jr. acquired a majority interest in the Santa Catalina Island Company from the Bannings in 1919, the destiny of the Island began to change forever. In 1972 members of the Wrigley family established the Santa Catalina Island Conservancy as a nonprofit organization dedicated to the conservation and preservation of the Island. In 1975 the Wrigley and Offield families deeded 42,135 acres of the Island to the Conservancy. With this gift the conservation and preservation of most of Catalina's interior and 48 miles of its coastline were given permanent status in perpetuity. This is the delightfully unspoiled area that these bicycle tours explore.

Editors' Note: At the time of book publication, the road between Eagle's Nest Lodge and Ben Weston Beach was closed due to extensive storm damage. This effectively blocks the middle part of the Middle Canyon/Cottonwood Canyon Loop. Before attempting this ride, contact the Catalina Island Conservancy as noted above to check the current road status.

TRIP #63 - AVALON TO AIRPORT-IN-THE-SKY

<u>GENERAL LOCATION</u>: Location (Topo) - Santa Catalina East and North

<u>LEVEL OF DIFFICULTY</u>: Up and back - strenuous to very strenuous
Distance - 20.6 miles; Time - 4-1/2 hours
Elevation gain - 2600 feet

<u>HIGHLIGHTS</u>: This is a rugged, sun-exposed adventure on paved road. From the Cabrillo Mole, a short tour of flat Avalon gives way to a rugged climb to Hogsback Gate, the departure point for the "outback." Another 1.7 miles of gritty climb leads to the East Summit. The remainder of this scenic ride plies the spine of the coastal

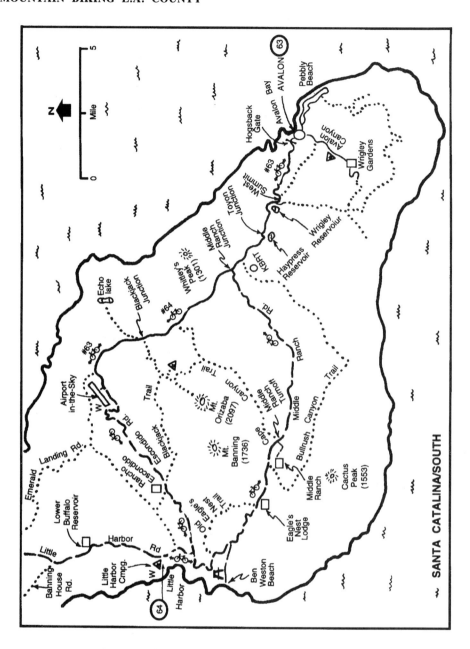

TRIP #63 - AVALON TO AIRPORT-IN-THE-SKY
TRIP #64 - MIDDLE CANYON/COTTONWOOD CANYON LOOP

range on an undulating road leading to Catalina's Airport-in-the-Sky. The one-way tour is strenuous. Although there is only about 500 feet elevation gain on the return segment, the added mileage places this trip on the "very strenuous" boundary.

TRAILHEAD: The trip starts at the ferry landing known as Cabrillo Mole in Avalon.

TRIP DESCRIPTION: **Cabrillo Mole to Hogsback Gate.** Fully paved, this is still no trick-or-treat ride. From the Cabrillo Mole, bike southwest on Pebbly Beach Rd. which becomes Clarissa Ave. beyond Crescent Ave. (aka Front St. -- no bikes). Turn right at Beacon St. and pedal northwest to Metropole Ave. and turn right again, returning to Crescent Ave. next to Avalon Bay (0.8). A left turn and then left again on Marilla Ave. (at The Landing) starts you on your steep, 500-foot climb to Hogsback Gate. A right turn at Vieudelou Ave., in a short distance, takes you up to a fork where you veer right on Stage Rd. (aka Old Stagecoach Rd.). A steady pumpathon past Camino Del Monte to the left leads to Hogsback Gate where you check to insure that a biking permit is in your possession (1.8).

Hogsback Gate to Middle Ranch Junction. Beyond the gate, the steep climb continues northwest and passes Wishbone Loop, a particularly sharp switchback. In another 1/2 mile the road almost makes about a complete loop before climbing to a road junction on the hard left. Just beyond is the east side of Wrigley Reservoir (3.6). This is the wonderfully flat East Summit area and the beginning of the much flatter and panorama-filled ride to Middle Ranch junction. In 1/2 mile is the Haypress Reservoir and Toyon Junction with one of the scattered telephones along the "main thoroughfares" of the backcountry. A mile beyond is the Bullrush Canyon Trail and KBRT radio tower to the left and the Middle Ranch Junction 0.3 mile beyond (5.6).

Middle Ranch Junction to Airport-in-the-Sky. In this area are superb views down the east-facing slopes to San Pedro Channel. In 2.5 miles of little ups and downs you pass a junction to Blackjack Mountain and its namesake campground on the left. This is also the hiker's entry to Mt. Orizaba, the highest peak on Catalina Island. Ahead, the road forks right to Echo Lake, while you bear left and make a testy 0.8-mile climb to the plateau with Airport-in-the-Sky at its zenith. The paved road swings left (west) and continues another mile to the airport entrance on the right (10.3). Unless you have a legal shuttle arranged, return the way you came and enjoy the blowout downhill south of the east summit.

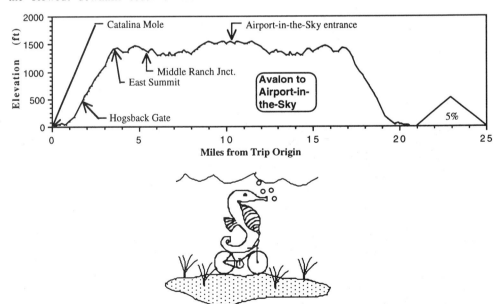

227

TRIPS #64 - MIDDLE CANYON/COTTONWOOD CANYON LOOP

GENERAL LOCATION: Location (Topo) - Santa Catalina North, South and East

LEVEL OF DIFFICULTY: Loop - strenuous
Distance - 21.1 miles; Time - 4 hours
Elevation gain - 2500 feet

HIGHLIGHTS: This is the least stressing of the loop directions of travel. The route passes Little Harbor, climbs to Little Harbor Overlook, then visits the lower reaches of both Cottonwood and Middle Canyons. A steep climb to Middle Ranch gives way to a five-mile modest upgrade and final steep dash through Middle Canyon to Middle Ranch Junction. A 4.7-mile, up-and-down transit along the coastal crest takes you past the Airport-in-the-Sky. This is followed by a refreshing 4.6-mile ridge run which includes a visit to El Rancho Escondido. The final 1.1-mile segment from Little Harbor Overlook returns you to the Little Harbor Camp and Picnic Grounds.

TRAILHEAD: The trip starts from Little Harbor Camp and Picnic Grounds. The route here from Two Harbors is described in the "Two Harbors to Little Harbor" trip.

TRIP DESCRIPTION: Campground to Middle Canyon. A 0.2-mile pedal takes you by Little Harbor heading south and past a junction to the left that is a back-door hiker's route to El Rancho Escondido (0.5) The road drops into the head of a canyon, climbs steeply south and east to Little Harbor Overlook and the Escondido Rd./Cottonwood Canyon junction (1.1) This is your loop outlet point. Middle Ranch Rd. drops down to the head of Cottonwood Canyon in 0.4 mile, climbs over a small crest and drops once more into Middle Canyon (3.2). The road to the right travels about 1-1/2 miles to Mills Landing and Ben Weston Beach, great destinations in their own rite. On the way you hit a "T" junction at (2.2), where the left junction leads to the Old Eagle's Nest Trail (hikers only) and a dead-end coastal trail right at (2.4).

Middle Canyon to Cape Canyon. The road climbs 0.4 mile in the canyon, then heads up the south face to a fork. Right heads south to Cactus Peak, while Middle Ranch Rd. bears left and returns to Middle Canyon (4.0). Switch over to the north side of the canyon on a steady climb and pass the Old Eagle's Nest Trail outlet near Eagle's Nest Lodge in another 0.3 mile. In 1/2-mile you find yourself at the opening of a broad canyon floor where you bike above Thompson Dam and expansive Middle Ranch to the right (south). A more gradual climb takes you to a crossroads at the impressive junction of Cape Canyon and Middle Canyon (5.5). Left leads up Cape Canyon to Blackjack Campground while right is the road entry to Middle Ranch .

Cape Canyon to Middle Ranch Junction. Follow Middle Ranch Rd. southeast another mile and enter a narrowing canyon. A moderate steady climb starts on the south side of the canyon, then takes you back and forth across the seasonal creek bed. At (9.0) the road begins a concerted climb for one steep mile before reaching its end point at Middle Ranch Junction at the paved road which transits from Avalon to Airport-in-the-Sky.

Middle Ranch Junction to Airport-in-the-Sky. Here are superb views down the east-facing slopes to San Pedro Channel. In 2.5 miles of little ups and downs you pass a junction to Blackjack Mountain and its namesake campground on the left. This is also the hiker's entry to Mt. Orizaba, the highest peak on Catalina Island. Ahead, the road forks right to Echo Lake, while you bear left and make a testy 0.8-mile climb to the plateau with Airport-in-the-Sky at its zenith. The paved road swings left (west) and continues another mile to the airport entrance (14.7).

Airport-in-the-Sky to El Rancho Escondido. A half mile on the plateau gives way to a downhill below the west side of the airport. At (15.8) the road transits above the upper reaches of a canyon enfolding the Buffalo Spring Reservoir and then switchbacks downhill for a mile. The road proceeds southwest above the same canyon (on the right, which outlets at Little Harbor), dropping steeply and following the ridgeline south of Peak 830 (17.6). Cottonwood Canyon is visible to the left and below. Another 0.6 mile of ridge running leads to a saddle with El Rancho Escondido (the old Wrigley Ranch) just ahead (west) and sitting below Peak 665. The saddle sits on a perch with canyons on both sides.

El Rancho Escondido to Little Harbor Camp and Picnic Grounds. Pass a fork, staying right (left goes down to Cottonwood Canyon), pass to the south of Peak 665 (18.6) and bike down another ridgeline 1.4 miles to a "T" junction at Little Harbor Overlook. Turn right (east) and retrace your incoming route 1.1 miles back to the campground (21.1).

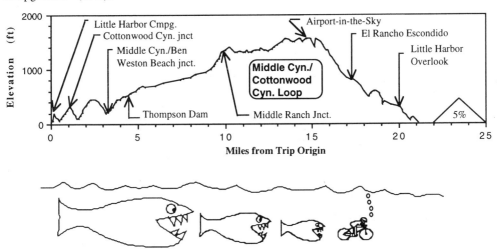

TRIP #65 - TWO HARBORS TO LITTLE HARBOR

GENERAL LOCATION: Location (Topo) - Santa Catalina North and South

LEVEL OF DIFFICULTY: Up and back - strenuous
                         Distance - 16.0 miles; Time - 4-1/2 hours
                         Elevation gain - 2200 feet

HIGHLIGHTS: The beach at Two Harbors was an old home to Spanish smugglers and more modern-day prohibitionists. Beyond Isthmus Cove is a 2.3-mile stair-step climb to West Summit and a super coastal viewpoint. From here Two Harbors heads south and inland, dropping down into Little Springs Canyon. The road climbs out of the canyon, drops down a ridgeline and rejoins Little Springs Canyon just before outletting at Little Harbor. A 1.3-mile extension takes you to Little Harbor Overlook and some excellent west coastal vistas.

TRAILHEAD: The trip starts from Isthmus Cove Beach.

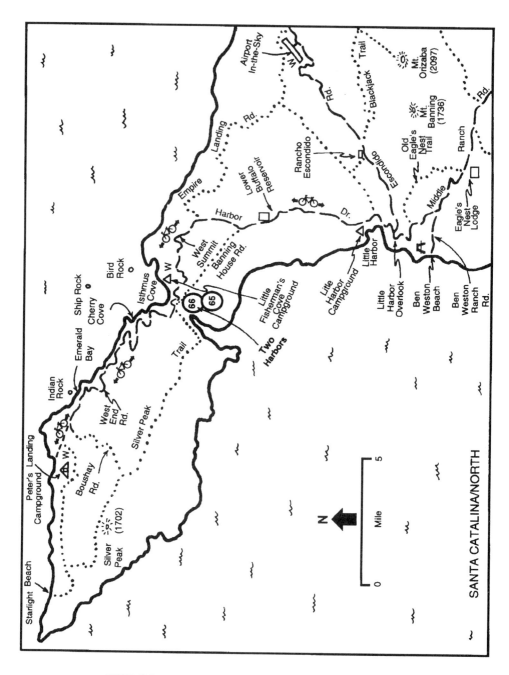

TRIP #65 - TWO HARBORS TO LITTLE HARBOR
TRIP #66 - WEST END ROAD

TRIP DESCRIPTION: **Isthmus Cove to West Summit.** Bike inland 0.2 mile to an east-west road and turn (east) (appropriately, west leads to West End Rd.). A steep climb leads to a fork at (0.7) with the road left returning to Isthmus Cove. Your route is right (north) onto Two Harbors Rd. as you follow a winding eastward-tending climb where there are views of Fisherman's Cove and Isthmus Cove below. The route passes Summit Reservoir (2.0) and finally peaks out after a 2.4-mile, 750-foot climb to West Summit in 0.7 mile.

West Summit to Little Harbor. Turn south with Peak 932 on your left and soon reach the head of Little Springs Canyon. The canyon narrows and the grade moderates as you pass Upper Buffalo Corral/Reservoir (3.5) and a road junction in 0.5 mile (stay south in the main canyon). At (4.2) the road crosses the canyon bottom to the east side and climbs above Lower Buffalo Corral/Reservoir (4.6). It follows a ridge downhill and passes below and east of Peak 570 before crossing a saddle. Look left (east) into Little Springs Canyon and right to a tributary canyon. Continue the steep downhill and reach the fusion point of the canyons (6.3), then dump out into a broad flat expanse above Little Harbor in 0.3 mile past the Little Harbor Camp and Picnic Grounds (water). This is the road's closest approach point just east of Little Harbor Beach (6.8). You can turn around here to cut 2.6 miles and 300-feet elevation gain off the ride -- at the cost of missing a popular scenic vista point.

On to Little Harbor Overlook. Continue south on the road, pass a road junction left in 0.3 mile (back-door hiking trail to El Rancho Escondido) and drop into a canyon outlet. From here is a 0.8-mile, 250-foot climb south and east to the grand Little Harbor Overlook and the Escondido Rd./Cottonwood Canyon junction (8.0). After gathering in the great coastal views, it is time to turn around and retrace your incoming route back to Isthmus Cove (16.0).

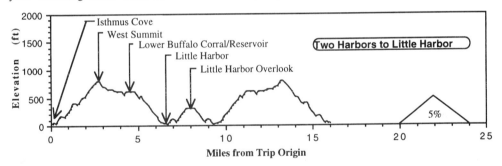

TRIP #66 - WEST END ROAD

GENERAL LOCATION: Location (Topo) - Santa Catalina West

LEVEL OF DIFFICULTY: Up and back - moderate
Distance - 13.6 miles; Time - 2-1/2 hours
Elevation gain - 1300 feet

HIGHLIGHTS: The ride starts from Isthmus Cove Beach at Two Harbors. From the center of the isthmus, pick up West End Rd. northbound. (Southbound leads to West

Summit and Banning House Rd.) For a shortcut from Isthmus Cove, look for a trail on the north hillsides which ascends 50-100 yards to an intersection with West End Rd. For either route, son after gaining this cliff-side road, you see Bird Rock, a stark white rock and more distant light-beaconed Ship Rock, both used as sailor's landmarks. Pass above Fourth of July Cove, head inland to the head of a canyon (1.3), then swing back toward the southern extent of Cherry Cove. An inland segment leads to V-shaped Cherry Valley with a grove of Catalina cherry (a shrub-like tree with cherry-like fruit) at its mouth. A transit through the valley takes you back for an extended cliff-side jaunt that reaches Howlands Landing in 4.3 miles from the start.

A short pedal leads to a point above aptly-named Emerald Bay and Indian Rock. Pass Boushay Trail, a dirt trail to the left, (5.7). In 0.5 mile West End Rd. swings to the left (west), while you take the trail on the right through grassland to a sharp drop down to Parson's Landing (6.8). The campground of the same name sports a small beach, restrooms, campsites and picnic sites. After a refreshing rest break (and maybe a dip) turn around and retrace the incoming route (13.6).

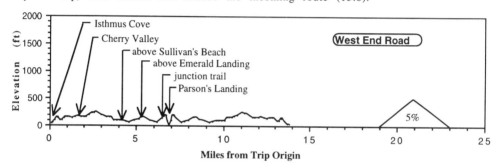

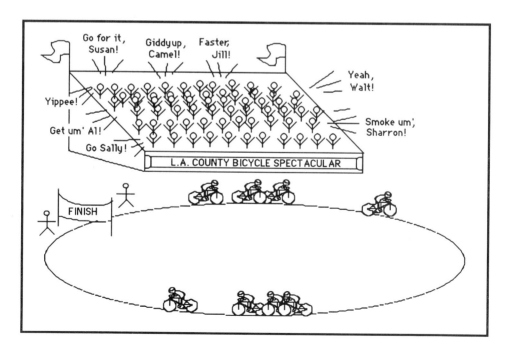

INDEX: SANTA MONICA MOUNTAINS

INDEX: MOUNTCLEF RIDGE/SIMI HILLS

INDEX: SANTA SUSANNA MOUNTAINS

INDEX: VERDUGO MOUNTAINS/SAN RAFAEL HILLS

INDEX: PUENTE HILLS

POTPOURRI

ATTRACTION, POINT OF INTEREST	TRIP NUMBER(S)
Cottonwood Canyon (Catalina)	64,65
Del Cerro Park (Palos Verdes Peninsula)	60
Eagle's Nest	60
Eagle's Nest Lodge (Catalina)	64,65
East Summit (Catalina)	63
El Rancho Escondido (Catalina)	64
Hogsback Gate (Catalina)	63
Isthmus Cove (Catalina)	65,66,67
"Jumper's Paradise"	62
Ladera Linda Park (Palos Verdes Peninsula)	60
Little Harbor (Catalina)	64,65
Little Harbor Camp and Picnic Grounds (Catalina)	64,65
Little Harbor Overlook (Catalina)	64,65
Lower Buffalo Corral/Reservoir (Catalina)	65
Middle Canyon (Catalina)	64
Middle Ranch Junction (Catalina)	63,64
Norm's Hanger	59
Palos Verdes Bluffs	61
Palos Verdes Shoreline Park	61
Parson's Landing (Catalina)	66
Point Vicente Lighthouse	62
Point Vicente Park and Interpretive Center	62
Portuguese Bend	60
Puddingstone Reservoir	59
Raging Waters	59
Santa Catalina Island	63,64,65,66
Two Harbora (Catalina)	65,66,67
Upper Buffalo Corral/Reservoir (Catalina)	65
Walnut Creek	58
Walnut Canyon	58
West End Rd. (Catalina)	66
West Summit (Catalina)	65

ODDs N' ENDS

THE BOOK REVIEW CREW:

Sam Nunez, Susan Cohen, and authors Sharron and Don Brundige

Jill Morales

Al Hook

Walt and Sally Bond

Trish Biancone (Honorary Member)

Most Honorable Crash & Burn (and some hamming up!)

NOTES:

NOTES:

NOTES:

NOTES:

NOTES:

NOTES:

NOTES:

NOTES:

BICYCLE RIDES
Santa Barbara & Ventura Counties

BY DON AND SHARRON BRUNDIGE

Published: 9/94; 68 Trips including 15 Best Mountain Bike Rides
ISBN 0-9619151-6-1; Library of Congress Catalogue Number 94-094025
 - City of Santa Barbara (Santa Barbara City, Hope Ranch, UCSB Campus Tour, Mountain Drive)
 - East County (Gibralter Rd., Upper Santa Ynez River, West Camino Cielo, Santa Barbara-Solvang)
 - West County (Jalama Beach, Solomon Hills, Los Coches Mtn. Loop, Point Sal State Beach)
 - Ventura Coast (Point Hueneme, Ventura to Ojai, Ventura to Santa Barbara, Coastal Century)
 - Inland/Urban (Agoura Hills, Westlake Village, Simi Valley, Rocky Peak, Potrero Rd.)
 - Mountains/Backcountry (Sycamore Canyon, Ojai-Santa Paula, Casitas Pass, Pine Mtn., Mt. Pinos)